MW01109877

Tragedy's Insights:
Indentity, Polity, Theodicy

Edited by Luis R. Gámez

Locust Hill Literary Studies No. 27

LOCUST HILL PRESS
West Cornwall, CT
1999

By arrangement with *Comparative Drama*
and with the permission of the Board of the
Medieval Institute.

ISBN: 0–933951–85–X

Contents

Tragedy's Insights:
Identity, Polity, Theodicy

Preface

When the old men of Argos tell us that we come to wisdom through suffering (τὸν πάθει μάθος), or when Creon cries that his sorrows have schooled him in the truth (οἴμοι,/ ἔχω μαθὼν δείλαιος),[1] we gather that the salutary complexities of the tragic stage may center not, as some have argued, on the representation of existential or ontological affliction,[2] but rather upon the insights gained through that affliction, however unwillingly we learn them. The essays assembled here, reprinted from the Spring 1999 issue of *Comparative Drama*, focus upon tragedy's insights from various perspectives: the redemption which atones for violence against the divine; the tension between individual strength and oppressive systems of political power; the negotiations which extend the dimensions of human identity; and the unique "interior antinomy" of the tragic drama, whereby action, scenic space, and words lead us to seek all-embracing answers to the bitterest questions.[3]

Reexamining the critical roots of that antinomy in "The Tragic Emotions," David Konstan (Brown University) argues for the inclusion of other audience responses than the pity and fear of Aristotle's *Poetics*, namely triumph and exultation. In fresh readings of Sophocles' *Ajax* and Euripides' *Hecuba* and *Bacchae*, Konstan draws our attention to the conflicting experiences of "compassionate terror" and "victorious confidence" in these tragedies. He notably focuses on the mechanisms by which playwrights encourage their audiences to identify with victims and victors; his argument suggests how this Aristotelian notion of identification realigns the emotional world of ancient tragedy.

In a particular application of the issue of identity to the most celebrated English tragedy, Robert C. Evans (Auburn University at Montgomery) examines "Friendship in *Hamlet*." His sustained, scene-by-scene analysis explores anew a social bond especially fascinating to Renaissance thinkers; by offering the reader a bracingly direct and minutely-attentive encounter with Shakespeare's text, Evans vividly presents the contrasts between dependence and independence, trust and betrayal, hatred and friendship. Brian Johnston (Carnegie Mellon University) pursues an inquiry as expansive as Evan's is intimate in "Ibsen's Cycle as Hegelian Tragedy." Focusing on the dialectical components of Ibsen's corpus, Johnston outlines a vast metaphoric project for the redemption of a modern collective identity, embracing unresolved spiritual conflicts as well as tragically transfiguring action. "The humdrum identities of modern urban life . . . are enlarged and galvanized by archetypal forces that extend the dimensions of human identity through individual, familial, communal, national, historical, cultural, natural, and supernatural circumferences of meaning."

Véronique Plesch (Colby College) investigates redemption within a medieval context in "Killed by Words: Grotesque Verbal Violence and Tragic Atonement in French Passion Plays." She looks at verbal abuse of Christ in the fifteenth-century cycles, closely recording a robust tradition of literally "adding insult to injury" with language drawn as readily from the kitchen as from game and farce. This carnivalesque and often shocking element in sacred drama is in her analysis ultimately regenerative, "since the Christian history of redemption is one of suffering and death that brings beatitude and eternal life." Hence God's justice is a tranquility born of violence.

Two essays in this collection place the *agon* within the context of the *polis*, linking the tragic drama with politics. The literary scholar David Bevington (University of Chicago) joins with the historian David L. Smith (Selwyn College, Cambridge) in presenting a binocular study of "James I and *Timon of Athens*." They set the wanton extravagance of the Jacobean court and of James himself against the world of Shakespeare's play, posing "an historically based reader-response" line of inquiry: what would an audience in 1605–8 have made of such reckless gift-giving as Timon's? The monarchy's bounty being a major political issue, does Shakespeare's characterization embody any sort of critique of James I? The abundant materials presented here compellingly argue for a fruitful correlation between play and historical event. Jerome Mazzaro, writing from Buffalo, New York, studies a neoclassical Biblical drama contexualized within American and European struggles for independence in "Alfieri's *Saul* as Enlightenment Tragedy." Alfieri related Aristotle's pity and fear to the essence of tyranny, to the sufferings and terror of the tyrant's oppression. "Alfieri's dominant central theme involves conflicts between this tyrant and a hero, the aim of their

struggle being 'political and personal liberty.'" Mazzaro finds in
this representation of the first Israelite king a reexamination of
the bounds of necessity and convention, turning what in classical
tragedy resides in powerful, external forces into internal psychological ones. Saul's self-divided warfare provides a Hegelian
"collision" leading to public and private catastrophe.

   "Some Late Reflections on Tragedy and Its Theatrical Chem-
istry," by J. L. Styan (now residing at Milford on Sea, England),
ends this collection by transcending the intellectual rubrics of
tragedy and focusing instead on the "pragmatic, testing theory
against practice." In a broad survey of the genre from ancient to
modern, Styan draws on a generous body of texts to discuss the
effects of tragedy in performance upon the spectator, and the crucial implications of the form for actor and director. His account
of the several metamorphoses of tragedy on the western stage—
from early ritual to the "dark comedy" of our time—is both wise
and authoritative, and a mirror for all students of the tragic art.

   These essay were originally gathered to mark the retirement
from *Comparative Drama* of editors Clifford Davidson and John
H. Stroupe. From 1967 to 1999 they nurtured the rich collegiality
which characterizes the journal's life, and which is reflected in
the offerings here. To sample the journal's treasury under their
leadership is to see with what regularity, and how wisely, John
and Cliff set us the example of industry and erudition seasoned
with humanity. This present volume is respectfully and affection-
ately dedicated to them.

> *"Se fosse tutto pieno il mio dimando,"*
> *rispuos' io lui, "voi non sareste ancora*
> *de l'umana natura posto in bando;*
>
> *ché 'n la mente m'è fitta, e or m'accora,*
> *la cara e buona imagine paterna*
> *di voi quando nel mondo ad ora ad ora*
>
> *m'insegnavate come l'uom s'etterna:*
> *e quant' io l'abbia in grado, mentr' io vivo*
> *convien che ne la mia lingua si scerna. . . ."*

Luis R. Gámez

NOTES

[1] Aeschylus, *Agamemnon*, Loeb Classical Library (1926), 177; Sophocles, *Antigone*, Loeb Classical Library (1912), 1271-72.

[2] See, e.g., George Steiner, "Tragedy, Pure and Simple," in *Tragedy and the Tragic: Greek Theatre and Beyond*, ed. M. S. Silk (Oxford: Clarendon Press, 1996), 534-46.

[3] Jovan Hristic, "On the Interpretation of Drama," *New Literary History* 3 (1972): 352-53.

The Tragic Emotions[1]

David Konstan

Among the critical ideas—such as imitation, catharsis, recognition, and peripety—that Aristotle's *Poetics* has bequeathed to the world is the thesis that tragedy engenders two characteristic emotions, pity (*eleos*) and fear (*phobos*).[2] Few scholars have quarreled with this proposition: but do these two feelings exhaust the range of responses typically evoked by tragedy? In what follows, I suggest that Aristotle's account is in fact deficient, and, more specifically, that Greek tragedies characteristically produce, alongside pity and fear, a sense of triumph and exultation in the audience. Furthermore, I argue that this question of the tragic emotions may have been in the air toward the end of the fifth century B.C., at a time when dramatists were experimenting with stories that simultaneously evoked the contradictory experiences of compassionate terror and victorious confidence.

I

Aristotle says little about why audiences feel pity and fear when they watch tragedies. In the *Rhetoric* (2.8.2), he defines pity as "pain arising from a perceived evil that is destructive or painful, in a person who does not deserve to meet with it—an evil that one may expect either to suffer oneself, or that someone of one's own [family] may do so; and this, when the evil appears near."[3] Aristotle goes on to say that those who have lost everything are, accordingly, incapable of pity, since they have nothing more to fear, as are those who expect that they will prosper exceedingly (2.8.3). He says too that one pities acquaintances unless they are too closely related, in which case a sense of horror (*to deinon*) drives out pity (2.8.12). Finally, he adds that people pity those who are similar (*homoioi*), whether in age, character, family, or whatever; "in general," he concludes, "one must presume that people pity just those things, when they happen to others, that they fear when they happen to themselves" (2.8.13).

Here, Aristotle seems to adumbrate a notion of identification, according to which pity arises when one is able to put oneself in

1

the place of the other. For identification to be possible, the other person must be similar in some respect to ourselves; furthermore, we must be liable to the same kind of suffering: one who believes himself to be wholly immune will not be capable of pity. On the other hand, pity requires a certain distance: if suffering touches one's children, for example, one shares in their pain directly and experiences horror, not compassion. Aristotle tends to regard members of a single family as sharing a common substance (*Nich. Ethics* 8.12.1161b17–19). Where there is identity, there is no scope for identification.

The account of pity developed in the *Rhetoric* explains why we feel this emotion in regard to characters in a tragedy, but seems to exclude the possibility that a work of art can arouse fear: pity is precisely what we experience in behalf of others when they suffer things that we fear in our own behalf. For this reason, I believe, Aristotle modifies his analysis of these emotions in the *Poetics*. Here, he explains that pity and fear are not excited when we see thoroughly bad men ruined: "for such a plot may involve sympathy [*to philanthrôpon*], but neither pity nor fear, for the one concerns a man who is undeservedly unfortunate, while the other concerns a man who is similar [*homoios*]: pity concerns the undeserving man, fear concerns the one who is similar" (13.1453a2–6). The idea that the object of pity does not deserve his fate is present in the definition Aristotle offers in the *Rhetoric*; in the *Poetics*, however, Aristotle exploits the concept of similarity in order to explain the terror that tragedy induces. If the characters on stage are enough like ourselves—the context indicates that the sense is morally similar—then we will experience their fear as our own.

Why only their fear, however? It is true that tragedy normally represents human suffering, but such suffering is usually the consequence of a conflict of wills between opposing parties. Perhaps Sophocles' *Oedipus the King* is an example of a tragedy in which the hero's agony results from the impersonal action of fate, but this is the exception, not the rule. Most often, where there are victims, there are victors as well. What is it that determines whether the audience identifies with the loser or the winner in such cases? We can state the point more sharply by availing ourselves of Aristotle's own categories. In the *Rhetoric*, Aristotle says that there is an opposite emotion both to fear and to pity: the opposite of fear is confidence (*tharsos*, 2.5), while the opposite of pity is *nemesis*, which we may perhaps translate as indignation.[4] What prevents the audience, then, from feeling confidence and indignation along with those characters in the drama who are safe and successful, as opposed to pity and fear with those who are defeated and humiliated?

There is an implicit answer to this question in Aristotle's thesis about similarity: if the victorious party does not resemble us, while the victims in the tragedy do, we will naturally identify with the latter. The context in the *Poetics* indicates, as we have seen, that the relevant point of similarity in the case of tragedy is moral likeness: it is, generally speaking, in character, rather than age, family, or profession, that we are analogous to the protagonists of a play. In those plays, then, in which the triumphant individuals are wholly bad, it may be that we will identify exclusively with the victim. But Greek tragedy does not usually represent the extreme, one-sided villains of Senecan or Jacobean drama, like the dreadful Atreus in Seneca's *Thyestes*. Thus, Aristotle's own theory leaves open the possibility that an audience may, in a given theatrical work, be induced to share the confidence of the conquerers rather than the terror of the defeated. Or else, they may be disposed to identify with both.

Aristotle gives us one last clue to the nature of emotional identification in tragedy: when the dramatic action (*praxis*) occurs on the part of an enemy toward an enemy, "there is nothing to move us to pity either in his doing or in his meditating the deed, except so far as the actual pain [*pathos*] of the sufferer is concerned; and the same is true when the parties are indifferent to one another" (14.1453b14–19).[5] Rather, the proper effect is produced when the conflict or *pathos* occurs among people connected by some positive affection (*en tais philiais*, 14.1453b18 –19), for example between brothers or parents and children.[6] From this we may surmise that in a good tragedy, according to Aristotle, the opposed parties are not vastly different in respect to virtue; it should follow, although Aristotle does not say so, that an audience can sympathize with both sides, provided that neither acts out of ignorance or sheer malevolence.

II

Sophocles' play *Ajax* may be read as almost a textbook application of the principles of tragic identification that Aristotle was to lay out a century later. The action begins with a scene in which Athena, presumably perched on the rear wall or *skênê*, beholds Odysseus sneaking cautiously toward Ajax's tent: "I always see you hunting down some opportunity to catch one of

your enemies [*ekhthroi*], and now too I behold you by the marine
tents of Ajax" (1–4). To this Odysseus replies: "Well have you
recognized that I am circling on the track of a foe [*dusmenês*]"
(18–19). That the action is to occur between enemies seems contrary to Aristotle's recommendation on the best way to arouse
pity, but Sophocles does not leave the matter here. After Athena
explains that she drove Ajax mad when he was on the point of
murdering the generals of the Greek army at Troy, she tells
Odysseus: "I shall reveal to you this visible sickness of his. . . .
Keep up your confidence [*tharsôn de mimne*], and do not consider the man to be a misfortune [*sunphoran*; i.e., to yourself].
For I shall prevent the twisted beams of his eyes from seeing
your visage" (66, 68–70). Inasmuch as Ajax is Odysseus' enemy,
Athena advises him to indulge in a sense of triumph, without
supposing that he has any part in the other's disaster. Odysseus,
however, reacts with alarm:

> OD. What are you doing, Athena? Don't call him out.
> ATH. Take it in silence and don't convict yourself of cowardice. . . .
>   What can happen? Wasn't he but a man?
> OD. And an enemy of mine, and still is.
> ATH. Isn't the sweetest laughter to laugh at enemies?
> OD. I'm satisfied that he remain inside.
> ATH. Do you tremble to see a madman in the open?
> OD. I'd not duck in fear if he were sane.
> ATH. But he won't see now though you stand near (74–83).

Athena pretends that Odysseus is physically afraid of Ajax, but
that is clearly not the reason why he wishes to avoid seeing him.
Rather, Odysseus is not disposed to enjoy the pleasure that
Athena offers him of rejoicing triumphantly in the complete destruction of Ajax, enemy or not. At this moment, Odysseus is in
the role of spectator to the action. Athena, who has humiliated
Ajax, is about to expose the insane hero to Odysseus' gaze and at
the same time to that of the public as well, and she offers everyone the opportunity to exult confidently in her total victory. But
Odysseus remains reluctant.

   After Ajax returns gloating to his tent, with the intention of
torturing the sheep that, in his madness, he confuses with Odysseus himself (105–13), Athena turns to Odysseus and says:

> ATH. Do you see, Odysseus, how great is the power of the gods? Who
>   ever had more foresight [*pronousteros*] than this man . . . ?
> OD. No one I know. Nevertheless, I pity him in his misfortune

[*epoiktirô de nin dustênon*], though he is my foe, because he has
been yoked by evil ruin [*atê*], and in this I have regard for my
condition no less than his: for I see that we who live are nothing
but figments, or a frail shadow.

ATH. Since you see this, never utter a proud word against the gods,
nor swell up for the weight of your hand or the depth of great
wealth. A day topples and restores again all human affairs
(118–32).

Athena and Odysseus agree that Ajax had been a good man, previous to his rage against the generals for awarding Achilles' arms
to Odysseus rather than to himself. Both his murderous fury, and
the god-inspired madness that causes him to mistake sheep for
men, are treated as a misfortune: Sophocles employs the archaic
term *atê* to capture the double sense of insanity and ruin. Because Odysseus recognizes the worth of Ajax, he is able to see
that he himself is also vulnerable to the kind of disaster that has
befallen him. To put it in Aristotelian terms, Odysseus perceives
Ajax as similar—*homoios*—to himself, his equal in forethought
and valor. Since he can thus identify with Ajax, the sight of his
wretched enemy does not fill him with empty confidence or induce him to gloat hubristically. For this reason, too, Odysseus is
capable of feeling pity, for, as Aristotle says, "people pity just
those things, when they happen to others, that they fear when
they happen to themselves."

Sophocles has created, in Odysseus, the model of an
Aristotelian spectator. As Odysseus watches, along with the actual audience, the spectacle of Ajax's misery, he responds with
just the right measure of identification—neither too close nor too
distant—that enables the feelings of pity for the other and fear in
his own behalf. In turn, he guides our own response, and human-
izes it, as opposed to the proud derision initially encouraged by
Athena: only the gods, it is implied, are in a position to enjoy
such confidence and security. The human condition is by nature
ephemeral, and subject to drastic alteration from one day to the
next.

In *Ajax*, Sophocles indicates that consciousness of our mortal
vulnerability to changes of fortune, and the capacity for empathy
with others that this inspires, are essential to social relations in a
democratic city-state. Ajax, in his famous deception speech, pretends that he has learned the need to accommodate to circumstances, since everything revolves in cycles: "For the future I'll
know to yield to the gods, and shall learn to revere the Atridae"
(666–67). But this is a lie, and Ajax, in his pride, kills himself

rather than endure the shame he has incurred. After Ajax's suicide, Menelaus and Agamemnon decide that his corpse should
remain unburied, because of his traitorous attempt to murder the
generals. Menelaus appeals to the need for stability in the *polis*:
"For never could laws in a city be decently sustained, where fear
[*deos*] is not established, nor could an army be wisely ruled if it
no longer had the shield of terror [*phobos*] and respect [*aidôs*]"
(1073–76).[7] Menelaus too appeals to the cycles in human affairs
(1079–88), but the fear he speaks of is fear of the authorities, not
the tragic fear of Aristotle, which depends on the understanding
that you are similar to the ruined man, and thus enables pity
rather than the haughtiness of Menelaus. Only Odysseus, aware
of his own vulnerability, is able to say of Ajax: "The man was
my enemy, but he was noble" (1355). Odysseus adds: "Many are
friendly now and hostile later" (1359), an insight that echoes the
words that Ajax himself uttered (679–83) in his deception
speech. Although Agamemnon in the end yields to Odysseus and
permits the burial of Ajax, he first exclaims: "It isn't easy for a
king to be reverend" (1350); the word I've translated as "king"
is, in the Greek, *turannos*, and the implication is clear: excessive
power leads to the kind of absolute confidence that, as Aristotle
understood, abolishes pity. In a democratic *polis* founded on
laws, citizens should recognize that they are, in principle, similar
to the others, save for differences in fortune.[8] The capacity for
tragic pity and fear is thus the basis, as Sophocles represents it,
of Athens' own civic life.

The setting of Euripides' *Hecuba*, which was probably composed in the late 420s, is Troy, immediately after the city has
fallen to the Greek army. Hecuba's condition is as wretched as
one can imagine. The great queen is reduced to slavery, her home
burnt to the ground, her male kin and fellow Trojans slain. In the
prologue, the ghost of her son Polydorus, who was sent to
Priam's ally in Thrace for his protection, explains that he has
been murdered by his host. Later, his body will wash up on the
Trojan shore, and Hecuba will have the opportunity to avenge his
death. In the first part of the action, however, she must helplessly
look on as her daughter, Polyxena, is led to slaughter. For Achilles' spirit has arisen above his tomb to demand that the girl be
sacrificed to his shade, thus to become his bride in Hades. As the
chorus of Trojan women relates, the Greek army was divided
about whether to make such a gruesome offering, but Odysseus
argued convincingly that doing honor to Achilles outweighs the
life of a mere slave (130–40).

Hecuba herself sings of her misery: "Oh wretched me, what shall I cry out, what howl, what lamentation?" (154–55). After she and Polyxena express their grief, Odysseus enters to lead Polyxena to the sacrifice (218). Hecuba reminds Odysseus of an occasion on which he was humble (*tapeinos*, 245) and in her power: though she had discovered his identity when he was spying inside the walls of Troy, Hecuba told no one and allowed him to escape. Then she admonishes Odysseus to take account of the changes in human fortunes: "It is not right that those in power use their power wrongly, nor that those who are lucky should imagine that they will always fare well; for I too once was what I no longer am" (282–84). Hecuba is appealing to Odysseus to recognize their common vulnerability, and on the basis of this perceived similarity to pity her. Odysseus, however, defends the necessity of honoring the fallen Greek soldiers in general, and Achilles in particular, in order to maintain the spirit of self-sacrifice that is required of soldiers. He then adds: "If you say that you are suffering pitiably, hear this: we have as many wretched old women and men as you, brides stripped of the finest grooms whose bodies this Trojan dust conceals. Endure!" (321–26). Hecuba turns to Polyxena and pleads: "Throw yourself pitiably at Odysseus' knees, and persuade him—you have a basis, he too has children—to pity your fate" (339–41). Polyxena, however, refuses to do so, for she proudly prefers to die rather than endure the pain and shame of slavery. Impressed by Polyxena's nobility, Odysseus concedes that he could wish her death did not have to be added to the rest (395), but he remains immune to Hecuba's entreaties. "You are pitiable, my child," Hecuba says to Polyxena when all hope is lost, "and I am a wretched woman" (417).

Unlike the Odysseus of Sophocles' *Ajax*, this Odysseus is invulnerable to pity for the fallen enemy. He bears no personal ill will toward Hecuba (she is not an *ekhthra*); indeed, he recognizes and is grateful for her earlier generosity toward him. But he does not feel enough of a connection or likeness to Hecuba to evoke deep compassion.[9] One may readily see why: he is a victorious Greek, she a defeated and enslaved foreigner; if it comes to pity for a woman's suffering, Odysseus is naturally inclined, as he says, to feel it rather for those mothers and wives who are related to him in nationality.[10] In spite of Hecuba's appeal to the changeability of fortune which affects all mortals, Odysseus does not fear for himself the kind of disaster that has overtaken the Trojan queen. As Aristotle says, pity arises "when the evil appears near"; nothing could be further from Odysseus' expecta-

tions for himself at this moment than the ruin that has befallen
Troy.

In Euripides' tragedy, Odysseus is not a spectator of
Hecuba's affliction, but part of the cause. The needs of his own
army, as he understands them, come into conflict with her well-
being, and in such a pass, Odysseus knows where his sympathies
lie. But what of the audience in the theater? Do we, or rather, did
they—the Athenians—feel pity for the unfortunate queen of
Troy? Let us consider the question in Aristotelian terms. Whom
did the ancient audience resemble? In the first place, they were
Greeks. In this respect, clearly, they were similar to Odysseus
rather than to Hecuba. In the second place, they were soldiers,
and at this moment in Athens' history undoubtedly confident of
their power, in the period following the Athenians' stunning victory over the Spartans at Pylos (425) which led in turn to the cessation of hostilities known as the Peace of Nicias (421). Finally,
they may have been men only: it is still debated whether women
attended the theater in classical Athens. Apart from a generalized
sense of the transience of human affairs, there is nothing that
would have induced in such spectators an identification with
Hecuba rather than with Odysseus. He is a fellow Greek warrior;
she a survivor among the conquered enemy; when, as Aristotle
says, the dramatic conflict is between enemies, or where there is
no *philia*, "there is nothing to move us to pity . . . except so far as
the actual pain of the sufferer is concerned" (14.1453b15–18).

"The actual pain [*pathos*]" can, to be sure, inspire pity in the
audience even when the characters in the drama, as enemies, are
immune to it. The Greeks may have found themselves identifying with Odysseus on the basis of their similarity to him; they
may very well also, as I believe, have approved his reasons for
insisting on the sacrifice of Polyxena.[11] The claims of a ghost are
normally to be respected in tragedy. Nevertheless, the vivid representation of Hecuba's suffering and the fall in her condition
can have aroused the pity of the Athenians, even if Odysseus,
who is immediately involved in the action, fails to be moved.
There are, indeed, grounds within the play for supposing that
Greeks might commiserate with Hecuba and Polyxena. The her-
ald Talthybius, when he accedes to Hecuba's request that he describe the sacrifice, replies: "You ask me to earn a double wage
of tears, lady, through pity for your daughter" (518–19). In the
very act of slaying the girl, Achilles' own son proves half unwilling to plunge the knife out of pity for her (566–67). In their empathy with Odysseus, then, the Athenians in the audience may

well have participated in the high confidence of the conquerors; like Talthybius and Neoptolemus, however, they may also have felt pity for Polyxena and perhaps for Hecuba as well, and the fear that is produced by the suffering of someone ultimately like oneself. Although Aristotle describes them as opposite emotions, moreover, there is no obvious reason why the Athenians should not have experienced both the confidence and the fear simultaneously.

In the second half of the play (beginning at l. 658), Hecuba discovers the treachery of her presumed Thracian ally,[12] Polymestor, and takes vengeance (cf. *timorein*, 749) by slaying his sons and blinding him into the bargain. Here, the audience is treated to a lively spectacle of revenge, with little obligation to identify closely with either party.[13] The basis of tragic pleasure lies elsewhere: as Aristotle says in the *Rhetoric* (1.11.13–14), "revenge is pleasant . . . , and victory is pleasant too, not only for those who are competitive but for everyone; for there arises a sense [or image: *phantasia*] of superiority, for which everyone has a passion, whether less or more."[14]

In an initial interview with Agamemnon, Hecuba describes Polymestor as a man who feared neither those below the earth nor those above in committing his unholy deed (791–92), and requests of Agamemnon: "Consider all these acts of his as shameful, and have respect for me, pity us—step back like a painter and look at me and observe the evils I endure; I was once a monarch [*turannos*] but am now your slave" (806–09). Agamemnon is thus invited to assume precisely the role of spectator, removed from the action. From this vantage point, he is able to respond to their common vulnerability, and he accepts Hecuba's supplication in pity, as he says, for her son and for her own misfortune (850–51). Later, when Polymestor, blind and childless, begs that Agamemnon avenge him, the Greek king refuses, in part because he violated his role as guest-friend or *xenos* (1244; cf. 1216, 774); his misfortune is deserved, and thus cannot, on Aristotle's definition, arouse pity. Neither is Polymestor ethnically related to Agamemnon. He is a pathetic spectacle, but there is no reason why he should arouse Agamemnon's fears: he himself broke no bonds of alliance with Hecuba or the Trojans. If there was anything to trouble his (or the audience's) aloof compassion for Hecuba, it can only have been the sight of a woman triumphing physically over a man—a barbarian man, however, and this materially softens the effect.[15]

In *Bacchae*, however, Euripides pushes to the furthest limit

the tension between triumphant confidence and pitiful abject-
ness. As the young Theban king, Pentheus, takes measures to
repress the worship of Dionysus (225–30), the chorus of Bacchants, in the first stasimon, celebrate piety, moderation, and
tranquillity as the highest values of their religion:

> Of unbridled mouths and lawless foolishness the end is misfortune,
> but thoughtfulness and a life of tranquillity remain stable and sustain a
> house. . . . Cleverness is not wisdom, nor is thinking beyond what is
> mortal. Life is short. For this reason, one who pursues great things
> cannot reap the present. These are the traits of mad and evil men, in
> my judgment. . . . What the most humble people think and practice,
> may I embrace (387–93, 397–402, 430–33).

While there is a large dose of escapism in the chorus' hopes for a
peaceful life,[16] their overall attitude is one of modesty and measure, to such an extent that, as Marilyn Arthur (now Katz) has
argued persuasively, they represent, at least in this phase of the
action, the ethical ideals of the Athenian audience itself.[17]

When Dionysus is imprisoned by Pentheus, the chorus are
shaken but retain their faith in his ability to save them. It is impossible to feel pity for Dionysus himself, because he is all-
powerful and has nothing to fear. It is Pentheus who, despite his
royal authority and bluster, is the vulnerable character in the
play. When Dionysus coldly seduces him into putting on
women's attire (828–36), and renders him mad, as Athena did
Ajax, so that he hallucinates a double sun in the sky, two cities
each with seven gates, and a bull in place of Dionysus himself
(918–23), the chorus thrill with triumph: "What is wisdom [*to
sophon*]? What finer reward from the gods among mortals than to
extend a conquering hand over the heads of one's enemies? What
is fine is ever pleasing" (877–8, 897–900). It is possible to see
their reaction as a sign of arrogance or barbarism, but they themselves continue to emphasize the importance of piety: "It comes
slowly, but divine might is trustworthy. It puts to the test mortals
who honor foolishness and, with mad beliefs, do not exalt the
gods" (882–87). This is more or less identical to what Athena
advises Odysseus in Sophocles' *Ajax*; as Carlos García Gual and
Luis Alberto de Cuenca y Prado rightly comment, "the chorus
takes refuge in traditional wisdom."[18] An exalted confidence at
the prospect of revenge and victory is, according to Aristotle, a
natural human sentiment. What is more, the chorus have no reason to feel pity at this moment for Pentheus: they see him as im-
pious and unjust, and, as barbarian women, they do not resemble

him in any of the ways that Aristotle regards as the basis for identification and empathy.

When a Theban messenger arrives on stage with the news of Pentheus' death, the chorus cry out in glee: "Lord Bromius, you reveal yourself to be a great god." The messenger soberly replies: "How's that? What have you said? Do you, woman, rejoice in the misfortunes of my rulers?"

> CHOR. I cry out as a foreigner in barbarian song. No longer shall I quiver in fear of bondage.
> MESS. Do you think Thebes unmanned?
> CHOR. Dionysus, Dionysus, not Thebes, has power over me.
> MESS. It's pardonable in you, but it is not good to rejoice over evils that have occurred (1031–41).

The chorus insist on their foreignness, and on the fact that they are not subject to the rule of Thebes. Though the messenger sounds a caution, he recognizes that the circumstances that arouse his pity and fear do not produce the same emotions in the hearts of these women, whom Pentheus had sought to punish and who are therefore his enemies. Even when they have heard the terrible details of Pentheus' slaughter, they react with elation: "Cadmean Bacchants, you have achieved a brilliant victory ode against groans and tears" (1160–62).

If the chorus are entitled to react with such uninhibited delight in their victory over Pentheus, what of the Athenian audience? Once we free ourselves of the belief that triumphal emotions are necessarily inappropriate to tragedy, we may suppose that the Athenians might well have shared the jubilation of the chorus, who after all are celebrating the success of a Greek god in castigating the irreverent disbelief of a mortal. True, these are barbarian women; but they speak, as we have seen, in the formulas of traditional Greek wisdom. Besides, Pentheus, as a Theban, is equally foreign to the Athenians, or nearly so: in the final years of the Peloponnesian War, there was little love between the two cities. The Athenians may very well have experienced a righteous pleasure at the humbling of an enemy king who had offended a god, and felt a deeper empathy with the restored confidence of the Bacchants than with Pentheus' misfortune.

At the same time, the grim spectacle of a mother dismembering her own son constitutes a case, if ever there was one, in which "the actual pain of the sufferer . . . moves us to pity." When Cadmus, at the end of the play, cries out before the lacerated pieces of Pentheus' corpse, "Now I am wretched, you [i.e.,

Pentheus] miserable, your mother pitiable, miserable your sisters" (1323–24), even the chorus leader is moved to say: "I suffer
your pain, Cadmus; your son's son has his deserved punishment,
but it is painful for you" (1327–28). But the Greek men in the
audience would have had an additional basis for identification
with Pentheus in their similarity to him as masculine, warlike,
and virtuous within his limitations: Pentheus' sin consists chiefly
in his resistance to introducing a new foreign cult into the city,
an event which the Athenians themselves had recently experienced with the importation of the Thracian festival of Bendis.[19]
Their view of Pentheus' death is thus likely to have had as much
in common with that of the Theban messenger as with the reaction of the chorus of Bacchants.

Euripides has produced, in *Bacchae*, a situation of conflicting identification: with one part of its psyche the audience enjoys
the triumph and high confidence of the Bacchants, while with
another it suffers with the doomed Pentheus. Aristotle speaks of
"the pleasure that pity and fear produce" (*Poetics* 14.1453b12),
but the tension in the self caused by contradictory simultaneous
emotions may be a more uniformly painful experience. When we
feel ourselves in the position of a victim, we are hostile to the
one who oppresses us; when we identify with the victor, we feel
contempt for the enemy we have defeated.[20] Normally, we locate
ourselves either in one position or the other; to experience both
exultation and pity at the same time is to feel hostility for that
part of ourselves that participates in the triumph of the winner
and contempt for that part that shares the defeat of the loser. I am
reminded of Aristotle's description of the psychological condition of wicked people (*phauloi*): "They neither rejoice nor con-
dole with themselves, for their souls are in a state of civil war
[*stasiazei*]" (*Nich. Ethics* 9.4.1166b18–19).

III

Aristophanes produced *Frogs* (405 B.C.) immediately after
the deaths of Euripides (406 B.C.) and Sophocles (405 B.C.),
which put an end to the great epoch of Athenian tragedy. In this
comedy, Aristophanes represents the descent to Hades of the god
Dionysus, patron of the Athenian theater, in order to resurrect
Euripides (66–67). When he arrives at Hades, however, Dionysus is asked to serve as judge of a contest (*agôn*) that was already
in progress between Euripides and Aeschylus (757–811), who
had died a half century earlier. Dionysus grants the victory to

Aeschylus, and it is he, rather than Euripides, whom he resurrects in the end.

Frogs thus presents a double image of the crisis of tragedy at the end of the fifth century B.C. On the one hand, the death of Euripides, followed shortly after by that of Sophocles, deprived the Greek theater, in Aristophanes' eyes at least, of its two greatest contemporary practitioners. The tragedians who survived these two are almost certain, Aristophanes suggests, to be of inferior quality. Without a doubt, this is a tribute to Euripides as a master of the tragic stage. On the other hand, Aristophanes evidently regarded Euripides himself as part of the problem that afflicted contemporary tragedy—a crucial part, given his preeminent status, along with Sophocles, in the second half of the century. It is for this reason that Aristophanes resurrects Aeschylus.

Of course, Aristophanes had made fun of Euripides in his earliest surviving comedy, *Acharnians* (425 B.C.), had put him on trial in *Thesmophoriazusae* (411 B.C.), and never tired of ridiculing phrases and themes from his plays. But what precisely did he find objectionable in Euripides' approach to tragedy? Various things, no doubt; but one point that has not received the attention it may deserve is the matter of tragic emotion and identification, which both pertains to the theme we are pursuing and offers, I believe, something of a new perspective on the nature of Aristophanes' critique of Euripides. Let us look first at *Acharnians*.

Dicaeopolis, the hero of *Acharnians*, wishes to dress up in the most wretched manner possible (*athliôtaton*) in order to convince the chorus of Acharnian charcoal sellers of his views concerning peace with Sparta (383–84); with this in mind, he approaches the house of Euripides to borrow some rags (393–94). Euripides emerges from his house dressed for one of his own dramas, and Dicaeopolis asks him: "But why are you wearing those rags from a tragedy, that pitiful [*eleeinên*] attire? No wonder you write about beggars. Anyway, I beg you by your knees, Euripides, give me some rag from an old play" (412–15). Euripides offers Dicaeopolis something worn by the unfortunate Oeneus, but Dicaeopolis insists on someone more wretched than he, more miserable than the blind Phoenix, more beggarly than the beggar Philoctetes, lame like Bellerophon, only a clever speaker as well. At last, Euripides realizes that Dicaeopolis is thinking of Telephus, the hero of a tragedy that Euripides had produced thirteen years earlier (438), and he gives him the desired garment.

To be sure, this is a caricature of Euripidean drama, and designed to be funny. But why should Aristophanes criticize the use of costumes that may arouse pity, as he himself acknowledges, in the audience? On Aristotle's criteria, one might have thought that Euripides was the perfect tragic poet. Now, Aristotle himself does offer some grounds for Aristophanes' attack on this aspect of Euripides' stagecraft (assuming it genuinely reflects a quality of his art). For in the *Poetics* he comments: "Those, however, who make use of the spectacle to put before us that which is merely monstrous [*to teratôdes*] and not productive of fear [*to phoberon*], are wholly out of touch with tragedy; not every kind of pleasure should be required of a tragedy, but only its own proper pleasure" (14.1453b8–11).[21] If Aristophanes means to convict Euripides of resorting to mere stage effects, Aristotle is with him on this point. But we must note, nevertheless, that Aristotle is not against the use of spectacle as such for the purpose of producing tragic emotion. Immediately before the passage just cited, he remarks: "The tragic fear and pity may be aroused by the spectacle; but they may also be aroused by the very structure and incidents of the play—which is the better way and shows the better poet" (14.1453b1–3). The story (*muthos*) itself, he explains, should, on a mere hearing, be able to arouse terror, like that of Oedipus. Aristotle, then, has no objection to use of spectacle, which is one of the six essential parts of tragedy, as he describes them. What he is evidently criticizing here is reliance on visual effects alone, when nothing in the plot produces the relevant emotional impact.

There is no reason to suppose, however, that the story of Telephus was a poor vehicle for pity and fear. Telephus had been wounded by Achilles while defending his city against the Greeks who, in one version of the myth, mistakenly attacked Mysia in the belief that they had landed at Troy. An oracle informed Telephus that he could only be healed by the one who had caused his injury; accordingly, he travelled to Argos to plead with Agamemnon, and disguised himself as a beggar in order to gain access to the palace. Why should Aristophanes have fastened on the pauper's clothing—a theme to which he returns several times in his comedies—as being particularly shocking or inappropriate to tragedy?[22]

Granted, kings dressed as beggars are easy to ridicule. Nevertheless, Aristophanes clearly found something offensive in Euripides' penchant for representing royal figures, and Greek ones at that—for Telephus turns out to be of Greek descent—in so abject a condition.[23] If this is the nature of tragic pity—and it is worth recalling that Aristotle called Euripides "the most tragic" (*tragikôtatos*) poet of all (*Poetics* 1453a29)—then Aristophanes parted company with Aristotle here, and felt that tragedy should ideally evoke a different emotional response.

To return now to *Frogs*: Euripides is represented in the poetry contest as excelling in "controversies, twists and turns" which thrill the worst element in Hades (774–76; cf. 954–57). Aeschylus, on the contrary, is portrayed as a figure of towering wrath, who responds to Euripides' challenge like an Ajax or an Achilles: "He rolls his eyes in terrible rage. There'll be helmeted contests of horse-hair crested arguments and the pin-slivers and parings of a mortal carpenter of wit defending himself against mounted phrases" (816–21). The contrast between Aeschylus and Euripides is reminiscent of that between the martial men of Marathon, as Aristophanes characterizes them in several comedies (e.g., *Wasps*), and the crafty sophists of his own time whom Aristophanes disparaged mercilessly in *Clouds*. To the fierce Aeschylus, Euripides appears as a "collector of phrases, beggar-maker and rag-stitcher" (841–42), a description that recalls Aristophanes' obsession with the *Telephus*. "A king covered in rags was something unheard of on the Attic stage at that time" comments Albin Lesky,[24] but Aristophanes is still harping on the theme more than thirty years after the original production.

Whereas Euripides affirms that he has taught the Athenians to speak and reason well (954–58), Aeschylus insists that he made the Athenians "breathe spears and lances and white-crested helms and helmets and greaves and seven-hided hearts" (1016–17). When Dionysus asks how Aeschylus achieved this, Aeschylus answers: "By writing a play that was full of Ares" (1021). "Which?" asks Dionysus. "The Seven Against Thebes," Aeschylus replies; "Everyone who saw it was fired with war-lust" (1021–22).

> DION. Badly done, for you gave the Thebans more heart for war. . . .
> AESCH. You too could have learned it, but you didn't pay it mind. Then I put on *Persians*, my masterpiece, and taught you ever to desire victory over your opponents. . . . This is what poets should make men practice (1023–30).

When Euripides defends his Phaedras on the grounds that such stories are true, Aeschylus admits as much, but says that "the poet should conceal what is vicious" (1053). Aeschylus then returns once again to Aristophanes' favorite topic, charging Euripi-

des with "draping kings in rags so that they may seem more pitiable [*eleinoi*] to the people" (1063–64). The result is, Aeschylus
says, that rich people now employ this tactic to evade their civic
responsibilities.

It is easy to imagine how Greek soldiers might have identified with Aeschylus' fierce and brave characters, but in what
way would his dramas have produced sentiments of fear and
pity? One has rather the impression that Aristophanes' Aeschylus
means to evoke the opposite emotions of indignation and confidence (*nemesis* and *tharsos*), as Aristotle defines them in the
Rhetoric: the Aeschylean audience seems invited to participate in
feelings of triumph rather than defeat, security and victory as
opposed to the compassion that derives from seeing a person like
oneself subjected to terrifying calamities to which all mortals are
vulnerable.[25] Of course, war is an ideal context in which to represent painful events. But Aeschylus, according to Aristophanes,
depicts his heroes responding not with a cry of anguish but with
a battle shout (cf. 1073). What Aeschylus objects to in Euripides'
account of Telephus is just the fact that Telephus is pitiable.

Aristophanes is a comic poet, and prone to satirical exaggeration. Is the simplistic picture he paints of the spirit of Aeschylean tragedy in fact fair to the great poet? Aeschylus cites, as we
have seen, his *Seven against Thebes* as an example of a "play full
of Ares," and claims that "everyone who saw it was fired with
war-lust." As it happens, Plutarch ascribes to the rhetorician
Gorgias exactly the same view.[26] Now, G. O. Hutchinson, in his
recent commentary on *The Seven* (xxxii), puts forward the view
that Aeschylus' tragedies, unlike those of his successors, may
each be characterized by a particular "atmosphere" that thoroughly pervades them: and, he adds, "when connoisseurs of the
fifth century called the *Septem meston Areôs*, they were responding to Aeschylus in the same sort of way."

To illustrate the martial character of *The Seven*, which
constitutes its dominant mood, Hutchinson comments: "On the
one hand, we have the Argives. The terrifying assault of the
whole army is forcefully described (59ff., 78ff., 287ff.). . . . But
still more terrifying are the furious passion and vigorous will of
the Seven to fight and destroy the city. . . . Their determination is
linked . . . with a superb and outrageous confidence in their own
powers, and defiance of the gods'" (xxxiii). Their impiety marks
the Seven as doomed to defeat, but since they are without fear
there is nothing in their demeanor to arouse the audience's pity.
"The other element in the martial atmosphere," Hutchinson con-

tinues, "is produced not so much by the Thebans as by Eteocles" (xxxiii), the son of Oedipus and brother of Polyneices, who is defending the besieged city with the intention of maintaining sole rule. According to Hutchinson, Eteocles is characterized by his shrewd and ironic language, his "contempt for frenzy and wild emotion, his self-control, his manly resolution and confidence," and his concern for the city and for moral excellence (xxxv).

Both the Argive attackers and Eteocles, then, are full of virile confidence. The element of fear is introduced by the chorus of Theban women, whose ethos, again in the words of Hutchinson, "is characterized especially by impassioned terror" (xxxvii). It is women who respond to danger with despair. Eteocles is firm and contemptuous of their anxiety. If the men in the audience identify more readily with Eteocles than with the panicky chorus, they will experience not the cowardly dread of the latter but the fierce indignation of the former.

The drama that Aristophanes' Aeschylus cites as his masterpiece is *Persians*. Here, the central figure of Xerxes does indeed cut a pathetic figure, as he returns to Persia defeated, humbled, and in torn robes (1019). The play ends with a long *kommos*, or song between chorus and actor, in which Xerxes laments his miserable fortune. But this apparent exception, in which Aeschylus puts on stage a king dressed in rags and wailing piteously, in fact proves the rule. For Xerxes is not a Greek but a barbarian or foreigner.[27] By the time he arrives, near the end of the play, his wife has already set the tone of womanish complaint, and by behaving in a similarly despondent manner Xerxes is subtly feminized as well.[28] Aeschylus may fairly claim that "with the Persians, my masterpiece, I inspired in you a burning desire always to conquer your enemies." As Dionysus says: "I was delighted when I heard of the death of Darius and the chorus clapped its hands and said, 'Wow!'" (1028–29), though Dionysus is confused about the story (Darius was long dead; his ghost appears) and the identity of the chorus, who are Persians and not Greeks.[29] The pleasure that Dionysus takes in this tragedy is anything but Aristotelian.

In advocating a style of tragedy that arouses *tharsos* or confidence rather than pity and fear, Aristophanes was, I suspect, taking part in a debate over the emotions proper to tragedy that was current in the late fifth century B.C.[30] In *Frogs*, Aristophanes posed the issue in polar terms: either compassion for the wretched, in the style of Euripides, or the Aeschylean mode of martial triumph. While Aristophanes came down on the side of

Aeschylus and the stimulation of a high spirits as the emotional
goal of tragedy, Aristotle preferred the evocation of pity. But
tragedy could be more complex than this, eliciting the conflicting
feelings of confidence and compassion simultaneously—and
thereby generating the kind of emotional *stasis* that Aristotle associated with the souls of wicked men.[31]

Brown University

NOTES

[1] This article draws extensively upon two previous papers of mine, published in
Spanish: "Las emociones trágicas," in Ana María González de Tobia, ed., *Actas del
Congreso: Una nueva visión de la cultura griega antigua en el fin del milenio, Synthesis*
vol. 5 (La Plata: Universidad de La Plata, forthcoming), and "Aristófanes sobre la com-
pasión y el temor," in Juan Antonio López Férez, ed., *Actas de las VI Jornadas Inter-
nacionales: Estudios Actuales sobre Textos Griegos (Comedia)* (Madrid: Universidad
Nacional de Educación a Distancia, 1998). Earlier versions of both papers were presented
as lectures for the course "La Crisis de la Tragedia Griega al Final del Siglo Quinto," held
under the direction of Professor Carlos García Gual at the Universidad Internacional
Menéndez Pelayo de Sandander in the summer of 1996. I am grateful to audiences at both
congresses and at the summer course for helpful comments and suggestions.

[2] See *Poetics* 6.1149b27–28; 9.1452a1–3; 11.1452a38–b1; 13.1452b32–53a6;
14.1453b1–5, 12–18; 19.1456b1; it is clearly a central topic in Aristotle's treatment of
tragedy. Cf. Plato's criticism of tragedy on the grounds that it undermines self-control
among citizens by legitimizing pity for the suffering of others (*Republic* 10.605C–606B);
cf. also *Philebus* 50B on emotion in drama. On the critical legacy of the *Poetics*, see
Amélie Oksenberg Rorty, ed., *Essays on Aristotle's Poetics* (Princeton: Princeton University Press, 1992). On Aristotle's conception of the emotions, see Alexander Nehamas,
"Pity and Fear in the *Rhetoric* and the *Poetics*," in David J. Furley and Alexander
Nehamas, eds., *Aristotle's Rhetoric: Philosophical Essays* (Princeton: Princeton Univer-
sity Press, 1994), 257–82, and the essays by John Cooper ("An Aristotelian Theory of the
Emotions"), Dorothea Frede ("Mixed Feelings in Aristotle's *Rhetoric*"), Stephen Leighton
("Aristotle and the Emotions"), Martha Nussbaum ("Aristotle on Emotions and Rational
Persuasion"), and Gisela Striker ("Emotions in Context: Aristotle's Treatment of the Pas-
sions in the *Rhetoric* and His Moral Psychology"), in Amélie Oksenberg Rorty, ed., *Essays on Aristotle's Rhetoric* (Berkeley: University of California Press, 1996).

[3] Unless otherwise indicated, all translations are my own.

[4] Cf. Leon Golden, "The *Poetics* for a Practical Critic" in Rorty, *Essays on Aristotle's Poetics*, 379–86. *Tharsos* commonly refers to a rush of confidence in combat, while
phobos indicates the collapse of self-possession that precedes a rout; the opposition between them was conventional, as in Thucydides 2.3.4, of the Plataeans attacking before
dawn the Theban force that had penetrated the city, "so that they might not fall upon them
in daylight, when they [the Thebans] would be more confident [*tharsaleôterois*] . . . , but
in the night when they were more in dread [*phoberôteroi*]."

[5] Trans. Bywater, in Jonathan Barnes, ed., *The Complete Works of Aristotle* (Princeton: Princeton University Press, 1984), 2326.

[6] For the meaning of *philia*, see David Konstan, *Friendship in the Classical World*

(Cambridge: Cambridge University Press, 1997) 9, 55–56, 68–70.

[7] One may compare Athena's remarks on the need for fear in civic society in Aeschylus, *Eumenides* 696–700.

[8] Compare the principle enunciated by Robert Reich, former Secretary of Labor of the United States, "Broken Faith: Why We Need to Renew the Social Contract," *The Nation* 266.5 (16 February 1998): 15, "any social compact is premised on 'it could happen to me' thinking." Reich adds, in reference to what he sees as the progressive disintegration of the compact in the United States: "Today's wealthy and poor, however, are likely to have markedly different life experiences."

[9] I am not persuaded by Judith Mossman (*Wild Justice: A Study of Euripides' Hecuba* [Oxford: Clarendon Press, 1995], 116) that "Odysseus appears arrogant and unjust," or that "Euripides ruthlessly undercuts his moral standing" (117).

[10] Cf. Ann Norris Michelini, *Euripides and the Tragic Tradition* (Madison: University of Wisconsin Press, 1987), 147: "For Odysseus, when Greek suffering is juxtaposed with Trojan suffering, the former alone is worthy of consideration. Further, unlike the other speakers, who profess pity at Hekabe's suffering, Odysseus alone is unmoved."

[11] See E. A. M. E. O'Connor-Visser, *Aspects of Human Sacrifice in the Tragedies of Euripides* (Amsterdam: B .R. Grüner, 1987), 66: "human sacrifice in general has been adopted by Euripides as a mythical theme, the rights and wrongs of which are not called into question"; O'Connor-Visser adds (67) that while the Greeks at large may be seen as free of blame in the *Hecuba*, "we are made to regard Odysseus as a wrongdoer in the first half" because of his trip to Troy where he received assistance from Hecuba. If the Greek audience, unlike the army represented in the play, was unambivalent about the sacrifice, Odysseus will not have lost its sympathies as a result of this single argument among the many that enter into Hecuba's plea to him.

[12] *Xenos*: cf. vv. 6, 19, 26, 710, 774, 1216, etc.

[13] On Greek attitudes toward revenge, see Mossman, *Wild Justice*, 169–77; Mossman does not cite the passage in Aristotle's *Rhetoric*.

[14] Cf. David Quint, *Epic and Empire* (Princeton: Princeton University Press, 1993), 18: "Ercilla's poem [*La Araucana*] belongs among the epics of the anti-imperial losers; but the passage [8.16.5–19.4] also suggests with clear-sighted realism that the losers who attract our sympathies today would be—had they only the power—the victors of tomorrow."

[15] That "Hecuba is all exultation" after taking her grisly revenge on Polymestor (Mossman, *Wild Justice*, 190) need not have alienated the Athenian audience, whatever its effect may be on modern sympathies; the question Mossman poses is: "What then do *we* think of Hecuba?" (my emphasis).

[16] Cf. Hans Oranje, *Euripides' Bacchae: The Play and its Audience* (Leiden: E. J. Brill, 1984), 108.

[17] See Marilyn Arthur, "The Choral Odes of the *Bacchae* of Euripides," *Yale Classical Studies* 22 (1972): 145–79.

[18] *Eurípides Tragedias*, vol. 3 (Madrid: Gredos, 1979), 385 n. 54.

[19] I do not see the need for the distinction drawn by Oranje, *Euripides' Bacchae*, 97–98, who concludes that in this scene Euripides "does not aim primarily at arousing

fear, but pity."

[20] Contrast Doris Adler, *Philip Massinger* (Boston: Twayne, 1987), 16: "[The] nature of drama and the primary purpose of dramatic satire . . . is ostensibly to effect change by persuading one either to identify with the victim or to face one's untenable role as an abuser, [although] the more prevalent function may well be to provide a moment of comforting and justifying escape."

[21] Trans. Bywater, in Jonathan Barnes, ed., *The Complete Works of Aristotle.*

[22] A. G. Geddes ("Rags and Riches: The Costume of Athenian Men in the Fifth Century," *Classical Quarterly* 37 [1987]: 313) notes that actors, especially in dramas that had an eastern setting, wore lavish garments (as opposed to the fifth-century Athenian preference for modest attire, in accord with the democratic emphasis on fitness and egalitarianism), and suggests (314) that for his Telephus Euripides may have cut expensive clothes into rags; the contrast with generic conventions, however, is quite enough to explain the effect that Euripides produced.

[23] On Telephus' nationality, see T. B. L. Webster, *The Tragedies of Euripides* (London: Methuen, 1967), 47; for the reconstruction of the play, Webster, 43–48; C. Collard, M. J. Cropp, and K. H. Lee, eds. and trans., *Euripides: Selected Fragmentary Plays* (Warminster: Aries and Phillips, 1995), 1.17–52; chapter 3 in Gregory W. Dobrov, *Figures of Play: Greek Drama and Metafictional Poetics* (New York: Oxford University Press, 1998). A fragment of Accius' adaptation (frag. VII Ribbeck) suggests that Euripides' play may have appealed explicitly to the pity of the audience: *nam huius demum miseret, cuius nobilitas miserias nobilitat*, which Webster (45) translates: "there is pity for him whose nobility ennobles his pitifulness." For Aristophanes' use of the *Telephus* story, see also Helene Foley, "Tragedy and Politics in Aristophanes' *Acharnians*," *Journal of Hellenic Studies* 108 (1988): 33–47; the bibliography for chapter 3 in Dobrov.

[24] *Historia de la literatura griega*, trans. J. M. Díaz Regañón and B. Romero (Madrid: Gredos, 1976 [orig. 1963]), 397.

[25] Jacqueline de Romilly (*L'évolution du pathétique d'Eschyle à Euripide* [Paris: Belles Lettres, 1980], 86) suggests that the contrast between Aeschylus and Euripides is that the former tended to inspire fear, the latter pity (cf. 16); but Aristophanes emphasizes valor rather than terror as the proper effect of Aeschylean drama.

[26] "Gorgias says that one of the tragedies by this author [Aeschylus], *The Seven Against Thebes*, is full of Ares" (Plutarch, *Quaestiones conviviales* 7.10.2, 715E); Aristophanes was presumably quoting Gorgias' comment, but G. O. Hutchinson suggests that "Plutarch's phrasing" may have been influenced by Aristophanes: Hutchinson ed., *Aeschylus: Septem contra Thebas* (Oxford: Clarendon Press, 1985), xxxii n. 13.

[27] See P. E. Easterling, "Gods on Stage in Greek Tragedy," in *Religio Graeco-Romana: Festschrift für Walter Pötscher*, Grazer Beiträge Supplementband 5 (Graz-Horn, 1993), 80; Christopher Pelling, "Aeschylus' *Persae* and History," in C. Pelling, ed., *Greek Tragedy and the Historian* (Oxford: Clarendon Press, 1997), 16–19.

[28] Shelby Brown, citing J. T. Sammons (*Beyond the Ring: The Role of Boxing in American Society* [Chicago: University of Illinois Press, 1988], 34–44) and G. Wills ("Blood Sport," *New York Review of Books* [18 February 1988], 6), reports that "American fight films were banned after 1910, largely in response to the racially charged defeat of white fighter James Jeffries by black fighter Jack Johnson, so that viewers could not see a black man beating a white. The spectator, assumed to be a white male or to share his values, could not be subjected to watching someone like himself lose": "Death as Decoration: Scenes from the Arena on Roman Domestic Mosaics," in Amy Richlin, ed., *Pornography*

and Representation in Greece and Rome (New York: Oxford University Press, 1992), 183. Brown explores the working of pity in connection with the Roman gladiatorial combats: "Most beasts of the arena, and many people, did not warrant any fellow feeling"; she notes that "on one recorded occasion when the crowd did pity the animals in the arena, the show was a failure" (cf. Cicero. *Ad fam.* 7.1.3, Dio Cassius 39.38.1–4).

[29] There are problems with the text of 1028. "Wow!" translates *iauoi*, which the *Oxford Greek-English Lexicon* (9th ed.), with this passage in mind, defines as a cry of grief (this is the only instance of the word cited); in that case, Dionysus is right about the identity of the chorus. Kenneth Dover comments that "clapping the hands usually expresses pleasure," but adds that "evidently one way of clapping could express grief, or could be regarded by Greeks as an Asiatic expression of grief": Dover, ed., *Aristophanes: Frogs* (Oxford: Clarendon Press, 1993), 321 and 1029.

[30] Neil O'Sullivan, *Alcidamas, Aristophanes, and the Beginnings of Greek Stylistic History* (Stuttgart: Franz Steiner Verlag, 1992), argues persuasively that Aristophanes exploits, in *Frogs*, a developed critical vocabulary; cf. also Maria de Fátima Sousa e Silva, *Crítica do teatro na comédia antiga* (Coimbra: Instituto Nacional de Investigação Científica, 1987), 301–62; Monica Centanni, "L'Eccitazione e la temperatura delle passioni: l'estetica del tragico da Platone ad Aristotele," *Annali dell'Istituto Universitario Orientale de Napoli* 17 (1995 [appeared 1996]): 76, "Ma la teoria estetica sugli sconcertanti effetti di terrore e commozione della poesia, soprattutto tragica, non è certo un'invenzione originale di Aristotele: la dottrina di *eleos* e *phobos*, già *communis opinio* nel dibattito culturale della fine del V secolo, era stata acutamente analizzata e descritta da Platone." For Aristotle's theory as a response to Plato's, see Olympiodorus *In Platonis Gorgiam* 1.172; Proclus *In Rempublicam comm.* 1.49 (ed. Wilhelm Kroll); Centanni 84–85; cf. also G. Cerri, "L'Apporto teorico del *Filebo* alla dottrina poetica dell'*eleos* e del *phobos*," *Filologia Antica e Moderna* 5–6 (1994): 9–37.

[31] There has been recent discussion concerning the emotions that Aristotle might have defined in the lost second book of the *Poetics*, as characteristic of comedy, corresponding to pity and fear in the case of tragedy (see, for example, Janko and Golden in Rorty, *Essays on Aristotle's Poetics*). I am of the opinion that he would have identified them precisely as *tharsos* and *nemesis*, the opposites of the tragic pair; these correspond well to the spirit of Aristophanic humor, which enjoyed presenting humble figures who are full of brash confidence and who overcome all challenges to achieve their goals. On the steadfast self-assurance of the Aristophanic hero, cf. Cedric H. Whitman, *Aristophanes and the Comic Hero*, Martin Classical Lectures 19 (Cambridge, Massachusetts: Published for Oberlin College by Harvard University, 1964) and Dana Ferrin Sutton, *Self and Society in Aristophanes* (Lanham, Maryland: University Press of America, 1980); see also David Konstan, *Greek Comedy and Ideology* (New York: Oxford University Press, 1995). In awarding the prize to Aeschylus in the poetry contest with Euripides, then, Aristophanes may also have been privileging the heroic resolution and militancy that were typical of his own art. (For a different view of how Aristophanes presents comedy as the solution to the crisis of tragedy, see Bruce Heiden, "Tragedy and Comedy in the *Frogs* of Aristophanes," *Ramus* 20 [1991]: 95–111.)

Killed by Words:
Grotesque Verbal Violence
and Tragic Atonement
in French Passion Plays[1]

Véronique Plesch

C'est la violence qui constitue le coeur véritable et l'âme secrète du
  sacré.
Violence is the heart and secret soul of the Sacred.[2]

In his classic essay *Violence and the Sacred* René Girard
explained that the sacrificial victim "unwittingly conjures up a
baleful, infectious force that his own death—or triumph—trans-
forms into a guarantee of order and tranquillity."[3] In the context
of the Christian theology of redemption, Christ's sufferings are
indeed directly connected to the atonement of humanity; and so it
could be said that the more Christ suffers, the better the atonement. I have had the occasion to study how in French Passion
plays of the fourteenth and fifteenth centuries the dramatic matter grows, from the earliest ones in the fourteenth century, in
which a few thousand lines suffice to tell Christ's story, to the
fifteenth-century cyclical monuments—not to say monsters—
which were performed over several days. I have shown how in
that textual expansion the sequences devoted to Christ's torments
are fundamental; indeed, I have argued that they are expanded
because they are important and the modalities of their expansion
are rooted in their meaning.[4]

In this essay I would like to take a closer look at the issue of
verbal violence against Christ. After all, even in the silent medium of pictorial arts, we find suggestion of words being uttered
through open mouths. In depictions of passion scenes the degrad-
ing nature of the words is implied by the ugly and caricatured
features of the henchmen, often reinforced by the offensive gestures they perform.[5] On the stage, even though torture is obviously of a primarily physical nature, the playwrights always
strive to include speech in scenes of torment. The reasons are

several. If left mute these scenes would no doubt be perceived as less important than spoken ones. Words can help convey to the public more information about the actions enacted on stage and thereby increase their suggestive impact. Dialogue can also indicate what gestures should be performed; stage directions are certainly insufficient means to orchestrate such complex choreographic events. But more important, the presence of verbal abuse, by literally "adding insult to injury," increases Christ's sufferings.

In the Gospels we find several passages in which Christ is verbally assaulted. There is of course the Mocking, when Christ is blindfolded, hit, and then asked to "prophesy"—to guess who hit him.[6] Luke reports how, before sending Christ back to Pilate, Herod clad him in a white garment "and mocked him."[7] Then comes the mock ceremony of the Crowning with Thorns, also accompanied by words: "And platting a crown of thorns, they put it upon his head, and a reed in his right hand, and bowing the knee before him, they mocked him, saying: Hail, king of the Jews."[8] At the Crucifixion passers-by "blasphemed him, wagging their heads, and saying: Vah, thou that destroyest the temple of God, and in three days dost rebuild it: save thy own self if thou be the Son of God, come down from the cross."[9] Christ is also mocked by the chief priests, along with the scribes and ancients; and finally, before giving up the ghost, either one or both thieves "revile him."[10]

In the spectacular textual expansion that characterizes French passion plays, verbal violence features prominently among the means used to develop the Gospel narrative. In elaborating upon this aspect the playwrights were certainly legitimated by the Gospels: Luke (22:65) wrote that during the Mocking Christ's tormentors were "blaspheming, many other things they said against him," thus encouraging exegetes and other writers on the Passion to flesh out the account. Kurt Ruh and Frederick Pickering were among the first to elucidate how medieval writers conducted this quest for details, and how the Old Testament provided a source.[11] Pickering explained how "important and revered metaphors and figures of prophecy could be translated into 'realistic' incident" from Christ's life.[12] Isaiah 1:6, for example, describes a male figure covered with wounds: "From the sole of the foot unto the top of the head, there is no soundness therein: wounds and bruises and swelling sores." This passage consequently leads to scenes in which henchmen take great care to hit Christ throughout his body, so as to realize Isaiah's prophecy.[13]

Old Testament sources likewise address the issue of verbal violence: Isaiah 53:3, for example, describes a man "despised and rejected of men."

When playwrights stage incidents of physical violence from the Gospels, they try, as much as possible, to include verbal abuse. During the appearance before Caiaphas when, as John recounts, Christ is hit by an officer, playwrights always develop the words which in the Gospel accompany the blow: "Answerest thou the high priest so?"[14] In the fourteenth-century *Passion Sainte-Geneviève*, not only does the officer give Christ two blows—and not just one, as in the Scripture—but he adds menaces, derides Christ's answer to the high priest, and finally concludes with irony:

> Demain en tel jour enterras!
> Garde a qui tu diz ces paroles,
> qui sont assez nissez et foles.
> Par fierté vas respondre trufes.
> Cy me garderas ces .ii. bufes;
> Je t'ay trouvé, tant t'é queru.[15]

> (Tomorrow you will be in quite a day,
> Beware of to whom you say these words,
> they are quite silly and insane.
> With pride you answer banter.
> Here, keep these two blows;
> I looked for you and found you.[16])

Of course, by the time we reach the fifteenth century and Gréban's *Passion*, the aspect of verbal violence combined with the blow is fully developed, with the officer (Dragon in this case) expanding the "Sic respondens pontifici," insisting on the interrogation by multiplying it:

> Et, villain, esse la maniere
> de respondre au pontife ainsi?
> A qui parlez vous, sire? A qui?
> Esse le bien que vous sçavez?
> Et pour ce que mesprins avez,
> vous en arez ceste soufflace.[17]

> (So, villain, is this the way
> to answer the pontifex?
> To whom are you talking, lord? To whom?
> Is this the best you know?
> And because you are so wrong,

you will have this blow.)

The blow provokes an ironically satisfied response from Annas:

> Tu dis vray, tu es en ma grace:
> c'est fait d'un tres gentil vassal. (G 19,563–64)

> (You are right, you are in my grace:
> this is the deed of a very nice vassal.)

Christ answers in four very dignified lines very close to the Gospels and his reply provokes yet more verbal abuse: he is called "villain maloustru" ("boorish villain," [G 19,569]) and "vieulx mastin" ("old dog," [G 19,571]) and is promised more torments (G 19,572–74).

Later, when Caiaphas orders torture—

> Oÿ, faictes lui hardiment
> du senglant pis que vous pourrés:
> ja tant de mal ne lui ferés
> que nous n'en soyons bien content. (G 20,791–94)

> (Yes, do to him
> the bloody worst that you can.
> You cannot harm him enough
> to content us.[18])

—the sequence that follows systematically matches physical and verbal abuse. The *rondeau-triolet* form rhythmically organizes the beatings,[19] while insisting on the insults:

Malcus	Ose tu semer telz langaiges, truant plus que ratruandi?
	(Dare you sow such lies, wretch who has become even more wretched?)
Dragon	Devant nos seigneurs haulx et saiges, ose tu semer telz langaiges?
	(In front of our high and wise lords, do you dare sow such lies?)
Gueulu	Au peuple presches et langaiges tout contre la loy.

(You preach to the people and speak
wholly against the law.)

Estonné   Truant, dy
ose tu semer telz langaiges
truant plus que ratruandi? (G 20,799–806)

(Say, wretch,
do you dare sow such lies,
wretch who has become even more wretched?)

Then the *tirans* take turns spitting upon Christ, and again words
and actions are coupled:

Bruyant   Fy du paillard rappaillardy!

(Fie on the rogue fallen into roguery!)

Malcuidant   Fy du faulx traïstre enchanter!

(Fie on the false, traitorous enchanter!)

Bruyant   C'est dommaige qu'on ne l'ardi
passé dix ans, ce faulx barter.

(It's too bad that he wasn't burned
ten years ago, this false deceiver.)

Dragon   Fy du larron!

(Fie on the thief!)

Goulu   Fy du menteur!

(Fie on the liar!)

Estonné   Fy du desloyal garnement!

(Fie on the disloyal rascal!)

Bruyant   Fy du plus mauvais seducteur
qui soit dessoubz le firmament! (G 20,807–14)

(Fie on the most evil deceiver
under the heavens.)

Passion plays also include new events not found in the Gospels, which are the product of exegetical elaborations. Such is the case of the night following Christ's arrest, which offers the occasion for the playwright to squeeze in more torture.[20] There too verbal violence comes to complement physical abuse. Already the *Passion des Jongleurs* stated:

> Einsi l'ont toute nuit gabé,
> Et escopi et deboute
> Tres qu'au demain que li jors fu.[21]

> (In that manner they mocked him throughout the night
> And spat upon and hit him
> Until the morning came.)

This is also the case in the *Passion d'Arras*.[22] After Caiaphas leaves the prisoner, ordering the guards:

> Esbatez vous jusques au jour,
> Et si vous gardez de dormir. (A 11,921–22)

> (Entertain yourselves until the morning,
> and beware of falling asleep.)

Christ is seated, as the three *Juifs de Sidon* along with Malchus proceed to torture him. Physical abuse is intensified by the derisive nature of the henchmen's remarks: they pretend Jesus is enthroned like a king, they ask him to tell jokes, they strike him by way of salute, they spit upon him, and compare their spittle to diamonds (A 11,941–12,082).

In Gréban as well, the prisoner's night of captivity is occupied by physical and verbal abuse. Roillart the henchman assures Annas:

> Nostre esbat est ja tout pourveu:
> a riens ne nous voulons esbatre
> sinon a le torcher et batre
> si nous en *mocquer* entre nous. (G 19,738–41; italics mine)

> (Our entertainment is all decided:
> we do not want to entertain ourselves
> in any other way but to beat and hit him
> and *to mock him* among ourselves.)

When later they are too exhausted to pursue physical torture, Dentart suggests:

Si nous reposons ung petit
icy et, en lieu de bastures,
combatons le de grans injures
tant que ceste nuit soit parfaicte. (G 19,841–44)

(Let us rest a bit
here, and, instead of beatings
let's fight him with great insults
until the end of this night.)

And indeed, twenty-seven lines of mockeries follow in which Gadiffer, Roillart, and Dentart mock Christ for pretending to be a prophet and the Messiah, for his preaching and his miracles, calling him "larron tant infame," ("such an infamous thief" [G 19,850]), "villain" (G 19,8553), "coquin" ("scoundrel" [G 19,869]), "putier" ("debauched" [G 19,869]), paillard," ("rogue" [G 19,870]), "vray fol" ("real madman" [G 19,870]), "villain papellart" ("hypocritical villain" [G 19,873]).

Another event not mentioned per se in the Gospels but developed by the exegetes is the *ductio Christi*, the leading of Christ from one place of his trial to another.[23] Again, in the staging of these episodes, the playwrights systematically include verbal abuse. As elsewhere during the Passion, we find purely gratuitous mockeries, as well as the promise for more torture. Specific to these scenes are the injunctions the henchmen hurl at Christ to make him quicken his pace—for example, suggesting that Christ is walking slowly because he is asleep,[24] or mocking his slow pace, comparing it to that of a clergyman, as in *Semur*: "Il me sanble que vous moignez" ("you seem to be walking like a monk")[25]; and in Gréban: "Ce paillard ne vueult cheminer:/ comment vient il a pas d'evesque!" ("This rogue does not want to walk: see how he walks like a bishop" [G 19,245–46]), or as a bride: "Allez vous a pas d'espousee?" ("Are you walking slowly, like a bride?" [G 20,232]). In all these instances, Christ's willingness to submit to his tormentors' will produces a contrast heavy with meaning. The prisoner appears as Isaiah's sheep led to slaughter (53:7) and Jeremiah's "meek lamb, that is carried to be a victim" (11:19–20). For whatever the abuse, Christ kindly responds, as in *Arras*: "J'iray debonnairement,/ mes amis, où il vous plaira" ("I will willingly go, my friends, wherever you want" [A 13,429–30]).

Of course insults represent a very important part of the verbal abuse inflicted upon Christ, participating in the extraordinary expansion of the dramatic matter.[26] In the *Palatine Passion* of circa 1300 *truant* (adjective and substantive, meaning "despicable," "rascal," "wretch") is the insult of choice. In several instances it is reinforced by ironic or insulting terms, as in "Sire truant" (P 273, 597, 609), or "faus truans ypocrites" ("false hypocritical rascal" [P 224]). Half a century later, in the *Passion Sainte Geneviève* some variety is introduced, as when Herod says to Christ: "tu es fol et meschant et nice" ("you are crazy and wretched and foolish" [SG 1,945]). Christ is often called *glout*, "scoundrel,"[27] and this insult is in many cases reinforced by adjectives, as in "faulx glout" ("false scoundrel" [SG 1,489]), "mauvais glous" ("bad scoundrel" [SG 1,500]), "glouton traïte" ("traitorous scoundrel" [SG 1,530]). "Deputaire" ("despicable") is also common, both as a substantive (SG 1,661) and as an adjective, qualifying Christ's heart (SG 1,553; 1,826; 2,016). By the time we reach the mid–fifteenth century and Gréban, not only does the amount and variety of verbal chastening reach new proportions, but in many instances one finds groups of two or three insulting terms, such as in "faulx traïstre enchanteur" ("false, traitorous enchanter" [G 20,808]), "vieulx truant detestable" ("detestable old rogue" [G 23,947]), "mauvais fol perilleux" ("evil, dangerous fool" [G 25,005]).

Despite their abundance, the corpus of insults hurled at Christ tends to be drawn from three main semantic fields. An important part refers to people at the bottom of the social scale, peasants and outcasts ("glout," "truant," "villain," etc.). Other prevalent sources for insults are hypocrisy and deceitfulness —reinforced by the repeated use of the adjective "false"—as well as stupidity and folly. The *Palatinus*'s overwhelming use of *truant* may be explained by the polysemy of the word. To the basic meaning mentioned above (despicable, rascal), it evolved into a secondary one of beggar or tramp, eventually reaching its modern French meaning of crook, gangster. In the *Palatinus*, Jesus is also accused of engaging in *truanderie*, a substantive derived from the verb *truander*, to beg. Derivations using the prefix *–erie* became popular in the fifteenth and sixteenth centuries, probably due to their affective value and their popular character. They are usually derived from verbs designating a reprehensible action and as a result, are likewise endowed with a pejorative meaning.[28] *Truant* thus belongs to the above mentioned category of outcasts, while also containing a notion of deceit. The element of mendacity and poverty is particularly interesting since a Franciscan influence has been detected in the *Palatinus*.[29]

In a way, none of these insults is purely gratuitous, for all three categories can be connected to textual sources. We have seen how the fundamental notion of poverty leads some characters to consider Christ and his disciples outcasts. The accusation of folly is of course derived from the Gospel scene of Herod clothing Jesus in the white robe of the mad,[30] while deceitfulness can be derived from his miracles and from the accusation that he had affirmed himself able to destroy and rebuild the Temple in three days.[31] This is forcefully stressed in the scornful words Christ receives on the cross:

Jheroboam	Vath du mauvais fol perilleux
	qui as voulu le peuple instruire
	de pouoir le temple destruire
	et en trois jours rediffier!

(Fie on the evil, dangerous fool
who wanted to tell the people
of his ability to destroy the temple
and rebuild it in three days.)

Mardocee	Tu t'es par trop voulu fÿer
	en ton faulx art, j'en suis tesmoing,
	car, quant c'est venu au besoing,
	le dyable, a qui tu as servy,
	te laisse a la mort asserv y
	tant qu'il n'est, par art de magicque
	ne par mal ou ton corps s'applicque
	que tu en saiches eschapper. (G 25,005–16)

(You wished to trust too much
your false art; I am a witness to this,
for now that you need help,
the devil, whom you served,
leaves you enslaved to death,
so that there is no magic art
nor evil that you can use
in order to escape.)

A recurring insult in the field of deceitfulness is that of being a sorcerer, hence the references in the passage quoted above to the "faulx art" and "art de magicque."[32] The suggestion of Christ's being a devil's devotee is also based on scriptural grounds, on episodes such as the Pharisee who declares, while witnessing a miracle, "This man casteth not out the devils but by Beelzebub the prince of the devils."[33] Miracles such as the raising of Lazarus and the curing of Malchus's ear are attributed to his activities as an enchanter.[34] In the *Passion Sainte Geneviève*, there is no irony in this accusation: Christ's enemies believe in that magic, even though they consider it to be of an evil nature. This is indeed the case when, during the Mocking, Haquin menaces Christ and affirms:

> Tu as resuscité le Ladre
> Par ton malvais enchantement;
> Mais se li evesques ne ment,
> Encor le comparras tu chier. (SG 1,652–55)

> (You raised the Leper [Lazarus]
> with your bad spell
> but if the bishop does not lie,
> you'll pay dearly for it.)

In the *Passion d'Arras*, on the other hand, the topic is always addressed in a sarcastic mode, as does for example "Le Premier de Sidon" when Christ is brought before Pilate:

> Et n'esse mie l'enchanteur
> Lequel juoit de passe passe?
> Il a fait mainte bonne farse
> En Nazareth et Galilée. (A 12,836–39)

> (Isn't this the enchanter
> Who did sleight-of-hand tricks?
> He made many good jokes
> In Nazareth and Galilee.)

I would suggest that "apoticaire" ("apothecary" [A 14,502 and 16,534]) and "maistre Ypocras" (A 14,508) should also be included in this discussion—whether the later is to be understood as "master Hippocrates" or "master Hippocras," as in the wine with spices, which was named after the Greek physician. As Léon Poliakov writes, "[W]hat is a physician? He was, in the past, a sorcerer, and is, even today, in the particular relation that links the patient to the doctor, a figure who detains an august and essential power. In fact, a physician always remains somewhat of a magician."[35] In this context we can also consider these two burlesque epithets: "maistre triacleur" ("master theriacker" [A 14,720])[36] and "maistre Aliboron" (G 22,890). Both are indeed related to medicine: a theriac is a preparation used as an antidote to bites of poisonous animals, while Maître Aliboron, a stock

figure of late-medieval French theater, is "the incapable learned,
the pedantic charlatan, the pretentious ignorant, the imbecile who
tries to pass as a scholar, sometimes pharmacist, sometimes physician."[37] The name Aliboron most likely comes from the helle-
bore, a medicinal plant, which was first thought to be able to cure
madness, but which ended up becoming in the Middle Ages the
proverbial panacea of the charlatans. However sarcastic, these
epithets are meaningful, for they call to mind the traditional metaphor of Christ as the physician who cures the illness of sin. It
recurs time and again in preaching,[38] and Gréban's characters
Joseph le Juste and Tubal, during one of Christ's appearances
after his death, say so: "Tu es medecin et mire" ("You are physician and healer" [G 31,963 and 31,975]).[39] Health, indeed, figures prominently among the imprecations hurled (directly or indirectly) at Christ, for most of these curses involve illness, as in
"Que la male fievre vous tienne" ("May the bad fever possess
you" [S 6,384]), "La mal passion l'abate!" ("May he be destroyed by the plague" [P 586 and 642]).

   Christ is also addressed with ironical titles. "King," for instance, is derived from the Gospels—in this case, from the derisive ceremony of the Crowning with Thorns,[40] although in the
Passion Sainte-Geneviève the vocative use of the title is found in
the mouths of Christ's enemies during many other Passion episodes: the *ductio Christi*, the Mocking, the Flagellation, the Way
to Calvary, the Nailing to the Cross, and the Crucifixion.[41] In
some of these instances *roy* is qualified, as in "faulx roy" ("false
king" [SG 1,604]), "bon roy" ("good king" [SG 2,110]),
"meschant roy" ("evil king" [SG 2,364]), "mauvais roy trahistes"
("bad traitor king" [SG 2,547]). In addition to the instances just
discussed of "maistre Ypocras," "Aliboron," and "triacleur," the
title "Master" recurs throughout the corpus of French Passion
plays. In the *Passion de Semur*, we find an interesting instance of
the ironic use of titles, their derisive effect being reinforced when
Christ is told: "Avant, maistre damp vavassour" ("Come on,
master viscount vassal" [S 6,377]).[42] "Maistre" is at times understood as master in theology: "Preschez nous cy de voz devis,/
maistre docteur de Gallillee" ("Do preach some of your precepts,
master doctor of Galilee" [G 19,861–62]). Ironical appellations
often refer to Christ's religious status, as in the examples quoted
above from *Semur* and Gréban when henchmen complain about
his walking too slowly. In Gréban, we also find a henchman designating the prisoner as "cest official" (G 20,171), a noteworthy
title because of its polysemy: an *official* being both an ecclesias-

tic judge and a chamber pot!

During the torments henchmen keep talking about their actions, deciding what they will do next, and commenting upon the state of their victim.[43] More often than not, their speech is exceedingly sarcastic and ironical, and as such constitutes yet another form of abuse.[44] When organizing their activities, the *tirans* often use ironic metaphors. A very common euphemism for torture is *jeu* (game), along with synonyms such as *esbat* (entertainment),[45] as can be seen in the quotations above, from both Arras ("Esbatez vous jusques au jour" [A 11,921]) and Gréban ("Nostre esbat est ja tout pourveu:/ a riens ne nous voulons esbatre/ sinon a le torcher et batre" [G 19,738–40]). When at the Mocking Christ is blindfolded and asked to guess who hit him, the game then more specifically becomes blind-man's buff.[46] Torments are also referred to as *feste* (feast), as when Claquedent calls Christ for the crucifixion: "venez a la feste" ("come to the feast" [G 24,578]). Also related is *noce* (wedding): "qu'oncque mais ne fut a telz nopces" ("that he's never been at such a wedding" [G 15,688]) promises Malchus while preparing for the arrest. This metaphor leads to comparing Christ to a bride, as in Arras: "Ce semble a voir une espousée" ("He looks like a bride" [A 11,851]), or in the already cited scornful question from Gréban: "Allez vous a pas d'espousée?" ("Are you walking slowly, like a bride?" [G 20,232]).

The ironic contrast between these ludibund, festive terms and the horror of the staged torments compels the viewer to an intense abhorrence of the henchmen. But as V. A. Kolve has shown, by "turning the tasks assigned by their masters into a sequence of formal games, into a changing metamorphosis of play. . . the *tortores* are dramatized as too self-aware, too conscious of their own need for amusement, distraction, and gratification, to be more than sporadically aware of the man they kill."[47] In so doing, the playwrights give a trenchant confirmation of Christ's words on the cross: "Father, forgive them, for they know not what they do."[48]

We have seen how Jesus behaves according to the Old Testament prophecies, a meek lamb brought to be sacrificed. Comparing Christ to an animal—and treating him like one—is yet another recurring way of demeaning him. And so Christ's body is referred to as "your filthy carcass" (G 20,185; G 19,748), his hands as paws (G 24,667), his face as a muzzle (A 14,611, 14,660; G 19,837, 20,843, 20,891–2) or a snout (G 20,902). As Jean-Pierre Bordier suggested, comparing Christ to an animal contributes to dehumanizing him.[49] Such remarks are, of course, yet another verbal torment; but they also are the result of physical torture, as bears witness this exchange in Gréban:

Malcuidant	Il est tant gasté de cracher amont et aval que le cueur me fait tres grant mal de le regarder en la face.
	(He is so smeared with spit from top to bottom that it turns my stomach to look at him in the face.)
Dragon	C'est tres mal dit, saulve ta grace: ce mot la luy est par trop beau.
	(That was badly spoken, saving your grace. That word is too good for him.)
Malcuidant	A le regarder ou museau, vueulx tu que je l'appelle ainsi?
	(To look at him in the muzzle: do you want me to call it that?)
Dragon	C'est bien dit. (G 20,837–45)
	(That's better.)

The loss of human features, and thus of human identity, is once again grounded on Old Testament prophecies, as in Isaiah 53:2 ("There is no beauty in him, nor comeliness: and we have seen him, and there was no sightliness"), Psalm 141:5 ("there was no one that would know me"), or Isaiah 52:14 ("As many have been astonished at thee, so shall his visage be inglorious among men, and his form among the sons of men").

In this process of disparagement by turning the prisoner into an animal, "dog" is a recurring insult: as in "villain matin" ("vile dog" [G 24,587]), "vieulx matin affaictié" ("hypocritical old dog" [G 23,944]), "faulx chien renoyé" ("false and traitorous dog" [G 22,221]). This may seem surprising, since in the Christological interpretation of Psalm 21:17 ("for many dogs have encompassed me: the council of the malignant hath besieged me"), the enemies of Christ are compared to dogs, an image often appearing in devotional literature and in the visual arts.[50] In these plays Christ's followers apply the insult to the Jews, as Saint John in the *Palatinus*: "mauvese gent cruëre,/ chiens enraignié" ("bad and cruel people, rabid dogs" [P 1,152–53]), or Saint Peter, who exclaims in Gréban: "Sont ilz bien chiens!" ("Are they dogs!" [G 16,379]). To accuse Christ of precisely what his enemies are constitutes another strategy to emphasize their infamy. We have seen how Christ is often called fool, another epithet associated with Christ's enemies and unbelievers, by reason of the Christological reading of Psalm 52 (53): "The fool said in his heart: There is no God. They are corrupted, and become abominable in iniquities: there is none that doth good."[51] Stéphane Gompertz aptly summarized the versatile ambiguity of insults: "insults define two antagonistic camps, at times excluding the person it is aimed at, at others the person who proffers it . . . : the 'good guy' confirms his value; the 'bad guy' stresses his downfall."[52]

The tormentors also use irony to justify violence, invoking a variety of reasons for hitting the prisoner. In a rather convoluted chain of metaphors, in the *Passion Sainte-Geneviève* Haquin suggests that Christ is sick and that he needs to sweat to be cured. Blows will be administered to that effect: "Nous te ferons sy fort süer/ Que ton mal se terminera" ("We will make you sweat in such a way that your illness will be over" [SG 1,634–35]). In this passage from Arras, Christ is hit to wipe his sweat, to keep him warm, to salute him, to kill a fly, to blow his nose:

Cayphas	Froictier lui fault le fronc, il sue,
	Gardez le de le reffroidier.
	(You need to wipe his forehead, he sweats,
	be careful not to let him get cold.)
Le Premier	Je te vuel mon hommage faire,
de Sidon	Car envers toy me sens tenus,
	T'aras de par moy une paire
	De beaux pinchons ou de cucus,
	Ten ton giron, les as rechus,
	Ne les laisse point envoller.
	Avise du fol, Cocquibus,
	Il les a laissiet eschapper.
	(I wish to pay you my homage,
	because I feel bound to you,
	I will give on your lap a pair

of nice finches and cuckoos,
Now you have got them
do not let them fly away.
What a fool, Cocquibus,
he let them escape.)

Le IIe de Sidon A aultre jeu nous fault juer,
Pour sçavoir s'il est vray prophete,
Vous verrez tantost belle feste. (A 14,515–27)

(We should play another game,
to know if he is a real prophet,
you'll soon see quite a party.)

[They proceed to decide that Christ will be blindfolded and will have
to guess who hit him]

Le Ve   Or, attent, je voy une mouche.
de Jherusalem

(O, wait, I see a fly.)

Le IIIe de Sidon Il fault que son nez je lui mouche.

(I need to blow his nose.)

Le Ve   Vecy la mousche, tien, je l'ay,
de Jherusalem Elle s'en va, car je frapay
Trop bellement de la moictie. (A 14,542–46)

(Here's the fly, I've got it,
it is flying away, because I hit it
far too gently.)

In addition to fulfilling all these ironical functions, blows are
also referred to by an array of metaphorical terms, in the passage
just quoted, for example, they are birds: *pichons* and *cucus*. Although we do find less colorful terms to designate blows (*coup*,
buffe, *horïon*) and the action of hitting (*ferir*, *battre*, *frapper*) the
dramatists seem to relish metaphorical language, and this particularly in later plays.[53] Many of these terms are derived from
verbs, often with a euphemistic meaning, as in *tatin* or *touche*
(from *taster* and *toucher*, to touch); others are derived from sub-
stantives designating body parts, as in *collée* (from *col*, neck),
oreillon (from *oreille*, ear).

A recurring theme among these metaphors is food.[54] During
the Way to Calvary in the *Passion d'Auvergne*, blows are succes-

sively called nuts, figs, pears, cake, eggs:

Malque	Or tien, Jhesus, prent ces deux noix et ceste figue mal rostie!
	(Here, Jesus, take these two nuts and this poorly roasted fig!)
Sirus	Mange ceste poere boulie et de ce guasteau mal prestit!
	(Eat this boiled pear and this poorly prepared cake!)
Cinelle	. . . Tien cecy, mange ces deux eufz! Tu n'aras meshuy aultre viande.[55]
	(. . . Take this, eat these two eggs! From now on you will have no other food.)

In Gréban, irony does not stop at the choice of "plum" to refer to a blow: it first becomes a *jorroise* (a plum from Jouarre), then the blows turn into food and the action of beating into that of feeding:

Goulu	Tout en jouant et esbatant, je luy asserray ceste prune. . . .
	(All in play and fun, I will give him this plum. . . .)
Malcuidant	Par les patins Dieu, quel jorroise! Oncques cop ne fut mieulx assis.
	(By God's shoes, what a plum! Never was a blow better placed.)
Bruyant	Luy en donrray je jusqu'a six d'ainsi faictes pour dejeuner?
	(Shall I give him up to six done like that for breakfast?)
Dragon	On le pourroit bien desjeuner de plus joyeulx metz pour l'amordre. (G 20,861–74)
	(One could regale him

with more delightful dishes to excite his appetite.)

Likewise, among the sarcasms remarking on Christ's state during torture, food is featured prominently. Here's what "Le Premier Juifz de Sidon" says about Christ's blood in *Arras*:

> Hau! qui veult faire des boudins,
> il s'en voise dire a ses voisins,
> qu'il viengne cy querir du sang. (A 14,472–74)

> (Hey! whoever wants to make blood sausages
> Should go tell his neighbors
> To come here and ask for blood.)

This truly offensive remark—the suggestion of making food with the blood of Christ, and a rather undignified one!—is, as are all the other sarcasms hurled at Jesus, meant to instill into the viewer an intense feeling of abhorrence for Christ's enemies. As Clifford Davidson has argued, Christ's blood was regarded quite differently from regular blood, a wholly sacred liquid.[56] In this particular case it also vividly expresses the abundant loss of blood provoked by the imposition of the crown of thorns. What's going on here can be understood in several ways, none of which excludes the others. The henchmen use metaphors derived from the domestic world, a down-to-earth and thus inglorious world, which produces a shocking contrast with the momentous actions taking place. The cross, for instance, the very instrument and symbol of redemption, becomes in the mouths of the henchmen a prosaic bed in which the Son of God will be "couchié moulle- ment" ("comfortably lying" [A 16,058]). But with the specific recourse to terms from the world of the kitchen, Christ becomes the object of the henchmen's culinary attentions. I will not go as far as the potential (and rejected) contributor to *Comparative Drama* whom Clifford Davidson recalls stating that the mass is ritual cannibalism,[57] although I think we can nevertheless agree that, after all, Christ's body *is* food—spiritual food—"pain de vie eternelle," ("bread of eternal life" [G 16,365]). As a matter of fact, when in the *Passion de Semur* Annas orders: "Frappéz sus con sus ung presseur" ("Hit him as on a wine press" [S 6,376]), the reference is to the prophecy of Isaiah 63:3, with the man from Bosra whose garments are red "like theirs that tread in the wine- press."[58] (I can't resist adding that the imagery of the wine press must have been particularly eloquent for the viewer from a wine- producing region such as Semur). This could explain why in the passage from Arras cited above, "Le IIIe de Jerusalem," asks: "Lequel preng tu ou rouge ou blanc?" ("Which one would you like: red or white?" [A 14,475]), and thus hints at the two types of wine, for *boudin* is never called *rouge*, red: it can either be *noir* (black, when made with blood) and *blanc* (white, when made with meat from pork or chicken). The choice between red and white calls to mind Christ's words at the Last Supper in Jean Michel's *Passion*: "le vin/ que vous prendrés, soit rouge ou blanc;/ c'est le calice de mon sanc" ("the wine you will take, either red or white, is the chalice of my blood").[59]

In using food metaphors to incorporate Christ's torments into kitchen activities, these henchmen call to mind the devils, and hence stress their malfeasance. Place of eternal fire and intense smells, Hell is traditionally envisioned as a gigantic kitchen, where the devils are the cooks.[60] One need only think about Villon's *Ballade pour prier Nostre Dame*, in which the poet's mother sees paintings of heaven and hell on the walls of her local minster, and in the latter "dampnez sont bouluz"[61] ("damned are boiled"). We can also think how the visual arts equip devils with flesh-hooks, medieval kitchen implements used to stir and sample meat cooking in a cauldron.[62] In addition to the image of the cauldron in which the damned are boiled,[63] the variety of torments leads to variety in the cooking preparations: roasting, stewing, braising, frying. In the Provençal *Jutgamen General*, Hell appears as a "rostisaria,"[64] while in the *Mystère des trois doms*, the devils plan to prepare a damned "a la sibolette" ("with chives"), "a la vineygrette," "a saulce lamproye" ("with lamprey sauce"), and to fricasee his liver.[65] In the *Mystère de Saint Martin*, Sathan asks Lucifer to give him as a reward the liver and the lungs of the Defenseur bishop to make a *pâté* with.[66] In Arras, Lucifer orders that the damned be put in a soup ("mettez les au potage" [A 18,178]), that they be fried (A 18,211), boiled (A 18,213), and roasted (A 18,218).

The damned are prepared in hell, but also devoured: a hell mouth being the traditional entrance, the digestive process starts right away.[67] When Judas dies, Lucifer declares:

> Or, le me baillez a sentir:
> je le vueil a coup engloutir
> et du traïstre larronceau
> ne vouldray faire q'un morceau
> puisque je le tiens de ma pacte. (G 22,048–52)

> (Now give him to me to touch,

> I want to swallow him quickly.
> Since I've got him in my paw,
> I want to gulp down the traitorous
> little thief in one piece.)

And the devil Astaroth comments:

> Vela ung deable de gargate.
> Comment il l'a tost devoré! (G 22,053–54)

> (That's a devil of a gullet!
> Look how fast he's devoured him!)

Jean-Pierre Bordier wonderfully expressed it: "hell is at the same time the kitchen, the dining room . . . and the guest":[68] not only are the damned prepared and consumed by the devils, but they are also fed, although not the most pleasant of dishes by far.[69]

As a matter of fact, the devils behave very much in the same way as the tormentors: they too think of their activities in terms of games. In the sequence that follows, Astaroth begs Lucifer to give him Judas's soul "pour nous jouer un petïot" ("so that we can play with it a little" [G 22,069]) and Lucifer agrees, encouraging them to "jouez en ung peu a la solle" ("go play football with it" [G 22,073]). And just like the *tirans* they argue about who will get to start the "game."[70] As in earthly torment scenes, a *rondeau* orchestrates their attacks:

Astaroth	Sus, deables, sus!
	(Come on, devils, come on!)
Fergalus	A luy, a luy!
	Temps est de commancer l'esbat.
	(At 'em! At 'em!
	It's time for the fun to start.)
Astaroth	Le traïstre soit assailly!
	Sus, deables, sus!
	(Let's smash the traitor!
	Come on devils, come on!)
Berich	A luy, a luy!
	(At 'em! At 'em!)

Cerberus	Puisque chascun y est sailly, il me fault courir au debat. Sus, deables, sus! A luy!
	(Since everyone else is joining in, It's time for me to jump into the fight. Come on, devils, come on! At 'em!)
Astaroth	A luy! Temps est de commancer l'esbat. (G 22, 089–96)
	(At 'em! It's time for the fun to start.)

Like the henchmen the devils are characterized by their colorful speech, constantly hurling insults at each other. Although "dragon," "turtle," "serpent," and other "chthonic creatures"[71] more specifically belong to the hellish environment, other insults are shared with the *tirans*. Consider the term *ribaudaille*, meaning "band of scoundrels": it is used both by the devils and by the henchmen and their chiefs. Compare these two *rondeaux-triolets*, one taking place in hell and the other during the Flagellation, with in each case "ribaudaille" appearing in the refrain.

Sathan	Ha, mercy, maitre!
	(Ha, mercy, master!)
Lucifer	C'est assez; je leur pardonne la fortune.
	(Enough; I forgive them the accident.)
Astaroth	Passez, ribaudaille, passez.
	(Come on, band of scoundrels, come on.)
Berich	Ha, mercy, maitre!
	(Ha, mercy, master!)
Lucifer	C'est assez; Les tuerés vous? Cessez, cessez!
	(Enough; Will you kill them? Stop, stop!)

Cerberus	Encor aront ilz celle prune.
	(They'll still have this plum.)
Sathan	Ha, mercy, maitre!
	(Ha, mercy, master!)
Lucifer	C'est assez; Passez, ribaudaille, passez. Les tuerés vous? Cessez, cessez! Je leur pardonne la fortune. (G 10,493–502)
	(Enough; Come on, band of scoundrels, come on. Will you kill them? Stop, stop! I forgive them the accident.) . . .
Pylate	Frappez fort, frappez; ribaudaille! Homme ne se mecte en doubly!
	(Hit, hit hard, you band of scoundrels. May no man forget what he's doing.)
Claquedent	Vous sembl'il donc que je luy faille?
	(Do you think I'm missing him, then?)
Barraquin	Frappez fort, frappez; ribaudaille!
	(Hit, hit hard, you band of scoundrels.)
Brayart	Nous le dessirons maille a faille: on ne voit riens que sang sur luy.
	(We'll tear him piece by piece. We see nothing but blood on him.)
Pylate	Frappez fort, frappez; ribaudaille! Homme ne se mecte en oubly! (G 22,755–62)
	(Hit, hit hard, you band of scoundrels. May no man forget what he's doing.)

Notice how in this scene the devils also refer to blows metaphorically, in this case as a "plum."

"Dog," along with its synonyms, is reinforced by adjectives frequently in the devils' mouths, as in the invectives Lucifer hurls at his colleague Sathan: "Faulx dragon, faulx matin famis,/ perverse tortue mortelle" ("False dragon, false famished dog, perverse and deadly turtle" [G 7,339–40]). We saw above that "mastin," "chien," and related terms are commonly addressed to Christ by the *tirans*. The tormentors also refer to dogs and other animals when addressing each other. Brutaumont says to Griffon: "tu as le museau rechigné/ comme le groing d'un vieulx limier" ("your muzzle grimaces like the snout of an old dog" [G 22,579–80]) and Griffon complains that Broyefort does not understand fast enough: "Tu n'es qu'un droit hours de Sçavoye." ("You are nothing but a bear from Savoie" [G 24,691]). We remember that some of the henchmen are endowed with names of fantastic animals, such as Griffon and Dragon, and that this latter appears among Lucifer's insults cited above. What the dramatists are thereby suggesting is the bestial quality of tormentors and devils alike. In the visual arts evil characters are often depicted with animal features,[72] while devils are characterized by the variety of their composite physiognomy, in which different animal elements are integrated.[73] This aspect is echoed in the text of our plays, when, for example, Cerberus speaks of his "museau" (G 24,476), Sathan of his "pacte" ("paw" [G 24,922]). Clearly a parallel is established—both by word and by action—between the devils and the henchmen. A continuity is suggested, with the henchmen carrying on the devils' work; we see that they belong to the same world of evil.

Now another point of encounter between the behavior of the devils and of the *tirans* is the comedy they generate.[74] We laugh at the expense of the devils, as when Sathan, who has managed to have Christ arrested, proudly returns to hell:

> Harau, comment joyeulx je suis!
> Harau, que j'ay joye atrainee
> confite de raige enflamee
> d'avoir si tres bien besoigné.
> J'ay tout gaignié, j'ay tout gaignié,
> j'ay fait un hault fait, ung chief d'euvre (G 23,305–10)

> (Hooray, how happy I am!
> Hooray! I've obtained such joy,
> nourished by fiery rage
> in having worked so well.
> I've won everything; I've won everything.

I've done a great deed, a masterpiece.)

His satisfaction is met by an unexpectedly furious Lucifer, who realizes that the death of Christ means loosing his tenants in hell. Similarly we laugh at the expense of the tormentors, and this even in dramatic scenes of torture. In the *Passion Sainte-Geneviève*, Marquin hits Haquin's thumb during the Flagellation,[75] while Claquedent stings himself with the crown of thorns:

Claquedent	Ay, dyablc!
	(Oh, the devil!)
Brayart	Qu'as tu?
	(What's the matter?)
Claquedent	Je me picque. Voicy ung tres mauvais abus.
	(I've pricked myself. This is a very bad mistake.)
Broyefort	Que vous estes bien coquibus et bien brustes et bestïaulx! N'y sçavez vous autres consaulx? Le remede y est cler et plain.
	(You really are a simpleton and a hick and stupid. Don't you have any other idea? The solution is obvious and simple.)
Orillart	Et quel?
	(And that is?)
Broyefort	Prenez en vostre main bons gros batons lourds et torçuz et frappez a puissance sus tant qu'elle y entre ou elle brise.
	(Take in your hand Very big, heavy, and gnarled sticks and strike him forcefully so that they gash him or break.)

Orillart C'est parlé de bonne devise:
nous en ferons en celle fourme. (G 22,909–18)

(That's a good plan.
We'll do in that way.)

Earlier on, Gadiffer was afraid of hurting himself by hitting Christ's head "Non feray, je me blesseroye/ a frapper: il y a trop d'oz" ("I won't do that, I would get hurt hitting him: there are too many bones" [G 19,706–07]). Despite their willingness to harm Christ, the *tirans* are depicted as lazy cowards, who are more interested in food than in performing their tasks, as Estonné, who declares that instead of going to arrest Christ,

J'aimasse mieulx a faire ung sault
pour aler garder la cuisine,
car, puisqu'on y frappe ou hutine,
j'ay tel paour que le cueur me part. (G 17,740–43)

(I would have preferred to drop by
to go guard the kitchen,
since there is striking and battling
I am so afraid that my heart rends.)

While Brayart, when asked "Vendras tu parler au prevost?" ("Will you come speak to the governor?" [G 21,512]), responds: "Esse pour escumer le rost?/ J'ay ma narine toute preste." ("Is it to smell the roast? My nostrils are ready" [G 21,513–14]).[76]

The comic character which graces the *tirans* and devils alike, along with the use of metaphors from the low and undignified domestic world and in particular that of the kitchen as well as from that of digestive functions,[77] are in turn very much comparable to what appears in contemporary comic theater.[78] The henchmen—through their names, their language, their use of metaphorical irony—present further significant parallels with farce.[79] Indeed, a lexical study of the insults and the names of the henchmen might begin with Halina Lewicka's seminal work on the language and style of comic theater, or Barbara Bowen's analyses of farcical metaphorical irony.[80]

With the expansion of secondary characters in fifteenth-century passions we find a series of names extremely suggestive of the function or character of the figure. Some, such as Dragon and Griffon, are names of fantastic animals; others, such as Estonné, Bruyant, Brayart, Claquedent, Groignart, and Malcuidant, evoke a certain behavior;[81] while Gueulu (also called Goulu), Dentart, and Orillart, suggest physical traits.[82] To this list one can add the name of a *valet* who helps at the Flagellation: Broyefort.[83] Such anthroponyms can be compared to those of emissaries: Maucourant and Trottemenu in Gréban, Trotim in Semur, and Marcherguay in the *Passion de Troyes*.[84] Many of these names end in *–art*, a particularly pejorative suffix.[85] The words formed by the addition of this suffix refer to individuals with a marked physical or moral trait, thereby exaggerated as in a caricature.[86] Evil qualities are reinforced by the presence of the prefix *mal–*, as in Maucourant, but also in Maliferas, Malbec, and Malegorge, the three men who in the *Passion d'Auvergne* mock Christ on the cross, and in the same play, Malembouchée, the wife of the smith who forges the nails for the crucifixion.[87] In so taking advantage of the evocative and connotative possibilities of anthroponymy, the playwrights follow a long tradition, most common in comic theater,[88] but going back to the *Chanson de Roland* with its Saracens Malbien, Malduit, Malquiant, Abisme, Falsaron, and so on.[89] As Jelle Koopmans recently argued, such anthroponymy participates in the "rituals of exclusion" which forcefully produce an image of the "Other."[90]

Christ is also referred to by such burlesque nicknames as "Mahuet" (A 14,670), as in the farcical character Mahuet Badin[91] or Gosset (A 14,669). Hypocoristic names in *–et* or *–ette* are legion in comic theater, and their value is more often than not ironic. Many are synonymous with fool.[92] Other nicknames include the already mentioned maistre Aliboron (G 22,890) and maistre Ypocras (A 14,508), as well as maistre Ongnon ("master Onion" [A 14,606]).[93] The already mentioned "maistre triacleur" ("master theriacker" [A 14,720]) should be included, if we think of the farce of "Le Pardonneur, le Triacleur et la Tavernière."[94] There is also "maistre Antitus" (A 14,716), the name, according to Jean-Pierre Bordier, of a famous author and actor of farces,[95] and several titles which allude to carnivalesque rituals, such as "evesque des folz" ("fools' bishop" [A 16,531]) and "roy des cornars" ("king of fools" [G 22,853]).[96] And since carnivalesque rituals are characterized by the inversion of values and status, we can now understand why Christ is called dog, fool, scoundrel, and so many other epithets which usually are associated with his tormentors. Hell too, is a world turned upside-down, where hierarchical values are inverted. It was marked since its inception by tumbling, with the fall of the rebel angels; and when the visual arts depict the fall of the damned, there too inversion is featured, for they fell headfirst into the hellish pit.[97]

We unquestionably have here a very popular discourse, suggestive of Bakhtin's spirit of the marketplace.[98] What of its insertion into the sacred context of the life and death of Christ? As we know these sequences and the contrast they create with the rest of the plays continue to shock the modern reader.[99] I am certainly not arguing in favor of a carnivalesque reading of these scenes —not in the sense that they would make the viewer feel any sympathy towards the executioners—and this especially in a volume honoring Clifford Davidson and John Stroupe. Davidson, when addressing the issue of conflict and violence in drama last year at the Medieval Congress, warned against the "temptation to interpret them as subversive, as bearing signs of social struggle, or as *irresponsibly carnivalesque.*"[100] What I am rather suggesting is the appropriation of carnivalesque modes into the tragic context of the economy of salvation. I fully agree with Jelle Koopmans when he states that the "*mystères* are rooted in a global symbolism, and the parodic and profane elements that enter in this construction are consciously integrated."[101] In the farce these elements are meant to delight the audience, who feels a mixture of relief and superiority, as if thinking, "We are not like that."[102] I would argue that, in this tragic religious context, the grotesque character of the henchmen similarly generates a feeling of alienation, although of a different nature, tinted in this case with revulsion and indignation. Strong feelings indeed, which would contribute to the lasting quality of the mnemonic mark left by the performance on the viewer's mind.[103]

I am thus lead back to my starting point, to sacrificial rituals in which the community has recourse to specific techniques to emphasize its disconnection from the executioner.[104] As Walter Burkert explained, the community engages in a "comedy of innocence" in order to deny any responsibility in the decision and the implementation of the murder. The executioner thus both belongs to the community and is rejected from it:[105] hence the fundamentally human nature of the tormentors in these plays, with their very down-to-earth reactions, of pleasure, fear, pain, tiredness—they truly are V. A. Kolve's "natural man."[106] At the same time, the playwrights emphasize their lowliness, and this in particular through comic and grotesque effects, which then contribute to induce alienation. The regenerative aspect of Bakhtin's parody[107] is also present in sacrificial rituals; Girard indeed writes that "derision of one form or another plays a large part in the negative feelings that find expression in the course of the ritual sacrifice and that are finally purified and purged by it."[108]

These plays assuredly express such a mutation; the regenerative aspect is at their core, since the Christian history of redemption is one of suffering and death that brings beatitude and eternal life.[109]

I started this essay by quoting from *La violence et le sacré*, and I now return to it. Concerning the sacrificial ritual in the Upper Nile Dinka culture René Girard noted that "it seems that the paroxysm takes place not at the death of the victim, but in the course of the ritual curses pronounced before its death. One gets the impression that these curses are in themselves able to destroy the victim; that it is, as in tragedy, for all practical purposes killed by words."[110]

Colby College

NOTES

[1] This essay is an expanded version of a paper delivered at the 33d Medieval Congress at Western Michigan University. My thanks to Luis Gámez, Molly Lynde-Recchia, and Graham Runnalls for their helpful suggestions. With this essay I wish to express my heartfelt gratitude to Cliff Davidson for his inspiration and mentorship.

[2] René Girard, *La violence et le sacré* (Paris: Bernard Grasset, 1972), 52; trans. Patrick Gregory, in Girard, *Violence and the Sacred*, (Baltimore and London: Johns Hopkins University Press, 1977), 31.

[3] Ibid., 87.

[4] Véronique Plesch, "*Etalage complaisant*? The Torments of Christ in French Passion Plays," *Comparative Drama* 28 (1994–95): 458–85.

[5] Véronique Plesch, "Walls and Scaffolds: Pictorial and Dramatic Passion Cycles in the Duchy of Savoy," *Comparative Drama* 32 (1998): 252–90, *passim*, and figs. 1 and 2.

[6] *Matthew* 26:67–68; *Mark* 14:65. Biblical citations are to the Vulgate (*Biblia Sacra iuxta Vulgatam Clementinam*, ed. Alberto Colunga, O.P. and Laurentio Turrado [Madrid: Biblioteca de autores cristianos, 1982]); translations are from the Douay-Rheims version.

[7] *Luke* 23:11.

[8] *Matthew* 27:29; see also *Mark* 15:17–20 and *John* 19:2–3.

[9] *Matthew* 27:39–40.

[10] In *Matthew* 27:44 and *Mark* 15:32 both thieves address Christ in a scornful way; in *Luke* 23:39, only one.

[11] Kurt Ruh, "Zur Theologie des mittelalterlichen Passionstraktats," *Theologische Zeitschrift* 6 (1950): 17–39; F. P. Pickering, "Das gotische Christusbild. Zu den Quellen mittelalterlicher Passionsdarstellungen," *Euphorion* 47 (1953): 16–37; translated as "The Gothic Image of Christ: The Sources of Medieval Representations of the Crucifixion," in

Essays on Medieval German Literature and Iconography (Cambridge: Cambridge University Press, 1980), 3–30.

[12] Pickering, "The Gothic Image of Christ," 19.

[13] Plesch, "*Etalage complaisant?*" 469–70.

[14] *John* 18:22.

[15] *Le Mystère de la Passion Nostre Seigneur du manuscrit 1131 de la Bibliothèque Sainte-Geneviève*, ed. Graham A. Runnalls, TLF, 206 (Geneva: Droz, and Paris: Minard, 1974), 1,386–91; hereafter abbreviated SG.

[16] Unless otherwise noted, all translations are mine.

[16] *Le Mystère de la Passion d'Arnoul Gréban*, ed. Omer Jodogne, Académie Royale de Belgique, Classe des Lettres, Mémoires, XII, 3 (Brussels: Palais des Académies, 1965), 19,557–62; hereafter abbreviated G.

[18] For translations from Gréban's *Third Day* (19,908–27,299) I quote (with amendments when necessary) from *Arnoul Gréban, The Mystery of the Passion: The Third Day*, trans. Paula Giuliano (Asheville: Pegasus Press, 1996).

[19] Plesch, "*Etalage complaisant?*" 462–3.

[20] Ibid. 459 and *passim*.

[21] *La Passion des Jongleurs. Texte établi d'après la Bible des sept estaz du monde de Geugroi de Paris*, ed. Anne Joubert Amari Perry (Paris: Beauchesne, 1981), 758–60.

[22] *Le Mystère de la Passion. Texte du ms. 697 de la bibliothèque d'Arras*, ed. Jules-Marie Richard (1891; rpt. Geneva: Slatkine Reprints, 1976); hereafter abbreviated A.

[23] See Plesch, "*Etalage complaisant?*" 459.

[24] "Avisez comment il sommeille" ("See how he dozes" [A 11,852]); "Fier ung cop pour le resveillier" ("Give him a blow to wake him up" [A 11,856]); "Passe avant; es tu endormis?/ Abrege toy appertement." ("Go ahead; are you asleep? Come quickly" [A 12,856]).

[25] I follow here Emile Roy's edition (*le Mystère de la Passion en France du XIVe au XVIe siècle: étude sur les sources et le classement des mystères de la Passion* [1903–04; rpt. Geneva: Slatkine, 1974], 6,580), rather than *The Passion de Semur* (ed. P.T. Durbin and Lynette Muir, Leeds Medieval Studies 3 [Leeds: The University of Leeds Centre for Medieval Studies, 1981], 6,580), which gives "Il me sanble que vous m'oignéz." ("It seems to me that you are anointing me"). Hereafter I use this later edition, abbreviated S.

[26] Plesch, "*Etalage complaisant?*" 464–68. On insults in general, see Stéphane Gompertz, "L'injure, le code, l'exclusion," *Senefiance 5: Exclus et systèmes d'exclusion dans la littérature et la civilisation médiévales* (Aix-en-Provence: Ed. CUER MA, 1978), 385–99.

[27] SG 1,553; 1,560; 1,834; 1,854; 1,878; 2,016; 2,040.

[28] Halina Lewicka, *La langue et le style du théâtre comique français des XVe et XVIe siècles* (Paris: C. Klincksieck; Warsaw: Panstwowe Wydawnictwo Naukowe, 1960), 103

and *passim*.

[29] Jean-Pierre Bordier, *Le Jeu de la Passion. Le message chrétien et le théâtre français (XIIIe –XVIe s.)* (Paris: Champion, 1998), 32; see also 473–76, in particular 474 for the use of "truant" in this context.

[30] *Luke* 23:11. For a list of plays with the scene of Herod accusing Christ of folly, see Bordier, *Le Jeu de la Passion*, 422 and 446.

[31] *Matthew* 26:59–67; *Mark* 14:55–65.

[32] See above for the insult of "faulx traïstre enchanteur."

[33] *Matthew* 12:24. See also *Matthew* 9:34, *Mark* 3:22, and *Luke* 11:15, as well as Bordier, *Le Jeu de la Passion*, 434–35, for accusations of Jesus being born of the devil, being a devil himself, or being devil-inspired.

[34] See for example P 277, SG 509, 1,313, and 1,317. For the accusation of magic, see Robert-Léon Wagner, *"Sorcier" et "Magicien": Contribution à l'histoire du vocabulaire de la magie* (Paris: Droz, 1939), who abundantly cites examples from French Passion plays. See also Bordier, *Le Jeu de la Passion*, 434–35.

[35] Léon Poliakov, *Du Christ saux Juifs de Cour*, Histoire de l'Antisémitisme, 1 (Paris: Calmann-Lévy, 1955), 167: "qu'est-ce qu'un médecin? Ce fut, jadis, un sorcier, et c'est de nos jours encore, dans la relation particulière qui unit le malade à son docteur, un personnage qui détient un pouvoir auguste et essentiel. En somme, un médecin reste toujours peu ou prou un magicien."

[36] See also A 14,482 ("esprouveur de triacle") and 14,719 ("Sces tu point esprouver triacle?").

[37] Paul Verhuyck, "Petite histoire littéraire de Maistre Aliborum," *La vie matérielle au moyen âge*, ed. Emmanuelle Rassart-Eeckhout, Jean-Pierre Sosson, Claude Thiry, Tania Van Hemelryck (Louvain: Institut d'Études médiévales de l'Université catholique de Louvain, 1997), 303–34; the quotation is on 304: "Le docte incapable, le charlatan pédant, l'ignorant prétentieux, l'imbécile qui cherche à faire le savant, parfois pharmacien, parfois médecin."

[38] Hervé Martin, *Le métier de prédicateur en France septentrionale à la fin du Moyen Age (1350–1520)* (Paris: Cerf, 1988), 452–53.

[39] "Mire" is just another form of "medecin." As a source for the tradition of Jesus as healer, V. A. Kolve (in *The Play Called Corpus Christi* [Stanford: Stanford University Press, 1965], 152) cites *Matthew* 9.12, when Jesus says to the Pharisees, "They that are in health need not a physician, but they that are ill."

[40] For the use of irony in the Crowning with Thorns, see Plesch, *"Étalage Complaisant?"* 465–66.

[41] *Ductio Christi*: SG 1,826; 2,072; 2,074; Mocking: SG 1,596; 1,621; 1,632; 1,640; 1,658; Flagellation: SG 2,295; 2,303; 2,312; 2,368; 2,464; Way to Calvary: SG 2,547; Nailing to the Cross: SG 2,611; Crucifixion: SG 2,634; 2,654.

[42] "Dam" is both a title and a nobility rank. In the feudal hierarchy, it came after the count and before the baron (hence my translation of "viscount"). It was also used as a honorific title, placed before the name. Cf. A. J. Greimas, *Dictionnaire de l'ancien français jusqu'au milieu du XIVe siècle* (Paris: Larousse, 1968), 156.

[43] Plesch, "*Étalage complaisant?*" 461.

[44] As with the variety of insults, the use of irony grows over time: almost absent in the *Palatinus*, it is paramount in fifteenth-century plays. See ibid., 465–68.

[45] See Randolph L. Wadsworth Jr., "The Bourreaux in Arnoul Greban's *Mystère de la Passion*," *Revue de littérature comparée*, 44 (1970): 499–509, esp. 502–04.

[46] See for example SG 1,583; S 6,433; A 14,540.

[47] Kolve, *The Play Called Corpus Christi*, 180.

[48] *Luke* 23:34. See Kolve, *The Play Called Corpus Christi*, 199.

[49] Bordier, *Le Jeu de la Passion*, 216.

[50] James H. Marrow, "*Circumdederunt me canes multi:* Christ's Tormentors in Northern European Art of the Late Middle Ages and Early Renaissance," *Art Bulletin* 59 (1977): 167–181; and *Passion Iconography in Northern European Art of the Late Middle Ages and Early Renaissance* (Courtrai, Belgium: Van Ghemmert, 1979), 36–40.

[51] I quote the first two verses of the Psalm. For the fool of Psalm 52 understood as enemy of Christ, see V. A. Kolve,"Psalm 52 and Medieval Passion Iconography: The Fool as Killer of Christ" (paper presented at the annual meeting of the Medieval Academy of America, 1993), *passim*. See also Ruth Mellinkoff, *Outcasts: Signs of Otherness in Northern European Art of the Late Middle Ages*, 2 vols. (Berkeley: University of California Press, 1993), 1:55, 136–37, 207–08.

[52] Gompertz, "L'injure, le code, l'exclusion," 390: "l'injure définit deux camps antagonistes: elle a pour fonction d'exclure, tantôt celui qu'elle vise, tantôt celui-là même qui la profère . . . : le 'bon' confirme sa valeur; le 'mauvais' souligne sa déchéance."

[53] See "Plesch, "*Etalage complaisant?*" 468.

[54] See Bernard Faivre, "Le sang, la viande et le bâton (Gens du peuple dans les farces et les mystères des XVᵉ et XVIᵉ siècles)," *Figures théâtrales du peuple*, ed. Elie Konigson (Paris: Editions du Centre National de la Recherche Scientifique, 1985), 29–47, esp. "Le bourreau et la nourriture," 38–41.

[55] *La Passion d'Auvergne. Une édition deu manuscrit nouvelle acquisition française 462 de la Bibliothèque Nationale de Paris*, ed. Graham A. Runnalls,Textes Littéraires Français, 303 (Geneva: Droz, 1982), 2,407–16. Hereafter abbreviated Auv.

[56] Clifford Davidson, "Sacred Blood and the Late Medieval Stage," *Comparative Drama* 31 (1997): 436–58.

[57] "Some Observations on Violence in the Medieval English Drama," paper read at the 33ʳᵈ International Congress on Medieval Studies, 1998.

[58] See Marrow, *Passion Iconography*, 83-94. The winepress motif also informs depictions of the Crowning with Thorns, in which "the crown is pressed onto Christ's head, usually by two staves arranged crosswise on top of the crown" (ibid., 92).

[59] *Jean Michel, Le Mystère de la Passion (Angers 1486)*, ed. Omer Jodogne (Gembloux: Duculot, 1959), 18,866–68.

[60] See e.g. Bordier, *Le Jeu de la Passion*, 577, 595; and Jelle Koopmans, *Le Théâtre*

des exclus au Moyen Age. Hérétiques, sorcières et marginaux (Paris: Imago, 1997), 48, 162.

[61] *Le Testament Villon*, ed. Jean Rychner and Avril Henry (Geneva: Droz, 1974), 80, l. 897.

[62] Barbara D. Palmer, "The Inhabitants of Hell: Devils," in *The Iconography of Hell*, ed. Clifford Davidson and Thomas H. Seiler, Early Drama, Art, and Music Monograph Series 17 (Kalamazoo: Medieval Institute Publications, 1992), 25, figs. 14 and 16. Palmer also shows how domestic implements in general are transformed into devilish tools. In this same volume Richard Rastall ("The Sounds of Hell," 112) recounts how the Harrowing of Hell play at Chester was performed by the Cooks, and the demonic background music was produced by banging pots and pans.

[63] See Clifford Davidson, "The Fate of the Damned in English Art and Drama," in *The Iconography of Hell*, 52–54.

[64] *Le Jugement dernier (Lo Jutgamen General). Drame provençal du XVe siècle,* ed. Moshé Lazar (Paris: Klincksieck, 1971), 205 and l. 2,432.

[65] *Le Mystère des Trois Doms joué à Romans en MDIX*, ed. Paul-Emile Giraud and Ulysse Chevalier (Lyons: Brun, 1887), 8,558–71.

[66] André Duplat, "Comparaison de quatre mystères de Saint Martin récités ou représentés aux XVe et XVIe siècles, en français ou en provençal," in *Atti del IV Colloquio della Société Internationale pour l'Etude du Théâtre Médiéval*, ed. M. Chiabò, F. Doglio, M. Maymone (Viterbo: Centro Studi sul Teatro Medioevale e Rinascimentale, 1984), 242. This appears in the play performed at St Martin-la-Porte, "Histoire de Saint Martin," ed. Florimont Truchet, *Travaux de la Société d'histoire et d'archéologie de Maurienne* (1881), 305.

[67] On the hell mouth, see Pamela Sheingorm, "'Who can open the doors of his face': The Iconography of Hell Mouth," in *The Iconography of Hell*, 1–19.

[68] Bordier, *Le Jeu de la Passion*, 595: "l'enfer est à la fois la cuisine, la salle à manger . . . et le convive."

[69] Davidson, "The Fate of the Damned," 56.

[70] See, for example, how in G 19,768–88 they end up casting lots in order to decide who will start hitting Christ during the night at Annas. For other examples of the tormentors quarreling over the prisoner, see Wadsworth, "The Bourreaux," 504.

[71] I borrow the expression from Sheingorm, "Who can open the doors," 7. On the biblical sources for "reptiles, snakes, and worms" in hell, see Davidson, "The Fate of the Damned," 52.

[72] See for example Wendelien A. W. van Welie-Vink, "Pig Snouts as Sign of Evil in Manuscripts from the Low Countries," *Quaerendo* 26 (1996): 214–28.

[73] Palmer, "The Inhabitants of Hell," *passim.*

[74] Moshé Lazar, "Les diables: Serviteurs et bouffons (Répertoire et jeu chez les comédiens de la troupe infernale)," *Tréteaux* 1.2 (1978): 51–69. The perception of the devils as comic is challenged by Koopmans, *Le Théâtre des exclus*, 23–24, 164.

[75] SG 2,366–67. Graham Runnalls notes in his edition (284) that this is one of the

few instances in this play meant to make the audience laugh.

[76] Paula Giuliano translates: "To get a slice of the action? My mouth is watering."

[77] Farting, for example, is another point of encounter between devils and henchmen. As Rastall suggests, "it is possible that farting was a not unimportant feature of the devils' stage business" ("The Sounds of Hell," 111). On the henchmen side, we can think about the Crucifixion scene in *Auvergne*, where they show their bottoms to Christ and Malegorge says: "Arregarde si le mien fume! / N'est ce pas la gorge d'ung four?" ("Look how mine is smoking! Doesn't it look like an oven?" [Auv 2,924–25]). Notice the oven metaphor, again pointing to the world of the kitchen.

[78] See Robert Garapon, "Le réalisme de la farce," *Cahiers de l'Association Internationale des Etudes Françaises* 26 (1974): 13–14.

[79] Hans Robert Jauss has insisted on the "non-interchangeability of the characters of the *chanson de geste* and courtly romance"—it seems that the barrier is less impervious between comic and religious theater ("Littérature médiévale et théorie des genres," *Poétique* 1 [1970]: 84) . On the relationship between *mystères* and other genres, see Jelle Koopmans, "Le Mystère de Saint Sébastien: Scénographie et théorie des genres," *Fifteenth-Century Studies* 16 (1990): 143–155.

[80] Halina Lewicka, *La langue et le style*; and, for example, Barbara Bowen's "Metaphorical Obscenity in French Farce, 1460–1560," *Comparative Drama* 12 (1978): 331–344.

[81] Estonné: past participle of the verb *estonner*, to surprise; Bruyant: gerund from *bruire*, to make noise; Brayart: from *braire*, to bray; Claquedent: from the verb *claquer*, to chatter and the substantive *dent*, tooth; Groignart: from *grogner*, to growl; and Malcuidant: from *cuider*, to think, thus meaning "who thinks in an evil way."

[82] Gueulu or Goulu: from *gueule*, mouth; Dentart: from *dent*, tooth; and Orillart: from *oreille*, ear.

[83] From the verb, *broyer*, to crush, and the adverb, *fort*, hard. All these examples are drawn from Gréban. Interestingly such names do not appear in the *Passion d'Arras*, where albeit we find great number of henchmen. Except for Malchus and a few others (Thare, Nacor, Goby, Gedeon, Othiarus), the tormentors are designated by their place of origin: *premier de Sidon, de Thiri, de Jherusalem.*

[84] Both Trottemenu and Trotim are derived from *trotter*, to trot; Maucourant from *courrir*, to run, and Marcheguay from *marcher*, to walk. For the *Passion de Troyes*, see *Le "Mystère de la Passion" de Troyes*, ed. Jean-Claude Bibolet (Geneva: Droz, 1987). Maucourant is one of the figures added to Gréban's *Passion*. On messangers' names, see Koopmans, *Le Théâtre des exclus*, 104–09.

[85] Kurt Glaser, "Le sens péjoratif du suffixe –ard en français," *Romanische Forschungen* 27 (1910): 938.

[86] Lewicka, *La langue et le style*, 214–15.

[87] Maliferas can be understood as "mal y feras," "you will do evil," while the two others put a negative stress on a body part associated with speech: *bec*, beak, and *gorge*, throat. Malembouchée, still used in modern French, means foul-mouthed.

[88] Jean Frappier, *Le théâtre profane en France au moyen-âge, XIIIᵉ et XIVᵉ siècles* (Paris: Centre de Documentation Universitaire, 1965), 42–44, 55, 62, 144.

[89] Malquiant is synonymous with Malcuidant. *La Chanson de Roland*, ed. Gérard Moignet (Paris: Bordas, 1969), 128–29. See also Carole Bercovi-Huard, "L'exclusion du sarrasin dans la chanson de Roland: Vocabulaire et idéologie: 'Co est une gent ki unches ben ne volt' (v. 3231),"*Exclus et systèmes d'exclusion dans la littérature et la civilisation médiévales, Senefiance* No. 5 (Aix-En-Provence: Ed. CUER MA, 1978), 345–61.

[90] Koopmans, *Le Théâtre des exclus*, 109–114.

[91] André Tissier, *Recueil de farces (1450–1550)*, 11 vols. (Geneva: Droz, 1986–97), X:117–181: "Mahuet Badin, natif de Bagnolet, qui va à Paris pour vendre ses oeufs et sa crème et ne les veut donner sinon au prix du marché."

[92] Lewicka, *La langue et le style*, 290.

[93] Frappier, *Le théâtre profane*, 17, cites a *Panégyrique de Saint-Oignon*, among examples of the parodic genre of the "sermon joyeux."

[94] Tissier, *Recueil de farces*, V:229–73.

[95] Bordier, *Le Jeu de la Passion*, 446. With "Antitus" Bordier proposes a lesson different from that of Richard's edition ("a Titus").

[96] Cf. Jacques Heers, *Fêtes des fous et carnavals* (Paris: Fayard, 1983), for example 177: "abbé ou pape des fous"; 202, 210–11: "abbé des cornards" and "prince des sots."

[97] See Barbara Obrist, "Les deux visages du diable," ed. Jean Wirth, *Diables et Diableries, La représentation du diable dans la gravure des XVe et XVIe siècles* (Geneva: Cabinet des estampes, 1976), 23.

[98] Mikhail Bakhtin, *Rabelais and His World*, trans. Helene Iswolsky (Cambridge, Massachusetts: M.I.T. Press, 1968).

[99] See opinions cited in Plesch, "*Étalage complaisant?*" 458 and 476–77 n. 3. See also Graham A. Runnalls, "Mystère Français: Drame Romantique?," in *Etudes sur les Mystères* (Paris: Champion, 1998), 18–19.

[100] "Some Observations on Violence," emphasis mine. See also Clifford Davidson, "Carnival, Lent, and Early English Drama," *Research Opportunities in Renaissance Drama* 36 (1997):123–42.

[101] Koopmans, *Le Théâtre des exclus*, 23: "Les mystères sont conçus à partir d'un symbolisme global, et les éléments parodiques et profanes entrent dans cette construction et y figurent comme éléments consciemment intégrés."

[102] Garapon, "Le réalisme de la farce," 19.

[103] Plesch, "*Étalage complaisant?*" *passim*.

[104] Hyam Maccoby, *Judas Iscariot and the Myth of Jewish Evil* (New York: The Free Press, 1992), 11.

[105] Maccoby, *Judas Iscariot*, 139, referring to Walter Burkert, *Homo Necans: The Anthropology of Ancient Greek Sacrificial Ritual and Myth*, trans. Peter Bing (Berkeley: University of California Press 1983). The term "comedy of innocence," which appears on p. 16, was coined by another scholar of Greek religion, Karl Meuli, "Griechische Opferbraüche," *Phyllobolia für Peter von der Mühl zum 60. geburtstag von Olof Gigon, Karl Meuli, Willy Theiler, Fritz Wehrli, und Bernhard Wyss* (Basel: B. Schwabe, 1946),

185–288.

[106] Kolve, *The Play Called Corpus Christi,* chapter 9, "Natural Man and Evil," 206–236.

[107] Bakhtin, *Rabelais and His World,* 21.

[108] Girard, *Violence and the Sacred,* 254.

[109] I don't go as far as Rainer Warning ("On the Alterity of Medieval Religious Drama," *New Literary History* 10 [1979]: 284), who argues in favor of "the possibility that the popularity of these plays was based less on their manifest function of moral instruction than on a latent aggressive function diverted into drama."

[110] Girard, *Violence and the Sacred,* 98.

James I and *Timon of Athens*

David Bevington and David L. Smith

Timon explores the lethal ambiguities underlying the gifts and loans through which power was brokered in the courts of Elizabeth and James.

—Coppélia Kahn[1]

It might be argued that Shakespeare's *Timon of Athens* presents a malign version of the dangers of prodigality, fitting a time when the monarch lived on credit and depended on others to manage his affairs.

—Jonathan Goldberg[2]

Kahn and Goldberg have laid before us the proposition that *Timon of Athens* needs to be understood in the context of Jacobean court politics, along with other plays like *Measure for Measure, Macbeth, Coriolanus, Cymbeline,* and *Henry VIII,* for which similar claims have been made. Whereas Goldberg mentions *Timon* only briefly in his absorbing study *James I and the Politics of Literature,* his argument that representation provides the essential link between politics and literature in the period has important implications for *Timon.* Kahn provides a substantial and fascinating analysis of the play in relation to Jacobean patronage, stressing the immense scale on which the Jacobean court indulged in "socially coded gift-giving." King and courtiers alike spent beyond their means, borrowing heavily without realistic hope of being able to repay. Kahn's anecdotes do indeed resonate with suggestive parallels to Shakespeare's misanthropic play about extravagant borrowing and ingratitude.

The present authors are especially indebted to Kahn's article and agree with its premises and conclusions. But whereas her methodological interest is in bringing together New Historicism, feminist criticism, and psychoanalytic theory to explore Timon's infantile need for identifying with a maternal but fickle figure of inexhaustible supply, our method focuses more on historical documentation and the vexed critical problem of determining whether it is possible to argue for a topical correlation between fiction and reality. One author of the present essay is a historian, the other a literary scholar. We have been trained in ways that

56

ought to be compatible, and yet acknowledge that the cross-over between the disciplines is notoriously difficult. Our hope is that we can at least establish in some detail the richness of materials available for such a comparison between the historical record and the play.

Our argument for a meaningful correlation between play and historical event rests ultimately on extensive parallels and chronological coincidences rather than on verbal similarities or on fictional details that can be explained only by topical identification. (This is true of Goldberg's and Kahn's arguments as well.) The parallels apply to many of James's courtiers as well as to the King; we focus on James not because he was unique but because he was indisputably the most visible and influential practitioner of large-scale extravagance. Granted these difficulties, we will argue that the parallel situations are pointedly similar in important respects: the epic scale of the giving, the lack of awareness on the part of the giver that disaster is lurking despite repeated warnings, and (as Kahn stresses) the complex and sometimes unflattering nature of the motivation for extravagance. We begin with the history, hoping to show that extravagance was not only a fact of life in James's early years (something that has long been known), but was the subject of intense political debate at the time when *Timon* was written.

I

When James VI of Scotland ascended the English throne in 1603 as James I, the English people breathed a sigh of relief to be governed still by a Protestant. In the opening weeks of his reign, "nothing was talked of but the religion, virtue, wisdom, learning, justice and many other most noble and worthy praises of King James."[3] From the time of his accession, contemporaries such as Bishop Andrew Willets frequently likened James to Solomon,[4] and he was indeed a major intellectual in his own right. The learned author of the treatise *Daemonologie* (1597), he had also shown himself well versed in the theories of divine-right monarchy and covenant theology in works such as *The Trew Law of Free Monarchies* (1598) and the *Basilikon Doron* (1603).[5] He was an internationalist eager to establish a reputation as a peacemaker: James's personal motto was *"beati pacifici"* ("blessed are the peacemakers"). His stern Presbyterian upbringing gave way in adulthood to a broad ecumenicism which promoted a greater degree of religious tolerance than England had known since the

Reformation. For all these reasons, James's stock as monarch, politician, and Supreme Governor of the Church is now receiving long overdue rehabilitation.[6]

Yet James's jubilant subjects were in for a shock when it came to his personal style; for, as John Morrill has remarked, "his main failings . . . were not intellectual but moral and personal."[7] His *Counterblast to Tobacco* revealed a quirky and self-righteous tendency. In personal demeanor he was scruffy, unkempt, earthy. He shambled. He could be vituperative. He disliked crowds, and once grew so exasperated at the constant presence of onlookers that he cried out: "God's wounds! I will pull down my breeches and they shall also see my arse."[8] Hunting so occupied his time that courtiers sometimes had difficulty in getting his approval for the ongoing business of government. In January 1605, for example, he left London to hunt at Royston "two days after Twelvetide." He was still there two weeks later, and told the Privy Council "to undertake the charge and burden of affairs, and foresee that he be not interrupted nor troubled with too much business."[9] To be sure, he encouraged the free exchange of ideas at court, and was capable of being brilliant, relaxed, and informal. He was a patron of intellectuals, a monarch whose "table was a trial of wits" and who "was as pleasant and fellow-like in all those discourses as with his huntsmen in the field."[10] Nevertheless he failed to distinguish between liberty and license. Decadence and corruption were bound to flourish by his example. In his drinking, James's physician Sir Theodore Turquet de Mayerne recorded, the King erred "as to quality, quantity, frequency, time and order."[11] His homosexuality became more overt as he grew older. As the Puritan antiquarian Sir Simonds D'Ewes delicately put it, "he had his vices and deviations."[12] James's personal style only encouraged the drunkenness and immorality that made his court a byword in Puritan eyes for Sodom and Gomorrah. Worst of all, he was extravagant.

An epic entertainment in celebration of the visit of King Christian IV of Denmark, in the summer of 1606, is a case in point. Sir John Harington's account captures the flavor of hedonistic excess, and is worth quoting in full:

> One day a great feast was held, and after dinner the representation of Solomon his Temple and the coming of the Queen of Sheba was made, or (as I may better say) was meant to have been made, before their Majesties. . . . The lady who did play the Queen's part did carry most precious gifts to both their Majesties; but forgetting the steps arising to the canopy overset her caskets into his Danish Majesty's

lap, and fell at his feet, though I rather think it was in his face. Much was the hurry and confusion; cloths and napkins were at hand to make all clean. His Majesty then got up and would dance with the Queen of Sheba; but he fell down and humbled himself before her and was carried to an inner chamber and laid on a bed of state; which was not a little defiled with the presents of the Queen which had been bestowed on his garments; such as wine, cream, jelly, beverage, cakes, spices and other good matters. The entertainment and show went forward, and most of the presenters went backward or fell down, wine did so occupy their upper chambers. Now did appear, in rich dress, Hope, Faith and Charity. Hope did assay to speak but wine rendered her endeavors so feeble that she withdrew and hoped the King would excuse her brevity. Faith was then all alone, for I am certain she was not joined with Good Works, and left the court in a staggering condition. Charity came to the King's feet and seemed to cover the multitude of sins her sisters had committed; in some sort she made obeisance and brought gifts, but said she would return home again as there was no gift which heaven had not already given his Majesty. She then returned to Hope and Faith, who were both sick and spewing in the lower hall. Next came Victory in bright armor and presented a rich sword to the King, who did not accept it but put it by with his hand; and, by a strange medley of versification, did endeavor to make suit to the King. But Victory did not triumph long: for after much lamentable utterance she was led away like a silly captive and laid to sleep on the outer steps of the ante-chamber. Now did Peace make entry and strive to get foremost to the King; but I grieve to tell how great wrath she did discover unto those of her attendants; and, much contrary to her semblance, most rudely made war with her olive branch and laid on the pates of those who did oppose her coming.

Harington concludes: "I ne'er did see such lack of good order, discretion, and sobriety as I have now done."[13] The fact that a representation of Solomon's Temple degenerated into this drunken chaos perfectly symbolizes the contradiction between James's high-flown theories of monarchy and the reality of his personal behavior.

The reasons for James's extravagance are not far to seek. Coming from the much smaller and less prosperous kingdom of Scotland in the far north, James experienced the sensation of entering a Promised Land when he arrived in the metropolis of London.[14] In Scotland, James had had to contend with the dour spirit of the Presbyterians. His childhood, following the murder of his father Darnley in 1567 and the deposition and exile of his mother Mary Queen of Scots the following year, was virtually barren of human love, a traumatic experience that left him desperate to "buy" affection. This craving has been plausibly linked to his later extravagance.[15] Although James handled the magnate-dominated polity of Scotland with considerable skill and success,[16] the English throne provided him with a sense of liberation and self-importance after a life of political turbulence and uncertainty. He reveled in opportunities for largesse, and the disparity between the Scottish and English currencies exacerbated this characteristic. Because the Scottish pound was worth but one twelfth of the English, James had only an uncertain appreciation of the worth of the money he now controlled. It was this combination of high intellectual gifts and a lack of practical good sense that earned James the sobriquet "the wisest fool in Christendom."[17]

Perhaps the best-known example of his inflationary recklessness is his creation of some hundreds of knights. Whereas Elizabeth had created only 878 knights during the whole of her forty-five-year reign, James created 906 in his first four months alone.[18] These were the "carpet knights" that Ben Jonson and other dramatists openly ridiculed. To be sure, Shakespeare's one use of the phrase, in which Sir Toby Belch of *Twelfth Night* characterizes Sir Andrew Aguecheek as a "knight, dubbed with unhatched rapier and of carpet consideration" (3.4.236–37), dates from 1600 or 1601 and thus shows the term to have been current before James came to the throne; the *OED* provides citations from 1576–80 by George Whetstone and others.[19] The phrase denotes scorn for one who "ever loves to be in women's chambers," as Cotgrave elegantly put the matter in 1611; a carpet knight excels in the boudoir rather than on the field of battle.[20] The term may also be derived from "knight of the carpet," from about 1547, used to describe those who knelt on a carpet or cloth spread before the sovereign as he sat in his regal chair of estate.[21] Whatever the derivation, a carpet knight bespeaks indolent luxury, not only in himself but in the sovereign who favors him. And however current the term may have been in the years just before 1603, James's unstinting largesse raised the visibility of carpet knighthood to new and undreamed-of heights. He also expanded the number of peers of the realm from fifty-five to one hundred and twenty by the time of his death.[22]

This "inflation of honors" went along with unprecedented financial expenditure. In the first four years of his reign, James gave monetary gifts of about £68,153 and pensions worth nearly £30,000 per annum. Wardrobe expenditure at court increased exponentially, from £9,535 per annum during the last four years of Elizabeth's reign to £36,377 per annum during James's first

five years. When Elizabeth died, the Crown's net debt stood at
£100,000 after fifteen years of war against Spain. By 1608 England had been at peace for four years, and yet the Crown's net
debt had soared to £597,337.[23] James's expenditures were in
large measure for entertainments at court and as a way of lavish-
ing money on his favorites. Masques at court were more frequent
than in Elizabeth's reign, and vastly more expensive.[24] The bills
of the Treasurer of the Chamber, which covered the ceremonial
side of the court, increased from £13,975 in Elizabeth's last four
years to £20,096 in the first five of James's reign. The historian
Arthur Wilson, who served as a clerk in the Exchequer Office,
wrote that the Court was "a continued maskerado, where [the
Queen] and her ladies, like so many sea-nymphs, or Nereides,
appeared often in various dresses to the ravishment of the be-
holders. The King himself being not a little delighted with such
fluent elegancies, as made the nights more glorious than the
days."[25] To celebrate James's first Christmas in England, several
masques were held at Hampton Court, the "apparels" for which
were thought to have cost £2,000–3,000, and the "jewels most
rich" a further £20,000.[26] The austere restraint of the Elizabethan
court gave way to what one contemporary called "luxury and
riot," and "an excess in apparel and expense."[27]

James's bounty was especially lavish during his first few
years in England, which he later justified as a necessary part of
establishing himself as ruler of his new kingdom. He told Parliament in March 1607: "My three first years were to me as a
Christmas. I could not then be miserable. Should I have been
oversparing to them? They might have thought Joseph had forgotten his brethren, or that the King had been drunk with his new
kingdom."[28] He reiterated this point in March 1610:

> That vastness of my expense is past, which I used the first two or three
> years after my coming hither; and, as I oft used to say, that Christmas
> and open tide is ended; for at my first coming here, partly ignorance
> of this state (which no man can acquire but by time and experience)
> and partly the form of my coming being so honorable and miraculous,
> enforced me to extend my liberality so much the more at the begin-
> ning. Ye saw I made knights then by hundreds, and barons in great
> numbers: but I hope you find I do not so now, nor mind not to do so
> hereafter.[29]

Even James's long-suffering Lord Treasurer, Robert Cecil, Earl
of Salisbury, acknowledged that "this is not strange at the first
coming of a prince to a kingdom."[30]

Unfortunately, James's largesse far outstripped the financial resources at his disposal, as he himself soon realized. He came to resent the incessant requests of importunate suitors, and once exploded at one individual: "You will never let me alone. I would to God you had, first, my doublet, and then my shirt; and when I were naked, I think you would give me leave to be quiet."[31] In late 1604, when Lord Sheffield pressed the King for a particularly large gift of money, James told him bluntly that "a king could not help a subject by the measure of the suitor's want but by the consideration of what himself might well spare; that my liberality ought not to be measured by his want, for I was bound to be no man's banker. What it would be in his account that received it I knew not, but sure I was that it was a fair gift for me to give."[32] Such encounters were extremely painful to James, and temperamentally he found it extremely difficult to say no. As he wrote to Salisbury in October 1605, "I cannot but confess that it is a horror to me to think upon the height of my place, the greatness of my debts, and the smallness of my means. It is true my heart is greater than my rent, and my care to preserve my honor and credit by payment of my debts far greater than my possibility."[33] Two years later, James informed the Privy Council that "the only disease and consumption which I can ever apprehend as likeliest to endanger me is this eating canker of want, which being removed, I could think myself as happy in all other respects as any other king or monarch that ever was since the birth of Christ."[34] Certainly "this eating canker of want" had structural causes that lay outside James's control: in particular, the fact that the English Crown was living on an inelastic income in an age of soaring inflation meant that the monarch's ordinary revenue had declined by about forty percent in real terms between the death of Henry VIII in 1547 and that of Elizabeth in 1603.[35] But politically James's pleas for financial help were not assisted by the fact that his own bounty undoubtedly worsened his financial problems. Contemporaries were quick to perceive the serious implications of James's gift-giving: as early as August 1604, the Archbishop of York lamented that "His Majesty's subjects hear and fear that his excellent and heroical nature is too much inclined to giving, which in short time will exhaust the treasure of the kingdom and bring many inconveniences."[36]

As a result, the monarch's bounty quickly became a major political issue in a way that it had never been under the parsimonious Elizabeth, and was the subject of vigorous debate within Parliament and the Privy Council. Discussion focused on the arguments for and against royal bounty, and especially on how far—and within what limits—it could be regarded as desirable. James always maintained that his position demanded some measure of generosity to his subjects. He reminded the Privy Council in January 1610 that "we shall be loath in the course of our life to come short of the greatness of our progenitors in any circumstances of ancient orders or magnificence, though we desire not to imitate any in tolerating any corrupt waste in officers or servants," and that "we desire not to hear of any such projects as may take from our servants or subjects all hope of reward or benefit; that were to possess benefit without love, or to be mastered by that servile creature, riches, which ought to be a slave to man, much more to princes."[37] Salisbury himself emphasized the latter point about the need to reward loyal service when he told Parliament the following month, "For a king not to be bountiful were a fault, for that duty is best and surest tried where it is rewarded, which is the cause and makes men the willinger to do service."[38] In another speech the next day, Salisbury stressed the irony that only a few years earlier English people had been criticizing Elizabeth for her frugality, and he concluded that if James "did not give, I should think his subjects lived in a miserable climate."[39] It was, however, a question of degree; and in practice, James found it extremely difficult to maintain his gift-giving within what many of his leading subjects regarded as reasonable limits.

From shortly after his arrival in England, James had received advice urging him to be mindful of the dangers of excessive largesse. Among the flood of poems, epistles, and panegyrics dedicated to James following his accession to the English throne was one of particular interest for the subject of the present essay, for it explicitly invokes the story of Timon as a warning to James. In his *Poeticall Essayes*, Alexander Craige advises the King,

> Give parasites enough, but not too much,
> And be not lavish, lest thy luck be such
> As Timon Coliteus, who outspent
> On Demeas and Gnatonides his rent;
> Of that unthankful number live anew,
> To promise much, and to perform but few.
> Be thou the stone (precellent Prince) of touch,
> For to discern the honest minds from such.[40]

Craige's warning was echoed repeatedly in the advice that Salisbury and the Privy Council offered to James between 1605 and 1610. In July 1605, the Privy Councillors urged James "to vouchsafe to forbear any more grants or promises by which your own receipts may be diminished or the profit growing by virtue of your commissions, until your Majesty have foreseen the end of your parliament."[41] They added that although some generosity was an essential attribute of kingship, if carried to excess this trait became harmful rather than beneficial: "this being a rule infallible, and better known to your Majesty than to us, that as liberality to well-deserving subjects doth multiply and confirm affection and duty to princes, so the benefits that are promiscuously bestowed and without convenient examination of merit or value do not only beget further importunity in those that lack, but breed contempt of the gifts and ingratitude to the giver."[42] In an extended treatise on James's financial position, Salisbury subsequently warned the King that "though the liberality and goodness that lieth in you are virtues, worthy of you as you are a great king, yet they are somewhat improper for this kingdom, which being compared with other monarchies may certainly be counted potent, but not opulent."[43] It was therefore "not possible for a king of England, much less of Great Britain, speaking regularly and not of vain contingents, to be rich and safe, but by frugality."[44]

Yet James seemed impervious to such counsel, and in the end Salisbury was forced to resort to more graphic ways of bringing home to the King the reality of his situation. Francis Osborne recalled an occasion when James wished to give £20,000 to his favorite, Robert Carr. Salisbury left the money

> upon the ground in a room through which his Majesty was to pass: who, amazed at the quantity, as a sight not unpossibly his eyes never saw before, asked the Treasurer whose money it was, who answered, "Yours, before you gave it away"; whereupon the King fell into a passion, protesting he was abused, never intending any such gift: and casting himself upon the heap, scrabbled out the quantity of two or three hundred pounds, and swore he should have no more.[45]

Regrettably, such warnings failed to work "a perfect cure upon his master's profuseness."[46] John Hacket wrote of James that "for thrift and saving, he could never be brought to think of them."[47] As early as 1605, an official commission warned the King, "the empty places of that glorious garland of your crown cannot be repaired when the garden of your Majesty's treasure shall be made a common pasture for all that are in need or have unreasonable desires."[48] James blithely ignored the searching questions he was asked, such as "whether the diet issued to himself and the Queen shall continue in as ample a manner for number of dishes. And if the same continue, then what abatements may be made in spice, napery, wood, coals, etc."[49] In 1610, Cecil's "Great Contract"—a radical attempt to overhaul royal finances by replacing feudal dues with a fixed annual income—was defeated, partly by James's own refusal to believe that such a reform was necessary.[50] Lionel Cranfield, Lord Treasurer from 1621, had a greater impact on royal debts, but still found it an uphill struggle to restrain what he termed "the King's inclination to thrive."[51] The combination of a desire to buy affection, a recognition of the arguments in favor of some bounty, and an inability to visualize how great his gifts actually were left James incapable of reducing significantly the scale of his largesse.

One dissident view in the debate may help explain why Timon, in Shakespeare's play, is so complacent about his extravagance and so ready to assume that his consequent financial need will generate a reciprocal generosity and thus redound to his ultimate benefit. Some of James's advisors took the optimistic view that in the long run James's gift-giving might actually strengthen his financial position. In November 1610, Sir Thomas Lewknor argued in the Commons that the recipients of royal gifts

> cannot be so ungrateful as in time of his Majesty's necessities, if they be required, not to express themselves in some thankful contribution. I remember I have read that Cyrus, when certain of his counsellors, that were faithful, told him that by excessive giving to his friends, he had impoverished himself and exhausted his treasure, he willed them to return after a few days and he would give them an answer to their contentment. In the meantime, he writes unto those friends, who in so full a measure that sometimes tasted of his bounty, required them to furnish him in his present expedition. He had undertaken that they should bring him such sums of money as they could conveniently spare. Within few days after, those men furnished him with an infinite mass of money, which Cyrus caused to be laid before him. He called there his counsellors and said, "See how much better a thesaurer am I than you. That which might have been unsafe in a treasury of lime and stone, I have caused to be safely kept in the hearts and hands of my friends." Now I doubt not but his Majesty, being a prince of admirable and unmatchable wisdom, hath used as much discretion in disposing of his wealth amongst friends as Cyrus did, and when he shall be pleased to make the like trial, I do not think but he shall find the like effect.[52]

Gift-giving, in other words, need not be viewed as wholly altruistic: it could be regarded as an investment that might one day yield a substantial return to the giver.

James certainly hoped, like Timon, that generosity would beget generosity. He envisaged a reciprocity in the giving that passed between a monarch and his subjects. As he told Parliament in March 1610, "I have spent much in liberality; but yet I hope you will consider that what I have given hath been given amongst you, and so what comes in from you goes out again amongst you."[53] Subjects had a reciprocal obligation to furnish the King's financial needs; James felt sure that "every good subject would rather choose to live more sparingly upon his own than that his King's state should be in want."[54] He even suggested that members of Parliament might emulate his own open-handed approach, for "freeness in giving graceth the gift, *Bis dat, qui cito dat*" [He gives twice who quickly gives].[55] Indeed, many of James's subjects in turn followed his example. Hacket was incredulous: "To what an immense riches in [James's] time did the merchandize of England rise to above former ages? What buildings? What sumptuousness? What feastings? What gorgeous attire? What massy plate and jewels? What prodigal marriage portions were grown in fashion among the nobility and gentry, as if the skies had rained plenty?"[56] One of the most extravagant of the Jacobean nobility was James Hay, later Viscount Doncaster and then Earl of Carlisle. Clarendon estimated his total life's expenditure at "above four hundred thousand pounds," and wrote that Hay was "surely a man of the greatest expense in his own person of any in the age he lived, and introduced more of that expense in the excess of clothes and diet than any other man."[57] Hay's favorite motto was "Spend and God will send"[58]; and in this respect, if in no other, James certainly lived up to his own maxim that "Kings are justly called gods."[59]

It will be clear from the above discussion that the desirability and consequences of excessive royal bounty emerged as an urgent public issue during the opening years of James's reign in England. The King's own behavior made this a subject of active political debate in a way that it had never been under his predecessor. Some of this debate took place behind closed doors, between the King and his Privy Councillors, but much of it, especially the lively debates in successive Parliaments, would have become known to a reasonably wide audience. All these developments form an illuminating context within which to locate Shakespeare's most searching exploration in drama of unwise generosity. For during precisely the years that *Timon of Athens* was most likely written, 1605–8, debate over the King's own bounty was at its height.

We do not wish to propose the Jacobean court as a "source" for *Timon* in the spirit of *quellen und forschungen*, or to argue topical analogies like those once used to "explain" the allegory of John Lyly's *Endymion* as a key to the complex relationship between Queen Elizabeth and the Earl of Leicester.[60] We would like to pursue the question, on the other hand, of the play's relationship to its historical context in 1605–8 or thereabouts. What prompted Shakespeare to write this bitter play about fiscal extravagance at a time when London was buzzing with rumors about James's latest follies? At about the same time as the play seems to have been written, the French ambassador Beaumont reported that "the English are for the most part little edified with the person or with the conduct of the King and declare openly enough that they were deceived in the opinion they were led to entertain of him."[61] What did Shakespeare suppose his audience might make of such a pronouncedly misanthropic dramatization of fiscal extravagance and its appalling aftermath? We do not know if the play was ever performed; the unfinished nature of the only text we have (the Folio text) may suggest that it was not. It may have been collaboratively written, with Thomas Middleton contributing a share, though the Folio editors, Heminges and Condell, appear to regard the play as essentially Shakespeare's. *Timon* was not published in quarto, and no contemporary records attest to performance or to anyone's opinion of the play (though it should be added that the same is true of a number of late plays like *Antony and Cleopatra* and *Coriolanus*). Whether or not performed or widely read, *Timon* raises questions about drama's role in its social setting, and we must assume that Shakespeare wrote it with a view to performance even if that goal was not realized. Our interest is not only in how the play's consciousness about fiscal extravagance may have been heightened by contemporary concerns, but also in how the play can be read in such a context.[62]

Does the characterization of Timon embody any sort of critique of King James, from however distant a perspective and filtered through an analogy that any audience would perceive as usefully imprecise? The question inevitably presents itself when we think about *Timon* in the historical context of extravagance at court, and yet the question raises serious issues about Shakespeare's professional relationship to the monarch. Shakespeare was, after all, a prominent member of an acting company that became officially the King's men after 1603. He was entitled to wear the royal livery in honor of the King's coronation. His plays were often acted at court before the King, as attested on the title page to the 1608 Quarto of *King Lear* and in various court records mentioning performances of *Othello* and *Measure for Measure* among other plays in 1604–1605.[63] *Macbeth* offers a tribute to James as the royal descendant of Banquo's line and even displays to Macbeth an "eighth king" at the end of a procession of Banquo's royal successors, "who bears a glass/ Which shows me many more; and some I see/ That twofold balls and treble scepters carry" (4.1.119–21). The "twofold balls" probably refer to the ceremonial orbs used at James's two coronations at Scone and Westminster as King of Scotland and England respectively. The "treble scepters" seems to allude to James's title as King of Great Britain, France, and Ireland, a style which he had adopted by royal proclamation on 20 October 1604.[64]

Would a playwright who authored what one scholar has called "The Royal Play of *Macbeth*"[65] turn his hand to another play about fiscal extravagance in such a way as to criticize, along with other members of the court, the playwright's own sovereign lord and master? The proposition as stated seems unlikely, and yet scholars have argued that *Coriolanus* and *Henry VIII* take up issues of factionalism at court that may also have seemed, by implication, critical of James and his favorites. Depictions of corruption and favoritism were of course commonplace in Elizabethan and Jacobean drama, from *The Spanish Tragedy* to *The Revenger's Tragedy* and beyond. Shakespeare wrote not simply or even primarily for James; his paying spectators were Londoners, never averse to decrying moral enervation among the rich and powerful.

Measure for Measure's Duke Vincentio has often been seen by critics as resembling King James in his wariness of crowds.[66] Is such a portraiture, if intended as topical, meant to be a flattering portrayal overall? Does it mix sharp observation with praise? Jonathan Goldberg has argued persuasively that the play does indeed explore a "special relationship" between James and Shakespeare himself as the playwright standing behind Duke Vincentio, in which we can perceive a parallel between the powers of the playwright and those of a sovereign, and in which Shakespeare's own independent authority is emphatically insisted upon. Even Ben Jonson, in an entertainment like *The Gypsies Metamorphosed* (James's favorite masque, presented in 1621), "managed to delight the sovereign and yet did not shirk criticism"; throughout his career, Jonson's praise for the Jaco-

bean era as a golden age was mixed with the wry observation that
"it is an age where all is bought and sold." Shakespeare, as writer
for a public acting company, enjoyed still greater artistic freedom with which to explore, through dramatic representation, the
essential link between politics and literature in the Jacobean period.[67]

Granted, then, that Shakespeare had the artistic license to
portray courtly extravagance in a way that his audience might
well recognize as familiarly close to contemporary court practice, need we insist on that contemporary model as a necessary
model for Shakespeare's play?[68] Timon's reckless generosity to
his followers is at once so clearly spelled out in Plutarch and Lucian, and so widely observable as a problem in English politics
generally (as in the often publicized examples of Edward II and
Richard II), that one must be wary of a too-easy assumption that
Timon would seem to score a hit on James's court in any specifically recognizable way. Richard Levin shows how easy it is to
pursue topical identifications and to argue, in a heads-I-win-tails-
you-lose style of debate, that the very mismatches in any purported correspondence between history and fiction can be as-
cribed to the author's need for tactful disclaimer of any direct
attack. Levin also warns us against the dangers of ascribing the
"platitudes of traditional wisdom" to any particular set of circumstances.[69]

Granted that there can be no single theoretical answer to this
problem, we wish to argue for a consideration of ways in which
events at court after 1603 and the presentation of extravagance in
Timon take on a complex and enriched meaning when examined
in juxtaposition. An historically based reader-response method
asks: assuming for the moment that the play may have been acted
or at least was written with a view to performance, what would
an audience in 1605–8 have made of Timon's reckless gift-giving? Such a focus draws attention, in both the political record
and in the play, to certain sharply drawn features: the monumental extent of the extravagance, the perception that the donor has
little idea of how much he is giving away, the problematic nature
of his motive for bestowing so much wealth on others, and the
ignoring of warnings. It is to these considerations that we turn
next in the play itself.

II

The first three acts of Shakespeare's play owe relatively little to the brief account in Plutarch, or to Lucian's satirical dialogue (which Shakespeare may have read in French). Both of these slender "sources" focus on the latter end of the story.[70] Plutarch's Timon is a misanthrope from the start, shunning human society except for Alcibiades, a "bold and insolent youth" whom Timon "made much of, and kissed him very gladly," and Apemantus, who shares Timon's gruff nature. The Athenians regard Timon as "a viper and malicious man unto mankind." Plutarch relates the story of Timon's mockery in offering his fig tree to any desperate Athenians who want to hang themselves (see the play, 5.1.204–11).[71] Plutarch concludes with the circumstances of Timon's death, and reports two versions of his epitaph, both of them bitter; they are closely paraphrased in the play at 5.4.70–73. Plutarch, after all, mentions Timon only parenthetically by way of illustrating Marcus Antonius' estrangement near the end of his life, "saying that he would lead Timon's life because he had the like wrong offered him that was afore offered unto Timon, and that for the unthankfulness of those he had done good unto, and with whom he took to be his friends, he was angry with all men and would trust no man." Plutarch's theme is embitterment through a sense of ingratitude, and he sees no reason to tell how Timon's bitterness came about or what his former prosperity was like. Lucian begins his dialogue after Timon has been abandoned to his impoverished estate, in order to focus on the irony of a renewed attentiveness toward Timon once people learn he has found riches in the ground. Lucian, or some redaction of him, seems to provide the material for Shakespeare's act 4.

In roughly the first half of the play, then, Shakespeare is working from a few hints in Plutarch and Lucian, along with some observations on gratitude in Seneca's *De Beneficiis*.[72] This first half is remarkably divergent from what follows. A number of recent productions have presented the play as divided into two parts that are visually and dramaturgically very contrastive. At Ashland, Oregon, in 1978, for example, the first half took place in the rich offices of Texas oilmen in their ten-gallon hats; their wives or women were sleekly dressed in a fashion-conscious way, while officious young men in expensively tailored suits spoke in the hushed whispers that testified to the awesomeness of wealth and power. In the second half, director Jerry Turner's set swung around 180 degrees to reveal a tangled landscape of Vietnamese strife, with Alcibiades and his molls outfitted as guerilla fighters carrying automatic weapons. More recently, in Stratford, Ontario, in 1991, Timon (Brian Bedford) appeared at first in an immaculate white suit and was surrounded by an adoring entourage in the midst of all the visible signs of plenty; in the second half, the landscape was reduced to that of Becket's *Waiting for Godot*, with Timon and Apemantus as alienated strangers glumly conversing in the shadow of a single, dead tree. As directorial interpretations, both productions spoke to the day-and-night contrast between Timon's days of prosperity and his days of ruin.[73]

The text of the play's first half plainly invites theatrical opulence. A key word is "bounty." Timon invites his guests to "share a bounteous time/ In different pleasures" (1.1.266), and his guests are nothing loath to "taste Lord Timon's bounty" (l. 287). Flavius, Timon's careworn steward, laments the fact that this "bounty had not eyes behind" to enable it to be more cautious (1.2.163). The flattering Lucius bids Timon's servant, Servilius, to "Commend me bountifully to his good lordship" (3. 2.53–54), while another sadly notes that "Doors that were ne'er acquainted with their wards [bolts]/ Many a bounteous year must be employed/ Now to guard sure their master" (3.3.39–41). The word in its various forms (bounty, bounties, bounteous, bountiful, bountifully) appears notably more often than in any other Shakespeare play, and is coupled almost invariably as in a fixed poetic epithet with Timon's name: he is a "bountiful good lord and master" and "a bountiful gentleman" (3.1.10, 40–41), "the very soul of bounty" (1.2.209), "bounteous Timon" (4.3.169), and the like. The related word "plenteous" is also more frequently used in *Timon* than elsewhere in Shakespeare; see, for example, Cupid's flattering reference to Timon's "plenteous bosom" at 1.2.124. "Ample" and "amplest" are used to characterize generosity and the gratitude it earns, as at 1.1.48 and 1.2.129. Most usages of these terms are from the play's first half; a few later instances recall with ironic effect his previous generosity or seek to awaken it once again.

This verbal emphasis on bounty is coupled with a hyperbole in language seeking to push to its limit the impression of endless largesse. The flattering lords who profit from the extravagance cannot find words to express their pleasure, so long as it is not at their own expense. "He outgoes/ The very heart of kindness," one lord marvels, and his partner replies in kind: "He pours it out. Plutus, the god of gold,/ Is but his steward" (1.1.287–90). This notion of the inadequacy of language to extol Timon as his sycophants wish points to an inflation in the rhetoric of flattery, but it also is part of the play's *ekphrasis* debate on the visual versus the verbal. Just as the Painter hopes to outdo the Poet with

"A thousand moral paintings" that can "demonstrate" truth "More pregnantly than words" (1.1.95–97), the theater can set forth visually and in nonverbal sound the splendor of Timon's entertainments. The play is unusually rich (as is *Henry VIII*) in elaborate stage directions, calling for "*Hautboys playing loud music,*" "*A great banquet served in*" (1.2.0), and the like. "*Trumpets sound*" as Timon first enters, "*addressing himself courteously to every suitor*" (1.1.99), or to announce the arrival of Alcibiades (l. 251). Timon's first great banquet features Cupid and "*a masque of Ladies*" as "*Amazons, with lutes in their hands, dancing and playing.*" Lords rise from table "*with much adoring of Timon*" to dance with the ladies, accompanied by "*a lofty strain or two to the hautboys*" (1.2.120–44). Jewels, coffers, and various other gifts and containers are a staple requirement in the way of props. Servants enter "*with wine*" (3.1.30). All this richness of theatrical paraphernalia is of course only a metonymy for the still greater wealth that it bespeaks, but seldom elsewhere does Shakespeare ask so much of his company's wardrobe and inventory of properties. The effect is distinctly reminiscent of court masques designed by Inigo Jones and Ben Jonson for the delectation of King James and his Queen.

Such visual extravagance has its negative side, of course. Flavius grieves that Timon's promises "fly so beyond his state/ That what he speaks is all in debt" (1.2.197–98). Apemantus' churlish presence serves to remind anyone who will listen of the vapidity of the spectacle at hand. "What a coil's here!/ Serving of becks and jutting-out of bums!" "What need these feasts, pomps, and vainglories?" (ll. 235–48). The masque especially is, in Apemantus' eyes, a "sweep of vanity" (l. 131). The senseless expense needed for such extravagance, says Flavius, is a "flow of riot" (2.2.1–3). Apemantus is a problematic figure, astute and yet repellent like Diogenes, given to hyperbolic vitriol just as Timon is given to hyperbolic bounty. The theatrical dialectic that brings together these divergent images of largesse encourages a dual view of Timon that is both admiring and critical, a duality that has much in common with early modern ambivalences about courtly splendor. In the context of King James's entertainments, the play's view of Timon reads at one moment like a poetic narrative of a courtly spectacle and at another moment like Puritan pamphleteering. Such a duality certainly invites curiosity as to Timon's motives for doing what he does.

"See, Magic of bounty," the Poet marvels, "all these spirits thy power/ Hath conjured to attend!" (1.1.6–8). From the very first, "power" is the key to understanding "bounty." The smell of power is what causes Timon's flattering dependents to "Follow his strides," fill his lobbies "with tendance," "Rain sacrificial whisperings in his ear,/ Make sacred even his stirrup, and through him/ Drink the free air" (1.1.85–88). "How this lord is followed!" exclaims the Painter, as he sees a flock of "certain Senators" trooping after Timon. "Happy man!" echoes the Poet (1.1.42–43). Timon repeatedly disclaims this "power," as when he refuses to silence Apemantus' criticisms (1.2.36), and yet his very exercising of restraint is part of what makes him so immensely influential and sought after. Even the paintings that are presented to him as flattering gifts speak with "mental power" (1.1.34). Power can quickly turn against Timon when his fortunes falter; Flavius is privately aware that Timon "has no power to make his wishes good" (1.2.196), and soon his fair-weather friends are regretting that they no longer have the "power to be kind" (3.2.55–56). Whether advancing up Fortune's steep slope or slipping downward, forgotten by those who followed him to the top, as in the Poet's allegory of the fortune-seeker (1.1.68–94), Timon is one whose power depends on his bounty. That he fails to understand the necessary connection is a major factor in his downfall.

Gift-giving can exercise a number of social functions, whether the giver is aware of that fact or not. Timon elaborates the conventions of gift-giving in some detail, and in terms not inappropriate to the lavish outlays of King James and his court. A donor is a patron. Cupid, preceding the masque of ladies, addresses Timon as such: "The five best senses/ Acknowledge thee their patron, and come free/ To gratulate thy plenteous bosom" (1.2.122–24). Patrons and petitioners need one another. Those who seek to serve Timon understand that their negotiations are to be conducted in a prescribed language of obligation: they are to flatter Timon for his "plenteous bosom" as a power to do good through his support of the arts, his befriending those in need of help, his assistance to those who have been victimized. Artists seeking his favor sense that their best move is to present works of art capable at once of flattering Timon and at the same time of seeming to offer criticism and thus affirm the sterling intellectual independence of the creative intellect. The Poet devises an allegory about Fortune's hill that is full of sententious truisms about the slipperiness and instability of Fortune but which can be read ambivalently as a tribute to one who, like Timon, demonstrates his natural superiority to other mortals by his ascent to Fortune's

throne. Fortune "wafts" Timon to her "with her ivory hand" even
as she "translates" his rivals into slaves and servants (1.1.68–94).

The Poet's thesis is that Timon's "large fortune . . . Subdues
and properties to his love and tendance/ All sorts of hearts" (1.1.
59–62). Huge wealth and grateful submission form a reciprocal
and symbiotic relationship; without one, one cannot expect the
other. "Love and tendance" are the *quid pro quo* of "large fortune." The Poet's observation that Timon's fortune is "Upon his
good and gracious nature hanging" (l. 61) is deftly ambivalent: it
appears to mean that Timon's wealth is a pleasant ornament to
his goodness, like rich raiment on a worthy person, but it also
suggests *sotto voce* that goodness of heart counts for little without a fortune to sustain men's loyalties. Reciprocity between patron and petitioner is similarly unstable: it uses a language of
loving assistance and dependency, but the contractual sense of
obligation puts a premium on what each party is to receive in
return for the giving or the receiving. The Jeweler knows how to
make repayment: in return for Timon's buying an expensive
jewel from him, the Jeweler stresses the way in which Timon's
largesse will be demonstrated by his gracious acceptance of it.
"You mend the jewel by the wearing it," he says (1.1.181).

Timon resists all such language of implicit empowerment,
turning aside the Jeweler's remark as if it were a jest: "Well
mocked." The Merchant, however, knows that the Jeweler has
expressed nothing more than a universal understanding about
human motives in being beneficent: "No, my good lord, he
speaks the common tongue/ Which all men speak with him" (ll.
183–84). The giving and receiving of bounty is a kind of commercial transaction, governed by rules of payment for something
received; indeed, in this transaction between Timon and the Jeweler, in which Timon will receive a jewel for his money but will
evidently pay a good deal more than he need do if he were to
drive a hard bargain, one is hard put to know where to draw the
line between commercial dealing and charitable donation.

Why is Timon so resistant to this language of commercial
exchange? In part it is because he wishes to think of his largesse
as a charitable act. The Merchant's formulation of common talk
about gift-giving robs Timon of the moral higher ground of altruism. One sort of gift-giving that seems to appeal especially to
Timon is the relieving of those in distress. His first act of charity
is to raise the fortune of his servant Lucilius so that a wealthy
older Athenian will not object to the marriage of his daughter
and sole heir to Lucilius and his modest means. The old Athenian

begs Timon to help him forbid the marriage; Timon instead discovers that providing Lucilius with an estate will remove the only material obstacle (1.1.116–60). Timon thereby becomes the patron of romantic love, the benefactor who paradoxically uses his wealth to protect the less privileged against the powerful control of those who have money.

The act appears idealistic, but is it selfless? Timon offers his own explanation based on a power relationship. "This gentleman of mine hath served me long;/ To build his fortune I will strain a little,/ For 'tis a bond in men" (1.1.151–53). Timon wishes to honor and reward the principle of the *comitatus*, that long-continuing loyalty upward of servant to master deserves an equal loyalty downward of master to servant. His view of this relationship as a "bond in men" is paternalistic; women are seldom given prominent roles in this play, especially its first half, and the daughter here in question is the subject of a three-way male negotiation between father, prospective son-in-law, and patron.[74] She does not appear in person even at the last stage of negotiation, and her presumed wishes are not even inquired into; Timon seeks to know only if Lucilius loves the daughter, and blandly accepts Lucilius' volunteered information that the daughter "accepts of" Lucilius' love in return (ll. 142–43). Timon's use of his wealth is a powerful gesture, however much vested on the side of youth and romantic attachment. As Terence Eagleton puts it, Timon's liberality "overwhelms, reducing other givers and their gifts to nothing beside itself."[75] It casts him in the role of savior, both in the eyes of others and of himself. It repays loyalty, and plainly asks for continued loyalty as an expression of gratitude.

Timon's gifts are not all directed toward those who are in distress, and accordingly the issue of motive becomes more complex. He also traffics in gifts with those who are his social equals. Recalling that a certain lord has recently praised one of Timon's finest horses, a "bay courser," Timon acts on that speech of praise by giving the horse to the praiser. "'Tis yours because you liked it" (1.2.210–12). Potlatch rituals in many traditional societies follow this convention,[76] as was illustrated when King Ibn Saud of Saudi Arabia met with President Roosevelt aboard a U.S. destroyer in Great Bitter Lake in the Suez Canal on February 14, 1945, right after the Yalta conference. Ibn Saud arrived in oriental splendor on another destroyer that was festooned with Turkish carpets, bodyguards armed with scimitars, a prayer tent on foredeck housing an astrologer and a food tester, and a flock of eighty sheep or goats penned on the ship's fantail. The King soon made it clear that he would be grateful to receive as a gift one of Roosevelt's personal wheelchairs and the companionship for the evening of Anna Roosevelt, who was accompanying her father. The president complied with the first request, not with the second. Roosevelt added the promise of a Douglas C–47 airplane, while the king responded with a solid gold knife, perfumes, Arabian attire for the president, and a sword encased in a diamond-studded scabbard, plus a promise that a complete harem attire for the president's wife and daughter would soon follow. Such a negotiation was proper, in Arabian terms, to Roosevelt's status as host and the King's as guest.[77] The comparable exchange in *Timon* suggests that the lord has spoken of the horse out of calculated awareness that his doing so should earn him the horse as a gift, and that Timon immediately recognizes his obligation under the terms of an agreed-upon convention. The obligation demonstrates his superiority in a contest of status, and acknowledges a kind of dependency in the lord even if Timon's rank and his are roughly equivalent.

Potlatch rituals can reach gigantic proportions, enough to bankrupt the giver, because the matter of status is of such overbearing social importance. The massive outlays in *Timon* arise from contests of this very sort between lords of rival station. "No meed but he repays/ Sevenfold above itself," an aristocratic observer marvels. "No gift to him/ But breeds the giver a return exceeding/ All use of quittance" (1.1.290–93). Investing in Timon, in other words, is better than what one can get from usual rates of interest. It follows, naturally, that Timon soon becomes an easy mark for wealthy men who understand the conventions of the potlatch and see how to put Timon repeatedly under the kind of obligation needed to maintain his exalted status. "If I want gold," explains a Senator with only slight exaggeration, "steal but a beggar's dog/ And give it Timon, why, the dog coins gold." Timon can be counted on to give a far better dog in return, not because he fails to know the value of his dogs but because his very status requires him to be more generous than the original donor. "If I would sell my horse and buy twenty more/ Better than he, why, give my horse to Timon—/ As nothing, give it him—it foals me straight,/ And able horses" (2.1.5–10).

Timon is similarly victimized when he practices other kinds of benefaction. Because he patronizes the arts so lavishly, artists cynically perceive that they need only flatter him in a seemingly edifying poem to be rewarded with a flow of generosity. One cannot be sure that Timon is unduly prone to flattery; the system itself requires him to be lavish as a way of showing his power of patronage. No doubt, too, his self-image as Maecenas is bolstered by what the poems written in his honor say (however ambivalently) about the greatness of his fortune. Even when he barters with jewelers and the like to make purchase of their creations, his role as patron demands that he act as benefactor, not simply pay what the market will bear. A jewel is hardly distinguished from a poem or painting; it is an investment in social status, and its acquisition must follow a certain code.

One striking resemblance we have already noted between Timon's extravagance and that of the Jacobean court is the failure to listen to warnings. We do not wish to press this resemblance as necessary evidence of direct copying from life, since the blindness to counsel is an integral feature of the entire system of gift exchange. Potlatch rituals often produce unbearable drains on the purse of the "winner" in a contest of epic gift-giving; since huge cost is the only pathway to success, the ruin of a fortune is to be expected. Still, the resemblance between Timon and King James and other members of his court may well have seemed a depressing reminder to those observers who wondered if anything could be done to avoid severe financial strain.

Timon responds in an oddly unstable way to financial warnings. The audience knows from the start that trouble is brewing. Fortune's fickleness is a truism known to all courtly observers, including the Poet and Painter (1.1.98–99). Flavius' worried aside that "There is no crossing him in 's humor" plainly bespeaks the loyal steward's attempts to make Timon understand that "When all's spent, he'd be crossed then, an he could" (1.2. 160–62). Apemantus' point is not simply that pomp is vainglorious, but that great lords and ladies eat one another and that the gods will ultimately confound "traffic" (1.1.216, 249). Even those who profit at Timon's expense know plainly enough what is going on and that it cannot last. Timon alone is blind to his own destiny and his own character.

Lack of self-knowledge is at the heart of his unstable condition. "So senseless of expense" is he, Flavius laments, "That he will neither know how to maintain it/ Nor cease his flow of riot." He "takes no account/ How things go from him nor resumes no care/ Of what is to continue." If his actions are "kind," they are certainly also "unwise" (2.2.1–6). Timon is at his most unattractive in his dealings with Flavius, even if he eventually concedes that Flavius is right (ll. 159, 177–79). His upbraiding of Flavius for insufficient warning of financial catastrophe is manifestly unfair. "You would not hear me," answers the steward, as he goes into damning details. When, "At many times," Flavius has presented his accounts to his master for audit, Timon has flung them aside. Flavius has had to endure "Not seldom nor no slight checks" in response to his tearful urgings that Timon be more prudent (ll. 128–46). Timon cravenly attempts to blame a servant for his own failings, until he eventually sees how unreasonable he has been. He is savage toward the servants of various lords who are sent to collect on their bills, as though these importunities were the servants' own doing.

This anger is occasioned in part by Timon's disillusionment, to be sure. Those who have sponged off him are heartless in refusing to help him, even if Timon is demonstrably by now a bad credit risk. Still, the fury is much more than the hurt idealism of a generous man. Shakespeare compassionately anatomizes the unstable mix of idealism and selfishness that are integral to Timon's view of himself as *generosus*. One telling moment occurs when Timon refuses to allow Ventidius to repay a gift that Timon made to him some time ago when Ventidius was in need. Ventidius has now received an ample inheritance from his father's will, and wishes to show his gratitude to Timon by giving the money back. Timon refuses. "I gave it freely ever," he explains, "and there's none/ Can truly say he gives if he receives" (1.2.12–13). Timon's presumably unconscious reformulation of Saint Paul's quotation of Jesus, "It is more blessed to give than to receive" (Acts 20:35), might well stagger a Jacobean audience. That familiar Pauline text[78] is central to the Christian paradoxes expressed in the Sermon on the Mount and the Magnificat: the mighty shall be pulled down from their seats, the meek shall inherit the earth, and so on (Matthew 5:1–12, Luke 2:46–55 and 6:20–23). It bespeaks, at its best, an intense and Utopian idealism of renouncing the world by giving all that one has to the poor and following Christ. Timon's inability to see what is potentially self-glorifying in his refusal to take back Ventidius' money smacks of hypocrisy. There appears to be no reason to accept Ventidius' offer of repayment other than that Timon's role in the potlatch ritual will be diminished. There are times, *pace* Saint Paul, when it is more self-effacing and generous to receive than to give.

Then, too, the play asks us to wonder if Timon isn't testing his friends with all this generosity. "O you gods," he exclaims, "what need we have any friends if we should ne'er have need of 'em?" (1.2.94–96). Timon says this as he is surrounded at his feast by grateful and flattering consumers of his substance. Once again the imagery compares Timon to Christ, and with blasphemous implications. "O you gods," says Apemantus, "what a number of men eats Timon, and he sees 'em not! It grieves me to see so many dip their meat in one man's blood" (1.2.39–41).[79] No Jacobean audience, surely, could resist seeing an analogy here to the Last Supper in this language of sacramental communion. Timon is to be the sacrificial lamb, and his ungrateful beneficiaries are to be the Judases at his crucifixion. Those friends are of course deplorably in the wrong, but Timon's distortion of the Golden Rule into a formula that will soon project a Lear-like fury at ingratitude is hardly admirable. It undercuts any claim he might make to altruism in his own conduct as patron. "Love's not love/ When it is mingled with regards that stands/ Aloof from th' entire point," says the King of France about Cordelia in a play that may be closely contemporary with Timon (*King Lear*, 1.1.242–44). By this standard, Timon's self-image of altruism is close to hypocritical.

Our point here is not to judge Timon and his pagan world of ancient Athens by the moral standards of the Christian commandments. We must observe, however, that Timon's actions are repeatedly framed in the context of the New Testament (as also are those in *King Lear*, which is similarly pre-Christian in its setting), however unaware the characters onstage may be of the resonances of what they say. The result is a thoroughly believable dramatization of gift-giving, one in which the benefactor's motives include much more self-aggrandizement than he is able to acknowledge. Timon's great rage may be as much the product of a conflicted view of self as it is a justifiable anger at the way he is treated. Timon's need to blame others is unquenchable. It masks in him any realization that his own approach to generosity has always been a reciprocal one, and that such a view of gift-giving is bound to lead to disappointment. Attempts to buy friendship, loyalty, and respect are doomed to last only as long as the wealth used for the purchase. Instead of coming to terms with this hard truth, Timon tears himself apart in rage.

The play's dominant image patterns, especially in the first half, underscore the ironies of Timon's search for self-esteem and popular acclaim through gift-giving. One such image pattern is that of gliding and slipperiness. The Poet speaks of poesy as a "gum which oozes/ From whence 'tis nourished" (1.1.23–24). Presumably he means to describe the creative process, but he does so in terms that characterize poetry as the sticky product of patronage. The Poet's Mount of Fortune features "glib and slippery creatures" tendering down their services to Lord Timon, "glass-faced" flatterers, treacherous slopes from which the fortunate soon fall, stoopings and bowings, and Fortune with her "ivory hand" (ll. 56–93). Jewels with their "luster" (1.2.148) repeatedly invoke the glitter of vainglorious pomp that belongs to the world of courtly masquing and entertainment. The commercial language of selling, value, price, "traffic," gold, Plutus, "meed," the "breeding" of money, "quittance" (interest rates), coffers, coining, expense, and the like, enforces a continual awareness of the economic basis of human transactions in this play (1.1.167, 178–80, and 289–93; 1.2.193; 2.1.6–7, etc.). When everyone's "business" is "money" (2.3.4–5), gift-giving becomes implicated as well. Shakespeare's apparent uncertainty as to the value of the so-called talent, and the resulting huge discrepancy between various debts amounting to "five talents" in one case and 25,000 in another (see 1.1.101, 2.1.1–3, 2.2.205, etc.), or simple vagueness at other times ("so many talents," 3.2. 12, "fifty—five hundred—talents," 3.2.39), quantifies the ambiguity that hangs over Timon's business transactions.[80] Repeated images of kneeling and bowing, of doffing the cap in deferential greeting, add to an atmosphere of obsequiousness. Connotations of coldness of demeanor, of "cold-moving nods" that freeze one into silence (2.2.218–19), serve as a bleak reminder that "'Tis deepest winter in Lord Timon's purse" (3.3.15). In the repeated motif of feasting and dining, the banquet of stones and water prepared by Timon for his fair-weather friends exposes the hypocrisy of hospitality and merriment in the play's opening extravaganza.

III

Our focus has been on the first half of *Timon*, not with a wish to demonstrate that Shakespeare consciously reworked the luxury of the Jacobean court into his dramatization of a misanthrope (though other sources for the play's first half are hard to find), but rather to ask what sort of contemporary resonance an English audience might have seen in this play. A mood of disillusionment nicely fits both play and Jacobean court scene. Gargantuan expense of entertainment and gift-giving may grow out of a desire to appear generous, but any dispassionate observer needs to realize that gift-giving can serve a political function. The giver defines his greatness by the amount he gives, and creates obligations that are essential to him for reasons of self-esteem and of power-seeking. The behavioral pattern can be partly infantile—a term used by some historians to characterize King James. In the psychoanalytic terms that Coppélia Kahn proposes, both Timon of Athens and James of Scotland may be attempting unsuccessfully to be self-sufficient and "maternal" without being beholden to others.[81] What we wish to stress is the intensity and immediacy of the public debate that erupted around the time of the writing of *Timon*, and the particularlity of that debate not just in relation to royal and aristocratic extravagance but in the way it deconstructed the supposed altruism of gift-giving into the kind of wry analysis of motive we find highlighted in Shakespeare's play.

University of Chicago
Selwyn College, Cambridge

NOTES

[1] Coppélia Kahn, "'Magic of bounty': *Timon of Athens*, Jacobean Patronage, and Maternal Power," *Shakespeare Quarterly* 38 (1987): 34–57, especially p. 35.

[2] Jonathan Goldberg, *James I and the Politics of Literature* (Baltimore: Johns Hopkins University Press, 1983), 268 n. 22.

[3] Quoted in D. H. Willson, *King James VI and I* (London: Jonathan Cape, 1956), 166.

[4] See, for example, Andrew Willets, *Ecclesia Triumphans* (London, 1603; STC 25676), sig. A3ʳ: "God hath given us a wise and judicial king, whose princely writings do give him preeminence before all his predecessors: another Solomon, a king and an Ecclesiastes, a learned writer." For another example, see Miles Mosse, *Scotland's Welcome* (London, 1603). We owe these references to Tim Amos. Throughout this essay, quotations from the early modern period have been lightly modernized for clarity and to provide uniformity of treatment.

[5] For a recent assessment of the last two works, see Jenny Wormald, "James VI and I, *Basilikon Doron* and *The Trew Law of Free Monarchies*: the Scottish Context and the English Translation," in *The Mental World of the Jacobean Court*, ed. Linda Levy Peck (Cambridge: Cambridge University Press, 1991), 36–54. The texts may be found in *James VI and I: Political Writings*, ed. Johann P. Sommerville, Cambridge Texts in the History of Political Thought (Cambridge: Cambridge University Press, 1994), 1–84. James's learnedness occasioned some resistance and even hostility; see Leah Marcus, *Puzzling Shakespeare: Local Reading and Its Discontents* (Berkeley: University of California Press, 1988), especially 113–14.

[6] For this, see especially: Jenny Wormald, "James VI or I: Two Kings or One?" *History* 68 (1983): 187–209; Maurice Lee, Jr., *Great Britain's Solomon: James VI and I in his Three Kingdoms* (Urbana: University of Illinois Press, 1990); Peck, ed., *The Mental World*

of the Jacobean Court, (especially the essays by Wormald, Sommerville, and Christianson); Kenneth Fincham and Peter Lake, "The Ecclesiastical Policy of James I," *Journal of British Studies* 24 (1985): 169–207.

[7] John Morrill, "The Stuarts," in *The Oxford Illustrated History of Britain,* ed. Kenneth O. Morgan (Oxford: Oxford University Press, 1984), 306.

[8] *A Royalist's Notebook: The Commonplace Book of Sir John Oglander, Knight,* ed. Francis Bamford (London: Constable, 1936), 197. One must be aware, of course, of the potential extent to which James's reputation as slovenly was a reflection of English xenophobic stereotyping and cultural misunderstandings, as well as the historiographic influence of the character assassination perpetrated by Anthony Weldon in his *Court and Character of King James* (London, 1650).

[9] John Chamberlain to Ralph Winwood, 26 January 1605, *The Letters of John Chamberlain,* ed. N. E. McClure, 2 vols. (Philadelphia: The American Philosophical Society, 1939), 1:201.

[10] John Hacket, *Scrinia Reserata: a Memorial Offer'd to the Great Deservings of John Williams, D.D.* (London, 1693), 1:38.

[11] Norman Moore, *The History of the Study of Medicine in the British Isles* (Oxford: Clarendon Press, 1908), 99.

[12] *The Autobiography and Correspondence of Sir Simonds D'Ewes, Bart.,* ed. J. O. Halliwell, 2 vols. (London: R. Bentley, 1845), 1:264. Cf. Bamford, ed., *A Royalist's Notebook,* 196.

[13] Sir John Harington to Secretary Barlow, 1606, *Nugae Antiquae: being a miscellaneous collection of original papers . . . by Sir John Harington, Knt.,* ed. Thomas Park, 2 vols. (London: Vernor and Hood, 1804), 1:349–52. The episode is discussed in relation to *Macbeth* by Alvin Kernan, *Shakespeare, The King's Playwright: Theatre in the Stuart Court, 1603–1613* (New Haven: Yale University Press, 1995), 71–88, especially 73–74.

[14] On this, see Willson, *James VI and I,* 159–74, and Menna Prestwich, *Cranfield: Politics and Profits under the Early Stuarts* (Oxford: Clarendon Press, 1966), 10.

[15] Derek Hirst, *Authority and Conflict: England, 1603–1658* (London: E. Arnold, 1986), 97.

[16] See especially Jennifer M. Brown, "Scottish Politics, 1567–1625," in *The Reign of James VI and I,* ed. A. G. R. Smith (London: Macmillan, 1973), 22–39; Wormald, "James VI and I"; and Lee, *Great Britain's Solomon,* 31–62.

[17] Anthony Weldon appears to have originated the phrase "the wisest fool in Christendom" (*The Court and Character of King James,* 186; see n. 8 above). See also Jenny Wormald, "James VI and I: Two Kings or One?", *History* 68 (1983): 187–209; and Bruce Galloway, *The Union of England and Scotland, 1603–1608* (Edinburgh: J. Donald, 1986), 59–60.

[18] Lawrence Stone, *The Crisis of the Aristocracy, 1558–1641* (Oxford: Clarendon Press, 1965), 71–74, 81–82.

[19] George Whetstone, *The Rock of Regard* (1576), 55; cited in *OED,* s.v. "carpet-knight."

[20] Randle Cotgrave, *A Dictionary of the French and English Tongues* (1611), s.v.

"Couchette, Mignon de couchette"; cited in *OED*, s.v. "carpet-knight."

[21] Sir John Ferne, *The Blazon of Gentrie* (London, 1586), 105; cited in *OED*, s.v. "carpet," 2c.

[22] Stone, *Crisis*, 97–104.

[23] For these figures, see Prestwich, *Cranfield*, 12–17. One must bear in mind factors beyond James's control contributing to extra expenditure, not least the need to support his family, set up a separate household for his wife, and the like. Then, too, Elizabeth's meanness made James's profligacy seem greater than it was.

[24] For the development of the Jacobean court masque, see especially Graham Parry, *The Golden Age Restor'd: The Culture of the Stuart Court, 1603–1642* (Manchester: Manchester University Press, 1981); and Stephen Orgel, *The Illusion of Power: Political Theater in the English Renaissance* (Berkeley: University of California Press, 1975). As to expenditure, it is important to remember that the 30 percent increase over Elizabeth's budget still amounted to a relatively small £7,000 per annum. See E. K. Chambers, *The Elizabethan Stage*, 4 vols. (Oxford: Clarendon Press, 1923), 3:280, for evidence of Jacobean saving by reusing costumes from Elizabeth's wardrobe in Daniel's masque of 6 January 1604.

[25] Arthur Wilson, *The History of Great Britain, being the Life and Reign of King James the First* (London, 1653), 53–54.

[26] "The Journal of Sir Roger Wilbraham," ed. H. S. Scott, in *Camden Miscellany* 10, no. 1, 3rd series, vol. 4 (London: Camden Society, 1902), 66.

[27] Godfrey Goodman, *The Court of King James the First*, ed. J. S. Brewer, 2 vols. (London: R. Bentley, 1839), 1:199–200.

[28] *James VI and I, Political Writings*, ed. Sommerville, 166 (31 March 1607).

[29] Ibid., 197 (21 March 1610). Cf. *Proceedings in Parliament, 1610*, ed. Elizabeth Read Foster, 2 vols. (New Haven: Yale University Press, 1966), 1:50.

[30] *The Parliamentary Diary of Robert Bowyer, 1606–1607*, ed. David Harris Willson (reprint, New York: Octagon Books, 1971), 44 (14 February 1606).

[31] Godfrey Goodman, *Court of King James*, 2:268 (Tobie Mathew to the Duke of Buckingham, 29 March 1623).

[32] James VI and I to Robert Cecil, October 1605, *Letters of King James VI and I*, ed. G. P. V. Akrigg (Berkeley: University of California Press, 1984), 243.

[33] Ibid., 261, James VI and I to Robert Cecil, October 1605.

[34] Ibid., 291, James VI and I to the Privy Council, 19? October 1607.

[35] Conrad Russell, *The Addled Parliament of 1614: The Limits of Revision* (Reading: University of Reading Press, 1992), 10.

[36] Historical Manuscripts Commission, *Calendar of the Manuscripts of the Marquess of Salisbury* 16 (1933), 220 (Archbishop Hutton of York to Robert Cecil, 10 August 1604).

[37] "A Collection of several speeches and treatises of the late Lord Treasurer Cecil

and of several observations of the Lords of the Council given to King James concerning his estate and revenue in the years 1608, 1609, and 1610," ed. Pauline Croft, in *Camden Miscellany* 29, no. 1, 4th series, vol. 34 (London: Camden Society, 1987), 298.

[38] *Proceedings in Parliament, 1610*, ed. Foster, 1:6 (14 February 1610).

[39] Ibid., 2:23 (15 February 1610).

[40] *The Poeticall Essayes of Alexander Craige, Scotobritane* (London, 1604), sigs. [B2ᵛ]–B3[ʳ]. We owe this reference to Tim Amos.

[41] "A Collection of several speeches," ed. Croft, 277.

[42] Ibid., 278.

[43] Ibid., 284.

[44] Ibid., 285.

[45] Francis Osborne, *Traditionall Memoyres on the Raigne of King James* (London, 1658), 85.

[46] Ibid., 85–86.

[47] Hacket, *Scrinia Reserata*, 1:225.

[48] Quoted in S. J. Houston, *James I* (London: Longman, 1973), 25.

[49] Prestwich, *Cranfield*, 13.

[50] Willson, *James VI and I*, 264–68. For James's attitude toward the "Great Contract," see *Historical Manuscripts Commission, Calendar of the Manuscripts of the Marquess of Salisbury* 21 (1970), 217 (Sir Thomas Lake to Robert Cecil, 30 April 1610).

[51] Prestwich, *Cranfield*, 204.

[52] *Proceedings in Parliament, 1610*, ed. Foster, 2:403 (16 November 1610).

[53] *James VI and I, Political Writings*, ed. Sommerville, 197 (21 March 1610).

[54] Ibid., 198 (21 March 1610).

[55] Ibid.

[56] Hacket, *Scrinia Reserata*, 1:224.

[57] Edward Hyde, Earl of Clarendon, *The History of the Rebellion and Civil Wars in England*, ed. W. D. Macray, 6 vols. (Oxford: Clarendon Press, 1888; reissued 1992), 1:77–78 (Book I: 135–36).

[58] Prestwich, *Cranfield*, 16.

[59] The phrase comes from James's speech to Parliament on 21 March 1610; quoted in J. P. Kenyon, *The Stuart Constitution*, 2nd ed. (Cambridge: Cambridge University Press, 1986), 12. Kahn, "'Magic of Bounty'," gives other instances of monumental extravagance among James's courtiers, including none other than Robert Cecil, Earl of Salisbury, James's long-suffering Lord Treasurer and counselor to the King on the need for fiscal

moderation. See also Wallace MacCaffrey, "Place and Patronage in Elizabethan Politics," in *Elizabethan Government and Society: Essays Presented to Sir John Neale*, ed. S. T. Bindoff, J. Hurstfield, and C. H. Williams (London: Athlone Press, 1961), 95–126.

[60] R. Warwick Bond, ed., *The Complete Works of John Lyly*, 3 vols. (Oxford: Clarendon Press, 1902), 3:9–13 and 81–103. Bond elaborates a thesis first propounded by N. J. Halpin, *Oberon's Vision in the Midsummer Night's Dream. Illustrated by a comparison with Lylie's Endymion* (London: Shakespeare Society, 1843).

[61] Quoted in Willson, *James VI and I*, 196.

[62] For a complementary reading of the play in terms of the decline of great feudal households that were faced with the traditional obligations of hospitality and patronage in a time of inflation and increasing burdens on landowners, see E. C. Pettet, *"Timon of Athens*: The Disruption of Feudal Morality," *Review of English Studies* 23 (1947): 321–36. Timon does at times give voice to the feudal ethos. Nevertheless, as Pettet concedes, Timon is too extravagant to be simply a representative of the old feudal order at its best. Our reading offers, we hope, one possible reason for the emphasis on excessive liberality. Kenneth Muir, *"Timon of Athens* and the Cash-Nexus," in *The Singularity of Shakespeare and Other Essays* (Liverpool: Liverpool University Press, 1977), 56–75, analyzes "the new domination of money" in the early seventeenth century as "clearly a threat to the conception of order Shakespeare shared with his contemporaries" because it supplanted traditional notions of order with one divorced from morality and based solely on self-interest. L. C. Knights touches briefly, in his "Timon of Athens," in *The Morality of Art: Essays Presented to G. W. Knight by His Colleagues and Friends*, ed. D. W. Jefferson (London: Routledge and Kegan Paul, 1969), 7–8, on the scramble for rewards at court and lavish expenditure in both the Elizabethan and the Jacobean periods. Richard Fly, *Shakespeare's Mediated World* (Amherst: University of Massachusetts Press, 1976), 119–42, astutely describes how in *Timon* an organic conception of a mediating body politic has given way to "a more rigid system of dialectical relationships, which compel individuals to struggle endlessly for a merely personal dominance."
Interpretations of *Timon* in the context of the economic crisis in the early seventeenth century that caused the financial ruin of many large estates are aptly summarized by Rolf Soellner, *"Timon of Athens": Shakespeare's Pessimistic Tragedy* (Columbus: Ohio State University Press, 1979), 114–28. Lawrence Stone's *The Crisis of the Aristocracy 1558–1641* (Oxford: Clarendon Press, 1965) is a major source of information, as is his earlier *Family and Fortune: Studies in Aristocratic Finance in the Sixteenth and Seventeenth Centuries* (Oxford: Clarendon Press, 1973). See also Christopher Hill, *The World Turned Upside Down: Radical Ideas during the English Revolution* (London: Temple Smith, 1972); C. B. McPherson, *The Political Theory of Possessive Individualism* (Oxford: Clarendon Press, 1962); W. K. Jordan, *Philanthropy in England 1480–1660* (London: Allen and Unwin, 1959); and Gail Paster, *The Idea of the City in the Age of Shakespeare* (Athens, Georgia: University of Georgia Press, 1985), 91–123.

[63] Chamber and revels accounts of 1604–5, reprinted in E. K. Chambers, *William Shakespeare: A Study of Facts and Problems*, 2 vols. (Oxford: Clarendon Press, 1930), 2:330–33.

[64] *Royal Proclamations of King James I, 1603–25*, vol. 1 of *Stuart Royal Proclamations*, ed. J. F. Larkin and P. L. Hughes (Oxford: Clarendon Press, 1973), 94–97.

[65] Henry Paul, *The Royal Play of Macbeth* (New York: Macmillan, 1950). See also Kernan, *Shakespeare, The King's Playwright*, 71–88; Kernan sees Macbeth as "making divine-right kingship identical with nature and sanity" (p. 88).

[66] E.g., Josephine Waters Bennett, *"Measure for Measure" as Royal Entertainment* (New York: Columbia University Press, 1966).

[67] Goldberg, *James I and the Politics of Literature,* especially pp. 128 and 136.

[68] See Marcus, *Puzzling Shakespeare,* especially pp. 108–48 on *Cymbeline;* and Stuart Kurland, "'A beggar's book Outworths a noble's blood': The Politics of Faction in *Henry VIII,*" *Comparative Drama* 26 (1992): 237–53.

[69] Richard Levin, *New Readings vs. Old Plays: Recent Trends in the Reinterpretation of English Renaissance Drama* (Chicago: University of Chicago Press, 1979), 171–93. Levin briefly discusses *Timon* not in terms of extravagance but in terms of purported Christ images in Shakespeare's plays.

[70] See E. A. J. Honigmann, "*Timon of Athens,*" *Shakespeare Quarterly* 12 (1961): 3–20.

[71] Citation references throughout are to *The Complete Works of Shakespeare,* ed. David Bevington, 4th ed. updated (New York: Longmans, 1997).

[72] See John Wallace, "*Timon of Athens* and the Three Graces: Shakespeare's Senecan Study," *Modern Philology* 83 (1986): 349–63.

[73] For other stage interpretations, see Gary Jay Williams, "Stage History, 1816–1978," in Soellner, ed., Timon of Athens: *Shakespeare's Pessimistic Tragedy,* 161–85.

[74] Kahn, "'Magic of Bounty'," 34–57.

[75] Terence Eagleton, *Shakespeare and Society: Critical Studies in Shakespearean Drama* (London: Chatto & Windus, 1967), 172.

[76] On potlatch rituals, see Marcel Mauss, *The Gift: The Form and Reason for Exchange in Archaic Societies,* trans. W. D. Halls (New York: W. W. Norton, 1990); Claude Lévi-Strauss, *The Elementary Structures of Kinship,* rev. ed. (London: Eyre & Spottiswoode, 1969); Helen Codere, *Fighting with Property: A Study of Kwakiutl Potlatching and Warfare 1792–1930* (Seattle: University of Washington Press, 1950); Abraham Rosman and Paula G. Rubel, *Feasting with Mine Enemy: Rank and Exchange among Northwest Coast Societies* (New York: Columbia University Press, 1971); Philip Drucker and Robert F. Heizer, *To Make My Name Good: A Reexamination of the Southern Kwakiutl Potlatch* (Berkeley: University of California Press, 1967); and Forrest E. LaViolette, *The Struggle for Survival: Indian Cultures and the Protestant Ethic in British Columbia* (Toronto: University of Toronto Press, 1961). For an analogy between the "Big Man" system of potlatch and Jacobean patronage practices, see Werner L. Gundersheimer, "Patronage in the Renaissance: An Exploratory Approach," in *Patronage in the Renaissance,* ed. Guy Fitch Lytle and Stephen Orgel (Princeton: Princeton University Press, 1981), 3–23.

[77] Frank Freidel, *Franklin D. Roosevelt: A Rendezvous with Destiny* (Boston: Back Bay Books, 1990), 593–94; Jim Bishop, *FDR's Last Year: April 1944–April 1945* (New York: Morrow, 1974), 443–47. The story is probably apocryphal that Ibn Saud, in praising the meal he was served, expected to receive the U.S. Navy cook as a suitable compliment in return, but it is at least in keeping with the known facts of this encounter.

[78] St. Paul may have had in mind Luke 6:34.

[79] This passage is from a scene attributed to Thomas Middleton by R. V. Holdsworth, *Middleton and Shakespeare: The Case for Middleton's Hand in "Timon of Athens"* (forthcoming), but this present essay is more concerned with the play's treatment of extravagance than with authorship of individual passages. The treatment seems reasonably uniform, as though agreed upon by the collaborators.

[80] See Kenneth Muir, "Cash-Nexus," cited in n. 62.

[81] Kahn, "'Magic of Bounty'," 34–57.

Friendship in *Hamlet*

Robert C. Evans

In 1958, Harry Levin reported that in the previous sixty years a new item of *Hamlet* commentary had been issued every twelve days.[1] By now the rate must be something closer to a new item every twelve hours or minutes. My chief justification for adding one more straw to the camel's back rests on the surprising fact that friendship—a crucial concern of classical and Renaissance thinkers—has not received much explicit or systematic attention as an important and pervasive theme in Shakespeare's great tragedy. Inevitably the topic is raised—usually in passing—in discussions of Horatio and of Rosencrantz and Guildenstern, but it has not received much sustained exploration.[2] My immediate purpose is merely to show that the theme of friendship does run throughout the entire play—that it appears even where it might seem present only slightly. While trying to establish its general importance, I also hope to focus on a few scenes and characters in some detail, as well as to discuss in broader terms how Shakespeare's concerns with friendship help enrich his tragedy.[3] *Hamlet* seems at least in part a play that is very much about friendship: a play about finding, making, losing, and keeping friends. It explores, from numerous perspectives, one of the most significant and inherently complex of human relationships—a relationship particularly fascinating to Renaissance thinkers, for many of whom friendship (in the words of Clifford Davidson) "is not only a radiant ideal but is also an expression of a most necessary kind of good will that makes society cohesive."[4]

I

The play's concern with friendship is sounded at once: "Who's there?" (1.1.1).[5] Quite literally, Barnardo wants to know not only *who* is there (whether the unseen figure is a friend or foe) but also *why* he is there (whether his intentions are friendly). This opening epitomizes the entire play and particularly Hamlet's position at court: surrounded by darkness, a lone figure needs to recognize his friends. Most humans can relate to this need, and the play probably exercises such strong psychological appeal partly because we all, to one degree or another, resemble Barnardo and Hamlet in wanting to know whether the persons nearest us are persons we can trust. Determining one's friends is only one dilemma the tragedy portrays and confronts, but it seems to be a dilemma immediately and forcefully relevant to most human lives.[6]

Barnardo's nervous question is answered by an apparently unfriendly and certainly formal challenge (1.1.2), which in turn elicits an equally formal, impersonal response that is also a pledge of public allegiance or political friendship (1.1.3). Only when Francisco uses a familiar personal name (1.1.4) do tensions relax: we realize, precisely when they do, that these men already know each other and perhaps are even friends. This intuition seems confirmed when Barnardo solicitously urges Francisco to get to bed (and thus to peace, quiet, and comfort). Like so much else in this play, however, these apparently caring words can also be interpreted in another way: as a calculated maneuver to dismiss Francisco before the ghost appears. Neither reading need (or perhaps can) have priority: here as elsewhere in *Hamlet*, exchanges even between apparent friends can have multiple significations, and just as it is sometimes hard but important to interpret the precise nuances of our own friends' speech, so it is usually difficult in *Hamlet* for either us or the characters to make absolutely unambiguous sense of anything said, not said, or implied. The play fascinates partly for this reason.

Further evidence of friendship between Barnardo and Francisco comes in the latter's response to the suggestion that he head to bed (1.1.8–9). Francisco's immediate willingness (once he knows he is speaking to a friend) to share not only his physical but especially his deepest emotional feelings seems significant in a play whose central character finds it so difficult to share true feelings openly, except in soliloquy. Francisco is lonely, cold, and sick at heart, but he at least has a comrade to whom he can confess these thoughts. Hamlet, at first, has no one with whom he can openly speak except the crowd of strangers who sit or stand off-stage.

As Francisco leaves, Barnardo bids him a solicitous "good night" (1.1.12) and asks him to urge his "rivals" to "make haste" (1.1.13–14). Here, with nice irony, the word "rivals" means not "foes" but "partners"—just one of many subtle touches of paradox in an immensely paradoxical play. Having briefly provided friendly relief to Francisco, Barnardo now seeks such comfort himself: throughout the play, the fear and danger of being left literally or metaphorically alone is stressed. In this work, many characters will eventually find themselves suddenly isolated.

Hearing Horatio and Marcellus approaching, Francisco now repeats Barnardo's earlier demand: "Who is there?" (1.1.15). It hardly seems an accident that Horatio's very first words are "Friends to this ground" (1.1.16). Horatio will later prove one of the play's best examples of friendship; his first word thus quite literally reflects his essential character. At this point, though, he uses the word "friends" more in a political than personal sense, thereby helping to remind us how the connotations of the term have evolved since the Renaissance. Today the word mainly refers to an inherently personal relation. In Shakespeare's time, however, it often carried associations of political or social allegiance. If a person was politically important, his "friends" were often his allies or followers, his dependents or entourage, his loyal citizens. Horatio, however, is a "friend to this ground" in more ways than one. Throughout the play, he seeks not only what is best for Hamlet as a person and prince but also what is best for Denmark. His opening words help make it seem entirely appropriate that at the very end of the play he becomes the designated spokesman not only for Hamlet but also for the entire Danish nation.

Marcellus echoes and endorses his friend's explanation by announcing that he and Horatio are "liegemen to the Dane" (1.1.16), although it seems subtly fitting that he (not Horatio) is the first to mention Claudius, the great rival of Horatio's future friend, the prince. It seems appropriate, too, that Marcellus uses a word ("liegemen") whose connotations are subtly formal and legalistic rather than intensely personal, for by the end of the play Claudius, although surrounded by friends in a superficial, political sense, will finally be abandoned by them all. Both Hamlet and Claudius lose friends during the course of the play, but in the final analysis Claudius is by far the more lonely and isolated figure.

The mutual solicitude all four men show in this opening scene helps establish an air of comradeship and community that not only helps counteract the very opening emphasis on isolation and fear but that also helps prepare, by contrast, for our later sense of Hamlet's isolation at court. Yet the small community no sooner forms than it begins to disintegrate: Francisco is eager to be gone, and his first words to Horatio and Marcellus (1.1.17) are at once a greeting and farewell. Even as he leaves he is bid adieu with conspicuously friendly words (1.1.18), while the heavy emphasis here on what seem to be first names also helps enhance the tone of friendship. Marcellus calls for "Barnardo," and Barnardo also seems already familiar with the man he addresses as "Horatio" (1.1.20–21). Horatio, in turn, adds to the friendly atmosphere by making a self-deprecating joke: to a question by Barnardo—"is Horatio there?"—he responds, "A piece of him," thereby telegraphing immediately his informality, his sense of humor, his tendency not to take either himself or situations too seriously, and also his ability to express personal discomfort without focusing excessive attention on himself (1.1.21–22). All these qualities would (and do) help make him an excellent friend, not only to these men but also, later, to Hamlet. Barnardo's enthusiastic greeting of the visitors, moreover, expresses more than merely formal courtesy: obviously he is sincerely glad that his friends have now arrived.

Horatio's first reference to the ghost as "this thing" (1.1.24) can be read in several complementary ways, all relevant to the friendship theme. The word "thing" already implies, perhaps, some slightly haughty skepticism, some gentle teasing and chiding. Horatio may already know Marcellus and Barnardo, but he is clearly not so close a friend that he is willing to take their mere testimony as absolute proof of the ghost's existence. His skepticism implies his mental distance, but his slightly mocking tone also suggests, paradoxically, that he feels comfortable enough to tease them. His question, then, establishes him as an outsider to their present bond, but also as someone capable of bonding. By calling the ghost a "thing," moreover, he suggests (unintentionally, perhaps) that it is the ultimate outsider, the ultimate "other": non-human, alien, and incapable (almost by definition) of normal friendship.

For the moment, then, Horatio stands apart from Marcellus and Barnardo. Like many friendships, theirs is rooted in a shared experience—one Horatio knows only by report. Perhaps there is wounded rebuke in Marcellus's comment that "Horatio says 'tis but *our fantasy,*/ And *will not let* belief take hold of him,/ Touching this dreaded sight *twice seen of us*" (1.1.26–28). It is as if Horatio even doubted their rationality, perversely rejecting their testimony even though they have twice witnessed the ghost together. Thus the ghost plays even here the double role it fulfills throughout the play: it simultaneously unites and divides. It binds Marcellus and Barnardo but separates them from Horatio, just as it will later bond Horatio and Hamlet while separating them from the court at large. The ghost proves a potent catalyst of both friendship *and* enmity.

Barnardo's invitation to sit (1.1.33) partly signals a relaxation of tension, an opportunity for physical comfort and psychological bonding. The guards' willingness to tell Horatio their story already implies their trust and respect (as does his willingness to listen). Even as the trio relax, however, an undercurrent of probably gentle enmity pervades Barnardo's request that Horatio should "let us once again *assail* your ears,/ That are so *fortified* against *our* story,/ What *we* have *two nights* seen" (1.1. 34–36). Barnardo implies that Horatio willfully rejects reliable testimony. Horatio responds with patient diplomacy: "Well, sit *we* down. And let *us* hear Barnardo speak of this" (1.1.36–37). His willingness to listen once more to a story he knows but doubts shows that his friends are more important than his comfort, time, or sleep; by merely listening, he affirms and repairs their slightly threatened bond.

Barnardo's leisurely, painstaking opening itself presumes patient, well-disposed listeners, but his narrative soon crumbles when the "thing" appears. Here as elsewhere, the ghost intrudes on genuine exchange, shattering a previously defined community. Marcellus's abrupt interruption of Barnardo (1.1.43) might normally seem rude, but here it signals both real friendship and narrow self-concern. There are, perhaps, touches of both triumphant sarcasm and genuine respect in Marcellus's injunction, "Thou art a scholar, speak to it, Horatio" (1.1.45), just as there seem both smug assurance and profound wonder when Barnardo asks, "Looks a not like the King? Mark it, Horatio" (1.1.46). The two friends are having both their worst fears and their personal veracity confirmed, and they cannot help feeling satisfied terror. Horatio, meanwhile, cements a new and deeper bond with them by confessing his own terror (1.1.47). Such ability to share so openly an emotion one might normally hide is often the sign or start of friendly relations.

When Barnardo and Marcellus urge Horatio to address the ghost, they acknowledge their fear, confess their own incapacity, and show respect for their educated friend. At the same time, Horatio's prompt willingness to challenge the ghost shows that he deserves their respect; this is one of the bravest acts in the play—an act soon repeated by Hamlet himself, and therefore one that helps establish Horatio's fitness as Hamlet's future friend. Perhaps Horatio feels specially obliged to confront the ghost because he had previously doubted his companions' word: his willingness to speak helps him make amends by retracting his earlier skepticism. Likewise, his speech may also help alleviate his friends' fear: he dares, quite literally, to stand between them and "this thing" (1.1.24), whom he now addresses with the respectful, familiar "thee" and "thou" (1.1.49, 52). Such potentially friendly phrasing is balanced, though, by his implication that the "thing" is lawless (*"What* art thou *that usurp'st . . ."* [1.1.49]), while his final words can be read either as an invocation of a shared ideal or as a threatening command: "By heaven, I charge thee speak!" (1.1.52). Horatio (like Hamlet later) cannot know whether the ghost is a friend or foe, and so he addresses it (to some degree) as both. In this sense the ghost symbolizes one of the play's most important issues: the difficulties of interpreting others' intentions and conduct. Horatio confronts a question we all, like Hamlet, repeatedly face: what exactly are the motives of this other being standing before me? Is this "other" a potential friend or not?

As so often happens in life, Horatio (like Hamlet later) must wait for an answer. The ghost stalks off. Marcellus thinks it "offended" (1.1.53)—a remark which may reflect either the ghost's sensitivity, Horatio's lack thereof, or both. Horatio responds with words perhaps motivated by fear, courage, desperation, wounded pride, apologetic humility, or all these feelings at once: "Speak, speak, speak, I charge thee speak!" (1.1.54). As elsewhere, such phrasing can be interpreted as a command and/or a plea. Although Barnardo cannot help teasing and chiding Horatio for his present fear and earlier skepticism (1.1.56–57), such mockery actually signals the beginnings of a deeper friendship among the astonished trio.

Horatio is now part of the fellowship of Barnardo and Marcellus because he has now shared the strange experience which earlier bound the other men together. In a sense, his experience is also ours, and, just as he now feels tied to the two guards in a way he didn't earlier, so do we. Here as so often, Horatio functions (in Bert States' clever phrase)[7] as "our man at Elsinore"—as a surrogate member of the audience, whose reactions guide and mirror our own. We trust him almost as much as Hamlet does, and so do many others. Barnardo, for instance, no sooner chides Horatio than he earnestly seeks the latter's honest opinion (1.1.58), and Horatio, like a true friend, answers without equivocation, in effect confessing his earlier error as he moves from real skepticism to total belief (1.1.59–67).

As Horatio recollects old King Hamlet (whose ghost has apparently just appeared), he emphasizes how the deceased monarch had once "th'ambitious Norway combated" and how he once "smote the sledded Polacks on the ice" (1.1.64, 66). Here as throughout, references to political alliances and national warfare help reinforce the play's parallel focus on private friendship and personal enmity. Indeed, because of their political roles,[8] neither old nor young Hamlet was (or is) capable of enjoying truly private relationships. All their connections are tinged by politics—which is one reason why Horatio, who seems almost totally uninterested in courtly power or large affairs of state, will attract Hamlet so much. He seems to treat Hamlet less as a prince than as a person. Little wonder that Hamlet will find Horatio himself so appealing.

The modesty of both Horatio and Marcellus (1.1.70–82) once again shows their capacity for real friendship, and the friendship theme is indirectly reinforced as Horatio recounts the foreign conflicts faced by "our last King" (1.1.83), who had been challenged to combat by the Norwegian monarch, Fortinbras. Such an open challenge meant treating even an enemy with a certain friendly honor (and therefore contrasts strongly with the secret, treacherous death King Hamlet later suffered at the hands of Claudius). Once again Shakespeare subtly lulls both his characters and us into a relaxed, comfortable mood, even while making Horatio describe such serious and open conflict. As Horatio ends, we know much not only about the old king but also about the currently unfriendly relations between young Fortinbras and the Danes. When the ghost suddenly reappears, he seems (thanks to Horatio's exposition) a less alien, more sympathetic figure, and Horatio addresses him as such. He offers to treat the ghost as a friend (1.1.133–35) and seems willing to assume that the spirit itself may be motivated either by friendly intents (1.1.136–38) or by a sincerely troubled conscience (1.1.139–42). Yet when the ghost fails to respond and begins to leave, he shouts (in either a command or a plea), "Stop it, Marcellus" (1.1.142), and when Marcellus asks whether he should strike the ghost, Horatio responds with poised, balanced reason: "Do *if it will not stand*" (1.1.144). In seconds, his treatment of the ghost has gone from hostile (1.1.130) to solicitous (1.1.131–42) to a complex blend of both (1.1.142–44).

Horatio does not disagree when Marcellus says, "We do it wrong, being so majestical, / To offer it the show of violence" (1.1.148–49). This comment can be read either as an implicit rebuke of Horatio for having urged him to strike or as the kind of frank, unembarrassed self-criticism (implicating them all) of which good friends are capable. Marcellus's troubled conscience in fact shows another aspect of his capacity for friendship, while his comment also reveals how much (in his mind) the ghost now seems sympathetic. Horatio, typically, reasserts balance by suggesting that it may yet prove a "guilty thing" (1.1.53), while Marcellus's subsequent reference to "*our* Saviour's birth" suggests another tie—common faith—that binds these friends (1.1. 164). As the scene closes, in fact, Shakespeare strongly emphasizes their new bond. Horatio urges, "Break *we our* watch up, and *by my advice,*/ Let *us* impart what *we* have seen tonight,/ Unto young Hamlet" (1.1.173–75). He speaks of them as a trio, advises (rather than dictates) their next step, and even asks explicitly whether the others approve his suggestion (1.1.177–78).

Here, as throughout the play, Horatio demonstrates his capacity as a true friend. By the same token, Shakespeare in this opening scene has already introduced, often quite subtly, many nuances of the friendship theme that will later become far more explicit. In this scene we have witnessed a lone, lonely man approached first by one friend and then by two others. We have witnessed the newly assembled group begin to bond and then watched their disturbed, distressed reaction when surprised by an alien "thing." We have witnessed one of the men bravely confront the thing, seen the thing depart, and then seen how the shared experience binds the group (and particularly two of them) even more tightly together. We have witnessed, in short, a detailed preview of what will happen when these men seek and find Hamlet himself.

II

Our own first glimpse of the prince occurs at the court of Claudius, who clearly holds center stage. Having just witnessed an old king who seemed silent, lonely, isolated, offended, frightening, and perhaps even frightened, we now see a new king who seems confident, voluble, friendly, and surrounded by personal and political friends. Here is the consummate politician, the man skilled at compliments, thanks, and hearty farewells (1.2.15–16, 41), an imposing glad-hander who knows all the social graces. But here, too, is Hamlet—standing aside, dressed in black, and immediately speaking the sardonic, biting, ambiguous language one never uses with truly friendly intent (1.2.65, 66, 74). Hamlet speaks like a person who feels threatened but who cannot lash out; his ambiguity both concedes and mocks his enemy's power. He speaks a private language, its true meanings known only to himself—a dialect at odds with the frank, friendly conversations of the play's first scene. That scene opened with our glimpse of a man alone and frightened in the literal darkness; the present scene shows Hamlet isolated in metaphorical darkness, though presumably surrounded by much literal light. His very first words may be an aside (1.2.65)—a technique that establishes his distance from the court while implying a connection with us. This aside (if that is what it is) thus foreshadows the great soliloquies, in which he will seem to speak to himself but will in fact bind himself ever more tightly in sympathetic friendship with the audience, winning our concern by privately baring his soul.

It is Hamlet's mother who first explicitly introduces the word "friend" here by urging Hamlet to "cast thy nighted colour off,/ And let thine eye look like a friend on Denmark" (1.2.69–70). Here as so often, Shakespeare squeezes maximum meaning from a few words, particularly (in this case) "like." The effect would differ if Gertrude had asked Hamlet to "be" a friend to Claudius; all she is asking, instead, is that he be "like" a friend. And even that, of course, is not the limit of her words' complexity. If she had asked Hamlet to "be" Claudius's friend, she would be implying that she knows he now *isn't* such a friend; instead, by asking him to look on Claudius "like" a friend, she may be suggesting that he merely needs to show more *obviously* the friendship she expects he inwardly and naturally feels. Yet her words are open to still other interpretations, since in saying "look like a friend on Denmark" she can be taken to mean, "look upon Claudius as *your* friend—realize that he is friendly toward you." And, if "Denmark" is taken to refer not simply to the king but to the whole country, her words can be understood to suggest either that Hamlet should treat his *nation* with friendship (by abandoning his self-absorption) or that he should realize the friendship his countrymen feel for *him*, or both of these meanings together. Ironically, all these possible meanings only help emphasize Hamlet's bitter isolation. He feels neither friendly towards Claudius nor genuinely befriended by him; and at the moment he feels no great affection toward (or from) his fellow Danes, who have so eagerly embraced the new king. Gertrude's soothing words (especially coming *from* Gertrude) only enhance his profound alienation. This feeling, in turn, is intensified by his realization that he cannot even fully express, at least outwardly, the true depth of his emotions (1.2.76–86).

Paradoxically, after delivering one of the most famous, powerful, and eloquent soliloquies in all of Western literature, Hamlet cautions himself to "hold [his] tongue" (1.2.159), and he says this just before the entrance of the man who will shortly become his closest friend and confidant, the future boon companion with whom he will finally be able to share some of his deepest concerns and most thoughtful ruminations. When Horatio does arrive, he greets Hamlet with decorous formality, and although the prince replies magnanimously, obviously he isn't at first sure whether he correctly remembers Horatio's identity (1.2.160–61). We first witness the pair, then, before their real friendship properly begins, and, just as the play will trace the steady growth of their connection, so it will trace the parallel decline of Hamlet's links with much older friends.

It is Hamlet, in fact, who first calls Horatio his "good friend" (1.2.163), but the words here imply just about everything except their usual meaning. Horatio is *not*, at this stage, Hamlet's "good friend": he seems at most an acquaintance. Yet Hamlet's willingness to *call* Horatio his "good friend" reflects well on the prince: in one deft phrase he cuts through layers of rank, reaching out to the humble inferior who has just called himself Hamlet's "poor servant" (1.2.162) and thereby showing genuine concern for the other's feelings. If the preceding soliloquy showed Hamlet depressed and self-absorbed, his conduct here seems graciously thoughtful. His gesture of friendship to Horatio—though perhaps at this point *merely* a gesture—shows him capable of a warmth, kindness, and fellowship hitherto lacking in our sense of him. Immediately after expressing his own deep pain in his bitter soliloquy, he can nonetheless reach out to others, putting them at ease when he himself is in turmoil. His words, moreover, may also suggest his own deep need at this point *for* friendship; perhaps he can reach out so magnanimously to Horatio because he now feels so totally isolated.

It is also possible, however, that Hamlet is so gracious to Horatio precisely because he knows that Horatio *is* both his social inferior and a relative stranger. Horatio, in short, poses no present or even potential threat; he can be welcomed as a friend because he is not a possible enemy. His distance from Claudius's court, in fact, probably makes him attractive to the prince. All in all, then, when Hamlet offers to exchange the "name" of "good friend" with Horatio (1.2.163), we cannot be sure whether the prince is motivated by mere courtesy or by potentially deeper feelings. Here as so often elsewhere in the play (and in our own social relations), we are left with possibilities to interpret, with ambiguous clues and unclear signals which we must struggle to read correctly, even when no single "correct" reading is probably possible.

The friendship theme is sounded explicitly again when Hamlet says he would be unwilling to hear even Horatio's "enemy" accuse him of a "truant disposition" (1.2.169–70). Both Horatio's humility and Hamlet's solicitous compliment show their potential as friends to themselves and others, while Horatio's brief and tactful comment about Gertrude's quick remarriage (1.2.179) shows at once his intelligence, discretion, moderation, and reasonableness—all qualities valuable in a good friend. Meanwhile, the friendship theme is reiterated when Hamlet mentions the possibility of confronting his "dearest foe" in heaven (1.2.182), while our sense of Horatio's fitness as a friend is reinforced when he recounts how Barnardo and Marcellus were willing to share with him "In dreadful secrecy" their original vision of the ghost (1.2.207). Similarly, Hamlet's request that all three of them keep the vision a secret (1.2.248) suggests that he has already begun to treat them as friends, yet once again this request also illustrates the uncertain status of numerous speech-acts in the play. Hamlet seems to speak as a friend, but since he is their prince his request also amounts to a command. Yet the fact that he does request (rather than order) their silence might seem, once again, to show his magnanimity. This rosy interpretation, though, is complicated by the fact that Hamlet is now dependent on these men—who may be potential friends, who are certainly social inferiors, but who also possess secret information that gives them power over him. His request for their silence, therefore, may demonstrate both graciousness *and* dependence, just as his promise to "requite [their] loves" (1.2.251) may indicate both generosity and power (including perhaps his financial superiority) and vulnerable need. Hamlet explicitly seeks their "loves" rather than the "duty" they offer (1.2.253–54), thereby suggesting a desire for an intimate rather than merely legalistic bond. He wants (and has apparently already to some degree achieved) their friendship rather than their simple political loyalty, and in less than three hundred lines we have seen him move from painful isolation to secret comradeship. He now heads a small community of seemingly trusting, trusted friends.

III

Friendship of a different sort is emphasized next. Laertes and Ophelia seem so attractive partly because they seem as much friends as brother and sister. Apparently they understand one another completely: they amiably tease, showing little sibling rivalry (1.3.1–52). Laertes shows real concern for Ophelia by warning her that Hamlet, because of his status, can never be a true friend or lover in the usual sense (once again underscoring Hamlet's special isolation). This advice also increases our respect for Laertes: a different kind of brother might seek to profit from his sister's closeness to the prince, but Laertes apparently values Ophelia more than any personal ambition. Meanwhile, Polonius's own friendly advice to his son (1.3.52–87) introduces some of the play's most explicit commentary on the friendship theme. Indeed, the fact that the father emphasizes friendship so much in these parting comments implies its crucial importance. He warns Laertes to beware of enemies who twist one's words; he counsels him to behave (as we have just seen Hamlet behaving) in ways that are familiar but not vulgar, since the excessive familiarity designed to win friends can often turn them away; he urges Laertes to be loyal to old and trusted friends and not abandon them for new friendships rooted in mere pleasure; and he advises his son about proper ways to conduct a quarrel (ironic advice in light of Laertes's later conflict with Hamlet). Nearly everything Polonius says here is relevant to dealings with friends, and nearly everything also implies the potential danger inherent in those relations. Ironically, even (or perhaps especially) the son of a powerful man needed to fear what and to whom he might speak and how he might behave, and Polonius's speech merely articulates many truisms of standard Renaissance friendship doctrines. (This fact makes it unlikely that Shakespeare intended Polonius here to seem merely ridiculous, as is sometimes suggested.) Much of his wisdom boils down to the standard teaching that one must first be a good friend to oneself in order to attract good friends and be one to others. As his son departs, Polonius implicitly concedes what any parent must: that a child's welfare depends as much on his friends as on his family.

After Laertes leaves, Polonius turns to Ophelia, seconding her brother's advice about becoming too friendly with "Lord Hamlet" (1.3.89, 123). Someone (a friend?) has warned Polonius of their connection. That Hamlet reaches out to this (non-threat-

ening) woman just after his father's death and his mother's
remarriage once again emphasizes his special need now for intimacy and affection,[9] and if Polonius were indeed an arch-court-
ier, he might see Hamlet's attentions as a splendid opportunity to
promote his own fortunes. Instead, like his son, he speaks to
Ophelia as a friend might, warning her to mistrust deceptive appearances and Hamlet's apparently amiable overtures. Here, as in
speaking with Laertes, he stresses the potential danger of apparent friendships. Personal ambition seems less important to him
than Ophelia's welfare—although here, as so often, we can never
be sure of the full complexity of a character's motives. Polonius
may realize the dangers of too close a connection with royal
power, especially given the current tensions between Claudius
and Hamlet. His advice, in some ways so apparently non-politi-
cal, may also be quite politic indeed. His concern for another
may also imply self-concern—a paradox which would only make
him typically human.

When Hamlet soon reappears, he is accompanied by his
friends Marcellus and Horatio. The trio's relative isolation is emphasized not only by their discomfort but by the noise made by
Claudius and his abundant friends of pleasure, whose revels trouble Hamlet far more than the cold. Such carryings-on, he feels,
will not win respect for Denmark but will damage the nation's
reputation, just as an individual may fail to win friends because
of a single private (but publicly known) defect. As Hamlet explains this point, however, the ghost appears, although it seems
not to trust the friendly intentions of Hamlet's companions
enough to share its secrets with them. It seeks, through "courteous action," a private conference (1.4.60), and although the attempt by Hamlet's friends to restrain him might ordinarily seem
highly unfriendly and disrespectful, in this case their willingness
to risk such *un*courteous action signals deep affection. Horatio's
words "You shall not go, my lord" (1.4.80) can seem both a command and plea, while Hamlet's reply (1.4.84) can seem the same.
His words are polite but forceful, while his willingness to
threaten them shows not genuine enmity but rather his desperation to satisfy both his curiosity and the demands of a relation
even more important than friendship. By the same token, their
decision to disregard his explicit order (1.4.88) shows no lack of
respect but the depth of their affection.

The friendship theme appears again when Hamlet finally
confers with the ghost, who reveals how he was poisoned with a
potion holding "an enmity with blood of man" (1.5.65). Hamlet

seems particularly disgusted that Claudius can pervert an obvious token of friendly feelings—smiling—while acting with such hypocritical hatred (1.5.106–08). When Horatio and Marcellus eventually find the prince, he shows himself his father's son by being unwilling to trust them with his newly discovered secrets—such trust being a conventional sign of true friendship. Ironically, and with typical ambiguity, Hamlet twice addresses Horatio and Marcellus as "friends" (perhaps with a tinge of sarcasm?) precisely while refusing to trust them (1.5.145–46) but also while requesting that they not reveal the little that they *do* now know.

Here again Hamlet is paradoxically more powerful than, but actually quite vulnerable to, his new friends. Both his real need and his probably genuine affection help explain why he humbles himself by making "one poor request" of them (1.5.148), but the fact that he swears them to secrecy also shows a lack of trust. He wants their public commitment to himself, each other, God, and even the ghost, knowing that to break such a public vow would reveal their unfitness for friendship, one of the chief private virtues. His use of his sword to confirm the vow is nicely ambiguous, for although it resembles a cross (thus symbolizing the religious dimensions of their oath), it *is* a sword, thus symbolizing an implicitly violent punishment if the oath is broken. The sword, often an emblem and instrument of hatred, here betokens one of the deepest possible bonds: violating this oath would make one an enemy not only to Hamlet but to God.

Ironically, although Hamlet himself plans to be (and already *is*) ambiguous in his own language, he makes his friends swear to avoid ambiguous hinting at court about what they already know (1.5.181–88). In short, he paradoxically urges them to be deceptive by acting and speaking as if they had nothing to hide. After they have sworn to all his conditions, he again tenders them his "love," but he immediately follows this emotional gesture with the promise of perhaps more practical rewards (1.5.191–94). Once more his complex position as a friend is implied: he is, after all, *not* "poor" or powerless, and so can handsomely reward these friends if they do remain loyal. If, however, one of them violates their vows and tells Claudius about the ghost and about Hamlet's plans, then the prince would indeed suddenly be far more vulnerable (or "poor"). Because of his relative isolation, Hamlet desperately *wants* friends, but now he also desperately *needs* them—facts which give added resonance to such words as "Let us go in *together*./ And still your fingers on your lips, I

pray" (1.5.194–95). Hamlet needs these friends to consider *him* a
friend if he hopes to keep his secret, and for that reason he needs
to convince them of his own sincerely friendly feelings. Thus the
word "pray" may be simultaneously a subtle command, a superior's magnanimous request, and a needy man's genuine hope.
Similarly complicated are the famous lines, "The time is out of
joint. O cursed spite,/ That ever *I* was born to set it right./ Nay,
come, let's go *together*" (1.5.196–98). Once again Shakespeare
juxtaposes Hamlet's desire for companionship with his political,
social, and metaphysical isolation. These lines show both his
need for friends and his realization of being, in the deepest
senses, utterly alone.

IV

The friendship theme seems especially prominent in act 2. It
is emphasized, for instance, when Polonius talks with Reynaldo
about Laertes's Parisian friends (2.1.6–15). He instructs
Reynaldo to portray Laertes as attracted by frivolous pleasures,
hoping thereby to detect whether Laertes is indeed associating
with the wrong people. Concerns with friendship become even
more prominent, though, when we meet Rosencrantz and Guildenstern, two of Hamlet's oldest and dearest chums (2.2.10–18).
Just as Polonius seeks to monitor his son by deceiving his son's
companions, so Claudius seeks information about his nephew by
employing friends of Hamlet's youth. Yet whereas Polonius is
motivated by genuine concern for his son, Claudius's motives are
far less benign. Incapable of genuine friendship, Claudius instead
constantly seeks "to use" others as instruments (2.2.3). He urges
Rosencrantz and Guildenstern to "draw [Hamlet] on to pleasures" and thus solicit information (2.2.15), but such phrasing
already (ironically) suggests the standard Renaissance distinction
between true friends (joined by a love of good) and temporary
friends (united by an ephemeral love of pleasure). Gertrude,
meanwhile, speaks with similarly unintended irony when she
says she is "sure" that "two men there is not living/ To whom
[Hamlet] more adheres" (2.2.20–21). She cannot know, of
course, that by this point his main allegiance is not to these
friends of his youth but to an elderly dead man—the ghost.

Although Rosencrantz and Guildenstern are often criticized
as ambitious, time-serving lackeys incapable of true friendship,
such a reading seems too simplistic. Shakespeare, after all,
makes even his obvious villain—Claudius—exhibit some real

moral complexity (particularly in the prayer scene [3.3.36–98]), and his depiction of Rosencrantz and Guildenstern is arguably far more subtle and sympathetic than is often supposed. Even their tendency to speak (and be spoken to) as a unit (e.g., 2.2.26–34) can be read not as mockery but as evidence of their close bond and mutual comfort: they know each other's minds and willingly share the spotlight.[10] Neither lords it over the other (as might be expected if ambition were their main motive). Instead they seem genuinely friendly and capable of serving as Hamlet's true friends. One minor tragedy of this great tragic play, in fact, is that their ancient friendship with him is soon ruined.

Rosencrantz and Guildenstern are another pair (like Barnardo and Francisco in 1.1, or Ophelia and Laertes in 1.3, or Horatio and Marcellus in 1.4, or Voltemand and Cornelius in 2.2, or Claudius and Gertrude throughout) whose very pairing helps emphasize Hamlet's isolation. They would need to be scheming hypocrites indeed if Guildenstern's closing words to Claudius are self-consciously ironic: "*Heavens* make our presence and our practices/ Pleasant and helpful to [Hamlet]" (2.2.38–39). Such words (like Rosencrantz's later comment to Polonius, "God save you, sir" [2.2.221]) suggest instead the relative sincerity of this pair in a play in which sincerity, ironically, is a trait Hamlet especially prizes. Of course, the fact that their motives have *been* so much disputed illustrates a central problem the play raises and confronts: the problem of ever being able to interpret another's intentions and behavior precisely, even when (or perhaps *especially* when) that person seems to be a friend. Hamlet himself never quite seems sure of his old friends' true intents, although he eventually chooses—wrongly, it would seem—to treat them as enemies (or at least as dispensably inconvenient). Paradoxically, one of the most unsettling aspects of Hamlet's own character is his easy dispatch of his two old friends and especially the relish with which he regards their eternal suffering (5.2.47). It is precisely his former friendship that makes his final hatred so intense—but to say this, of course, is to jump too far ahead.

Hamlet's first encounter with Rosencrantz and Guildenstern is one of the longest and most interesting scenes in the entire play, especially in its bearing on the friendship theme.[11] Already Shakespeare begins to distinguish subtly between them: Rosencrantz seems closer to Hamlet, a distinction implied by the pair's first words. Guildenstern calls Hamlet his "honoured lord," whereas Rosencrantz terms the prince his "most dear lord" (2.2.222–23). Hamlet immediately greets them as his "excellent

good friends" and as "Good lads," words echoed when Rosencrantz describes them as "indifferent children of the earth"
(2.2.224–27). Such language not only subtly underscores their
childhood connections with the prince but also becomes increasingly ironic. If Rosencrantz and Guildenstern really are ambitious hypocrites, then emphasizing their childhood links with
Hamlet makes them seem true schemers who betray both their
friend and their former innocence. If, on the other hand, their
motives are sincere and they thus retain some of their youthful
idealism, then Hamlet's own later treatment of them seems
shockingly brutal. In either case their relationship with him will
now no longer be what it once was, as soon becomes clear.

The trio's easy, light-hearted banter implies the age and intimacy of their friendship, but their jokes about Fortune already
introduce a darker note. Meanwhile, their bawdry (2.2.228–36)
implies a friendship ultimately rooted in ephemeral pleasures and
thus lacking the serious substance of Hamlet's new connection
with Horatio. The off-hand allusion to the rarity of honesty (2.2.
237–38) helps remind us that honesty is especially prized in a
friend, but the reference also seems ironic since *dis*honesty is
precisely what Hamlet will come to suspect in (and even display
toward) his old friends. Meanwhile, Hamlet's description of
Denmark as a "prison" (2.2.241) helps stress his isolation, since
a prison deprives one (almost by definition) not only of freedom
but of true friends. Once again Hamlet's alienation is emphasized
by the closeness of the pair he addresses: their intimacy is implied even in Rosencrantz's simple disagreement with an opinion
Hamlet has just expressed: "*We* think not so, my lord" (2.2.248).
Rosencrantz can confidently assume that he knows his companion's mind; Hamlet can rarely feel confident enough to assume
this about anyone (except, perhaps, Horatio).

Hamlet's growing separation from his erstwhile friends is
subtly emphasized by his pronouns when he responds to the
comment just cited: "Why, then 'tis none to *you*; for there is
nothing either good or bad but thinking makes it so. To *me*
[Denmark] is a prison" (2.2.249–51). Rosencrantz's rejoinder—
"Why, then your ambition makes it one; 'tis too narrow for your
mind," 2.2.252])—tries playfully to echo Hamlet's syntax and
phrasing, but it introduces the topic of ambition in a way that
inevitably seems ironic. Ambition, after all, is the flaw Hamlet
later suspects in *them*. If his suspicion is wrong, then it seems
doubly ironic that Rosencrantz should here falsely (if jokingly)
accuse Hamlet of the fault. If, however, Hamlet's suspicion is

correct, then it seems ironically smug, daring, and/or foolhardy for Rosencrantz to accuse Hamlet. Indeed, the fact that Rosencrantz can accuse another so comfortably of ambition suggests that ambition is *not* one of this pair's major motives. There is, of course, another possibility: that by raising the issue, he seeks to trap Hamlet into confessing his own aspirations—in which case Rosencrantz would paradoxically be demonstrating his own ambitiousness. (The multiple ways in which even this one brief exchange might be read illustrates the difficulty of making clear, unambiguous interpretations of others' motives—a difficulty quite relevant to the friendship theme.) In any case, this exchange helps remind us that although *shared* ambitions can cement a friendship, conflicting ones can help tear it apart.

By playfully debating Hamlet, Rosencrantz and Guildenstern seek the kind of amiable disagreement and conflict that often, ironically, build or reveal friendship. Their banter shows how well they know him—how much older friends they are with him than is Horatio. It is almost as if (in this scene) we witness them reenact old routines. Of course, the visitors completely miss (at least at first) the more serious implications of Hamlet's words: while they play an old game, he has left such play behind. The trio converse but do not really communicate, and although Hamlet rejects considering them his "servants" and insists on calling them "friends" (2.2.267–74), treating them as true friends is precisely what he refuses to do.[12] Indeed, his claim that he is "most dreadfully attended" may even be a sarcastic gibe, in which case his claim to speak "like an honest man" is itself a bit dishonest, and perhaps also sarcastic (2.2.267–70). Sarcasm, of course, is complicated: it expresses contempt but perhaps also fear, superiority but perhaps also weakness, hostile aggression but perhaps also a hope for reform. It may insult (by mocking the target's dull imperception) but may also pay understated tribute to the target's ability to take a subtle hint. Sarcasm can prick a target without severing a relationship completely. Once again, the problem of correctly determining precise motives in ostensible friends becomes apparent here.

This problem surfaces again when Hamlet bluntly asks his visitors to tell him, "in the beaten way of friendship, what make you at Elsinore?" (2.2.269–70). Rosencrantz blatantly lies (2.2. 271), although his response is less easy to judge or condemn than it might at first seem. It raises the difficult issue of whether it can ever be right to lie to a friend, especially if motivated by sincere concern for the friend's welfare. Hamlet's visitors may truly believe, after all, that they can help him by discovering his secret[13]—although they obviously know, too, that such a discovery will also please Claudius and Gertrude. Once again Shakespeare refuses to simplify, especially when dealing with friends. Particularly resonant, for instance, is Hamlet's response to the lie: "Beggar that I am, I am even poor in thanks, but I thank you. And sure, dear friends, my thanks are too dear a halfpenny" (2.2.272–74). If this is sarcastic, then his true meaning is precisely the opposite of what he seems to say. The claim of inferiority and poverty would then mask his strong sense of moral superiority and of greater political power, and his apparent graciousness would barely disguise his growing frustration and anger.

Hamlet's elaborate self-depreciation is immediately followed by blunt, plain words that may simultaneously express a hostile challenge, impatient contempt, and a genuinely heartfelt, even pained plea to old, beloved comrades: "Were you not sent for? Is it your own inclining? Is it a free visitation? Come, come, deal justly with me. Come, come. Nay, speak" (2.2.274–76). Critics who see Rosencrantz and Guildenstern as practiced, hypocritical courtiers pay insufficient attention to Hamlet's own immediately ensuing admission that "there is a kind of confession in your looks, which your modesties have not craft enough to colour" (2.2.279–80). He seems to concede that they are too innately honest to lie effectively to a friend. The visitors seem richer, truer characters (and less like cardboard stereotypes) if we see them as true but cornered friends: do they continue to lie (thus seeking to help Hamlet) but thereby destroy their friendship with him, or do they confess and thus jeopardize assisting him (while also betraying their obligations to the king and queen)? They are trapped between duty and friendship, and, to complicate matters even more, their own self-interests are inevitably involved. If they alienate the prince, they lose not only a friend but a powerful ally; if they disappoint the king and queen, they not only fail in a serious obligation but also risk angering the royal couple. As always, Shakespeare makes things difficult—or rather, he imitates the complexities of real human dilemmas. It is precisely this refusal to simplify that makes his plays—and his treatment of the friendship theme—so rich.

In a moment that echoes Horatio and Marcellus's earlier being forced to swear secrecy on Hamlet's sword, the prince now forces Rosencrantz and Guildenstern to swear openness by "conjur[ing]" them "by the rights of our fellowship, by the consonancy of our youth, by the obligation of our ever-preserved love, and by what more dear a better proposer can charge you withal, [to] be even and direct with me whether you were sent for or no" (2.2.283–88). The anaphora is ringingly effective, and Hamlet's words can imply both strength and vulnerability, both power and weakness. He speaks as he would be spoken to: with directness. He abandons subtle sarcasm, and although his words still seem full of suppressed anger, they may also express a pained and deeply injured plea. When his visitors hesitate, Hamlet himself says, "Nay, then I have an eye of you. If you love me, hold not off" (2.2.290–91). The first sentence has been read either as an aside or as direct address, and the difference shows how even slightly altering one apparently simple phrase can complicate interpretation, especially in exchanges between friends. If Hamlet *does* here speak an aside, then that decision already suggests his distance from (and even contempt for) his old friends. If, however, he speaks directly to them, then he once more shows a friendly, open willingness to appeal to their good natures and "ever preserved love" (2.2.285–86). Guildenstern's brief, monosyllabic reply—"My lord, we were sent for" (2.2. 292)—is wonderfully, paradoxically eloquent, implying at once reluctance, shame, sincerity, and reticence. It is just the kind of simple but complicated language one friend might use to another.

Hamlet's offer to explain *why* they have been sent for (2.2. 293–95) can be seen as contemptuous, solicitous, or both, since he anticipates their discomfort with telling the reasons themselves. Significantly, he then shuts off any genuine discussion of his own feelings, telling them he doesn't know precisely *why* he has lost his earlier mirth (2.2.295–97)—although in saying so he obviously lies. Having just urged them to be honest, he is now dishonest himself, but only because he suspects *them* of possible dishonesty: as always, motives and their interpretation are complex, especially between friends. Paradoxically, he describes with supreme effectiveness earthly wonders he claims he can no longer even recognize, and his image of earth as a "sterile promontory" is particularly relevant to the friendship theme, implying isolation amidst vast surrounding space (2.2.297–303). Rosencrantz and Guildenstern are treated to another small soliloquy: Hamlet has not yet completely shut them out or off, and although he refuses to share his chief secret with them, he does share some of his deepest, sincerest feelings (2.2.303–310).

The visitors even seem comforted by Hamlet's willingness to share his gloom. Certainly the earlier tension now begins to

subside—a change signaled by Rosencrantz's smile (2.2.310).
Hamlet interprets the smile as a reversion to their earlier youthful
bawdry (2.2.309–10). Rosencrantz's insistence, however, that
Hamlet has misinterpreted his reaction (2.2.311) simply raises
once more a chief theme: whether we can ever really know another's motives, even a friend's. Yet the smiling and the shift of
topic, following Hamlet's profound and eloquent words, may
also suggest that Rosencrantz and Guildenstern simply cannot
operate on the prince's intellectual or spiritual level, that they
cannot truly comprehend him, that they haven't really been *listening*. Rosencrantz's very smile, which seems to signal a re-
sumption of their earlier friendly relations, may instead suggest
that these men are now too shallow (or rather that Hamlet, having been chastened by his father's death and the ghost's visit, is
now too deep) for the trio ever to resume a real friendship. Alter-
natively, the smile may perhaps indicate some real subtlety and
perceptiveness in Rosencrantz. Perhaps, recognizing the prince's
deep pain, he solicitously seeks to change the subject, to brighten
the mood, to give his old friend happier things to think about.

V

   Significantly, when Rosencrantz tells Hamlet of the players'
approach, he says that they travel partly because they have been
abandoned by city audiences. Once again unstable friendship is
implied, especially since the players have been rejected for a
competing children's group. Hamlet explicitly likens the disloyal
audiences to the fickle courtiers who once mocked but now flatter Claudius. All this behavior, of course, is relevant to the
friendship theme—a theme also reiterated when the prince
finally welcomes Rosencrantz and Guildenstern, even offering
them his hands (2.2.366–71). The trio's old friendship seems mo-
mentarily restored, as does Hamlet's mood, but even this moment is ambiguous. Some critics see Hamlet's gesture here as
just that: a gesture, not a real reconciliation, and his famously
puzzling comment that he can distinguish "a hawk from a hand-
saw" (2.2.375) can be read as warning, threat, friendly advice, or
all three at once. His friendship with his old chums is, like so
much else in the play, continually open to interpretation. Ironically, however, Hamlet and his two old friends (now positioned
at each ear) do seem united by contempt for Polonius. Rosencrantz even joins Hamlet in mocking the old man (2.2.376
–81)—neatly illustrating the aggression latent in friendship, the

way friends can bond by turning on someone else. The irony, of course, is that Hamlet will eventually also turn on these two and eventually kill both them *and* Polonius. The trio's current alliance will not last.

Toward the players, however, Hamlet seems immediately and unfailingly friendly—though even this moment is complex, since he had earlier said he planned to greet them with a zeal therefore partly planned (2.2.368–71). Yet there seems real warmth in his words "Welcome, good friends" and "O, old friend" (2.2.418–19) and in his playful demeanor. His warmth seems particularly striking after his coldness toward Polonius (and, before that, toward Rosencrantz and Guildenstern). Indeed, perhaps these encounters with possibly false friends help make his feeling for the players so enthusiastic. Although the actors, paradoxically, are professional deceivers, to Hamlet they seem more trustworthy than almost anyone else. Their relative power-lessness and dependence means that he can also comfortably treat them as friends: like Horatio, they are too impotent to pose any threat, so he can relax with them in ways he can't with most others. He can even joke with them about their *not* being friends (2.2.420), while his generally friendly treatment of them, and particularly his teasing of the younger players, winningly demonstrates his underlying capacity for real affection and generosity. In such scenes, as in those with Horatio, we glimpse Hamlet's normal character. We see who he has been (and is capable of being) when unburdened. We see a Hamlet whose capacity for affection makes him seem, in turn, eminently lovable.

Another reason Hamlet can relax with the players is that they are *openly* suitors. They obviously seek favor and money, without hidden motives. Paradoxically, he can welcome them as friends partly because he knows they need employment, and their abandonment by their own former friends (and paying customers) makes them even more dependent on friendly patrons. Given the actors' importance to the larger friendship theme, therefore, it hardly seems surprising that the chief player's speech deals so explicitly with open hatred (2.2.464–514).[14] The familiar lines stir tearful compassion even in the actor, and his empathy with the sufferings of long-dead, fictional persons seems particularly striking when ironically followed by Polonius's smug intention to treat the players "according to their desert" (2.2.523). Hamlet's wonderful response—"God's bodkin, man, much better. Use every man after his desert, and who shall scape whipping? Use them after your own honour and dignity . . ." (2.2.524–25)

—memorably encapsulates two chief principles of true friendship: charity and the Golden Rule. Yet Hamlet's rebuke of
Polonius for being insufficiently friendly also constitutes (as he
seems to realize) an implicit rebuke to himself. Thus, having
mercilessly mocked the old man earlier, he now cautions the
players, "look you mock him not" (2.2.539). These words, like
the explicit references to friendship with which this interlude
concludes (2.2.530–31, 540), help emphasize once more a crucial
theme.

2.2, one of the play's longest and most interesting scenes, is
in fact particularly significant to the friendship theme, which is
soon sounded again. As Hamlet commences another lonely soliloquy, he upbraids himself for being incapable (unlike the player)
of true compassion for another's sufferings, especially those of
his own father. Yet he also reveals one reason he has not already
avenged his father's death: he is not yet sure whether the ghost is
a true friend or a tempting foe (2.2.594–600). Like all of us, in
short, he confronts the problem of interpretation, of trying to determine whether another's apparently beneficent motives are
truly friendly or not.

VI

Just as friendship had surfaced explicitly in 2.2, so it arises
again in 3.3, when the long-absent Horatio reenters. Significantly, he appears just as Rosencrantz and Guildenstern (whom
Hamlet now considers false friends) are leaving (3.2.52). This
juxtaposition seems deliberate: Shakespeare faced no need to
bring Rosencrantz and Guildenstern back so briefly (especially
with Polonius, whom Hamlet also considers no friend) unless to
contrast them with Horatio, whom the prince greets enthusiasti-
cally. He is answered, in turn, with more obvious affection and
less formality than Horatio has previously used (3.2.52–55).
Clearly their friendship has deepened, as Hamlet confirms in a
speech centrally important to the friendship theme.[15] Horatio has
humbly offered "service" (3.2.53), but Hamlet instead extols him
as being "e'en as just a man/ As e'er my conversation cop'd
withal" (3.2.54–55). "Just" can imply that Horatio is not only
personally ideal and well-balanced[16] but is also a perfect human.
In all these senses Hamlet's praise looks back both to his earlier
commendation of mankind (at 2.2.303–08) and to the moderation
he had just been celebrating when instructing an actor
(3.2.1–45). Like the ideal man Hamlet had earlier called "the par-

agon of animals" (2.2.307) and also like the ideal actor who never oversteps "the modesty of nature" (3.2.19), Horatio strikes just the right proportion and balance—qualities Hamlet himself may feel he now lacks (although this very speech shows how much he still possesses them and how much they remain his ideals).

When Horatio tries to demur, Hamlet cuts him off (3.2.56), but the interruption isn't rude. Instead, Hamlet protects both his and Horatio's dignity by claiming he doesn't flatter: why, he asks, should he flatter the poor? The question might normally seem ungracious, insulting, or condescending, but Hamlet's mere asking of it shows how comfortable he feels with Horatio, how much he trusts Horatio's perception. That Hamlet can mention Horatio's relative poverty so blatantly shows how little he prizes such matters, how much he values Horatio for better qualities than wealth or power. Although a cynic might note that Horatio is in fact far from totally powerless (because apparently only he knows the full secret)[17], and that Hamlet therefore has *some* reason to "flatter" him (3.2.56), this exchange mainly shows Hamlet's mutual confidence in himself and his friend. What might normally seem awkward or impolite instead illustrates their easy friendship. The very blatantness with which Hamlet risks insulting Horatio instead helps guarantee the sincerity of the enthusiastic commendation that now follows.

Hamlet's extended praise of Horatio amounts, in effect, to another soliloquy. It thus helps intensify (almost as much by form as content) our sense of Horatio as Hamlet's true friend, a man with whom (and to whom) he can speak frankly. To no one else has Hamlet earlier spoken so intensely, for so long, about matters so obviously important—except to himself. His praise of Horatio even recalls the soliloquy in which he had wondered whether it was "nobler in the mind to suffer/ The slings and arrows of outrageous fortune . . ." (3.1.57–58).[18] Here he extols Horatio as one who, "in suff'ring all, . . . suffers nothing,/ A man that Fortune's buffets and rewards/ hast ta'en with equal thanks" (3.2.66–68). As elsewhere, this speech links—while implicitly contrasting—friendship with Fortune. True friendship is Fortune's opposite: a true friend is as stable, trustworthy, and certain as Fortune is not. A true friend is not "a pipe for Fortune's finger,/ To sound what stop she please" (3.2.70–71), and Horatio is just such a friend. But before Hamlet continues, he abruptly stops himself (3.2.74). Perhaps he ends so suddenly for fear of embarrassing Horatio; perhaps he stops because both understand that deep friendship need not be verbalized; or perhaps he stops partly because he realizes he is slipping into self-absorption—that even his praise is falling into monologue. Whatever his reason for stopping, his words clearly reflect well on himself; by commending Horatio,[19] he wins our own respect. And the fact that he has apparently shared with Horatio his deepest secret—the ghost's allegation against Claudius—shows that Hamlet's trust is more than merely verbal.

The play's tendency to link friendship and fortune is reflected also in Hamlet's *Mousetrap*. Thus the Player King observes how love fluctuates with fortune, and how "*The great man down, you mark his favourite flies*" while "*The poor advanc'd makes friends of enemies*," so that "*who not needs shall never lack a friend,/ And who in want a hollow friend doth try/ Directly seasons him his enemy*" (3.2.195–204; italics in original). The taut syntax mimics the quick mutability it describes, while the sudden shifts between total opposites imply how superficial such changes are. Similarly intriguing is the ambiguity of "needs": in one sense the word suggests that the highly fortunate will never lack friends, but in another sense it implies that whoever doesn't *need* a friend will always have one. The latter meaning suggests superficiality on both sides—as if friendship were merely a matter of need. Here as in other respects, the language of the play-within seems more subtle than we might first suspect. Thus "hollow" nicely suggests an inner emptiness invisible from without, while "seasons" perverts the normally pleasant associations of that word. When false friendship is the topic, even the language used to discuss it seems perverse.

Ambiguity of a different sort arises when, after the play upsets Claudius, Hamlet exults with Horatio, whom he calls his "Damon dear" (3.2.275). When editors gloss the reference at all, they usually assume that "Damon" alludes to a shepherd from conventional pastoral literature. Even this meaning would suggest a close friendship between Hamlet and Horatio, but another possibility is that "Damon" might also suggest the legend of Damon and Pythias, two of the most famous classical friends.[20] They united against a tyrant—a detail that gives the possible allusion all the more relevance to *Hamlet*.[21] Indeed, just when the prince links Horatio with Damon, Horatio offers a clear (if typically subtle) criticism of Claudius by sarcastically implying that the new king is an "ass" (3.2.279). And immediately after Hamlet and Horatio reaffirm their bond by agreeing about Claudius, Rosencrantz and Guildenstern (whom Hamlet now considers false friends) appear. As before, Shakespeare here juxtaposes the true friend with the alleged imposters, thereby enhancing our awareness of both.

Significantly, Hamlet converses mostly here with Guildenstern, from whom the prince has always seemed more distant than from Rosencrantz. Their quick, staccato, back-and-forth exchange underscores their mutual impatience, and Guildenstern soon feels Hamlet's contempt. Twice, seeking better treatment, he utters either a plea or a demand or both (3.2.300–01, 306–10). Yet because he and Rosencrantz represent Hamlet's mother, the unfriendly treatment they receive also amounts, in part, to sublimated rage at Gertrude. They, of course, cannot know this, and there seems genuine hurt in Rosencrantz's stung comment, "My lord, you once did love me" (3.2.326). He now (ironically) shares the same emotions as Ophelia, and his plain-spoken sentence comes with all the more force after all the earlier edgy ambiguity. His comment can be read as pained, defiant, or both; it can seem at once an assertion of dignity, dependence, and protest. Although Hamlet offers his hand, this normally friendly gesture can now seem either empty or contemptuous. Likewise, Rosencrantz's request that Hamlet share his "griefs" with his "friend" (3.2.330) can seem either genuinely solicitous (and therefore all the more generous, especially if he does feel rejected and insulted) or as dishonestly prying and probing. Hamlet, of course, *is* willing to share his griefs with his friend—but that friend is now Horatio.

Just as Hamlet's earlier praise of Horatio had echoed the "to be or not to be" soliloquy, so his rebuke of Guildenstern echoes the speech to Horatio. (The allusion is especially significant if Horatio hears it: Hamlet thus implicitly commends the true friend before the allegedly false.) The prince had earlier praised Horatio for not being "a pipe for Fortune's finger" (3.2.70). Now, after offering Guildenstern a recorder, Hamlet accuses him of treating the prince himself as a pipe (3.2.355–56). Normally the offer of the instrument would seem friendly; here, though, it seems muted physical aggression that concretizes the very metaphor Hamlet now explains. His repeated emphasis on pronouns such as "you," "me," and "my" (3.2.354–63) underscores his new distance from his former friends, while his closing request (or command—"Leave me, friends" (3.2.378)—nicely illustrates the complex ambiguity of the key word, since "friends" here presumably includes not only Rosencrantz and Guildenstern but also Horatio. Hamlet, at this moment, is surrounded by "friends," but to him only one seems a friend in the deepest sense.

VII

Friendship remains important in the rest of act 3 and throughout act 4. Thus Hamlet no sooner departs than his chief enemy enters, flanked by Rosencrantz and Guildenstern. Claudius' first words—"I like him not" (3.3.1)—can refer to Hamlet's recent conduct, the prince himself, or both, just as Guildenstern's concern to "keep those many bodies safe/ That live and feed upon your Majesty" (3.3.9–10) can seem public-spirited, self-serving, or a combination. Rosencrantz (predictably) echoes his friend (3.3.11–23), and although their words can be seen as merely parasitic, what they say is also simply true: threats to kings *can* threaten commonwealths. As usual, Shakespeare leaves his characters' motives unclear, and Rosencrantz and Guildenstern can indeed be seen as acting as sincere friends to Claudius, Denmark, Hamlet, and themselves—all at once. Their willingness to accompany Hamlet to England after his obvious recent hostility suggests that self-concern is not their only motive, though of course they inevitably now recognize that if Hamlet defeats Claudius they will also likely lose. They exemplify the peculiar instability of friends to the powerful: as Hamlet's intimates, they once stood to gain the friendship of many others. Now, as men he deems enemies, they risk losing the friendship of many—except for Claudius and Claudius's friends. Friendship, normally thought a buffer against the world's uncertainties, here seems to be just the opposite, no matter which perspective they adopt.

Similar ambiguities arise in act 4. There Claudius, learning that Hamlet has killed Polonius, addresses Rosencrantz and Guildenstern as friends (4.1.33), although—as usual—it isn't clear whether he thus shows diplomacy, real certainty of their loyalty, desperate need, or a combination thereof. Likewise, when he says he plans to consult his "wisest friends" (4.1.38), he can seem motivated by heartfelt need and/or clever cunning, especially since, by consulting them, he hopes to head off potential enemies who may include the "friends" themselves (4.1.40–45). Meanwhile, further ambiguity seems inherent in Hamlet's ensuing treatment of Rosencrantz and Guildenstern, especially when he calls the former a "sponge" (4.2.11). Obviously the word expresses contempt, but in explaining it Hamlet may also be warning his former intimate about Claudius's true motives (4.2.

14–20).[22] And Rosencrantz's uncertain reaction to the accusation (4.2.13) can seem either pained, indignant, or both.

Claudius must deal cautiously with Hamlet partly because the latter has too many friends among the people (4.3.4), and so, speaking with the prince, he uses friendly diction to disguise unfriendly motives (4.3.40–46). Ironically, he calls Rosencrantz and Guildenstern Hamlet's "associates" (although they are now more nearly his; 4.3.35), and he plans to rely on his friendship (or "love") with "England" (4.3.61) to help eliminate the prince. Many paradoxes inherent in the friendship theme are implied here: "England" is not merely the country but the brother king— a friend whom Claudius hopes he can count on. Yet their connection is not merely one of friendship but of intimidating "power" (4.3.62), and Claudius's hope for Hamlet's death—"Do it, England" (4.3.68)—can seem both a demand and a desperate plea. Such political dimensions of friendship are then immediately reinforced when we see Fortinbras—who started the play as Claudius's enemy—seeking the Dane's friendship so he can attack the Poles, his new foes (4.4.1–6). Juxtaposed with this, however, are Rosencrantz's gentle words urging the prince to board ship: "Will't please you go, my lord?" (4.4.30). This question can seem tenderly solicitous, calculatedly ingratiating, cautiously diplomatic, or some combination of these. Even in such simple words Shakespeare captures the complexities of dealings between (former?) friends.

Politics and friendship intersect again near the end of act 4, when Claudius fears that "buzzers" will "infect" the newly returned Laertes' "ear" with slander against the King (4.5.90). Although "buzzers" implies that such people are true friends neither to Laertes, Claudius, nor the state, Claudius is obviously motivated less by concern for Laertes or Denmark than for himself, and it is indeed Claudius who will soon pose as Laertes' friend and "infect" his "ear." When Laertes bursts in with a mob whom he courteously treats as friends (4.5.112–15), Gertrude and Claudius themselves respond with friendship that seems partly genuine though mostly fake (4.5.116, 122, 125–27, 129, 137, 139). Had the King responded with anger or force (as he might if Laertes had not come with so many friends), he probably would only have stirred up enmity. Instead, by responding with apparently calm friendship, he disarms his potential rival. He cautions Laertes not to allow intended revenge to harm "both friend and foe," thereby prompting the young man to say that he seeks only his father's "enemies" and will welcome and reward

his father's "friends" (4.5.142–47). Later Claudius asks Laertes
to put him "in your heart for friend" (4.6.2)—words that can
seem deceptively hypocritical or that may reveal a genuine desire
and need. When Claudius appeals to Laertes' "conscience" (a
valuable quality in a friend) he implies that he has one, too
(4.6.1), while his nervous reference to Hamlet's many friends (4.
6.16–24) seems particularly ironic since it was (and is?) a similar
concern that determined his treatment of Laertes. Claudius now
seems to share his secrets, worries, and even his self-love with
Laertes (4.6.30–35). Normally such openness would characterize
a good friend, but his apparent frankness is part of a ruse. Likewise, his willingness to praise Hamlet as "Most generous, and
free from all contriving" (4.6.134) seems ironic in more senses
than one. His praise may be sincere; or it may be calculated; but
(as we will soon learn from Hamlet's own mouth) it may also be
naive.

VIII

Act 5 opens with the famous exchange between the two
grave-digging clowns, who seem to be old friends or at the very
least old acquaintances. Their easy barbs suggest, ironically,
their amity. Soon they are confronted by another pair of friends
(Horatio and Hamlet). As the latter inspects a nearby skull, he
even imagines it as having once been a false friend or flatterer
(5.1.81–85). The grave-digger, appropriately, speaks with neither
false friendship nor flattery; instead, he addresses his social superior with the same insouciance he had just used toward his associate. Shakespeare thus underlines the ultimate lack of human
distinctions (a main theme of this scene): the clown treats the
prince as little more than another man (and thus as a potential
friend). A similar familiarity now also characterizes Hamlet's
relations with Horatio (whom he addresses frequently here by his
first name), although Shakespeare effectively contrasts the banter
between the clowns (and between the clown and Hamlet) with
the more thoughtful conversation between this other pair of comrades. Indeed, Horatio's willingness here even to criticize Hamlet's thinking (5.1.199) implies their present closeness: as he will
demonstrate repeatedly in this final act, Horatio is often willing
to disagree with his companion—a willingness which often signals true friendship.

The ensuing fight between Hamlet and Laertes in the grave
emphasizes the friendship theme in a different way: these men

who might have (and ultimately will be) friends (5.1.217) battle to show who bears greater affection for Ophelia. Yet Hamlet is also angry because he feels wrongly accused by the man he earlier considered a friend: "Hear you, sir,/ What is the reason that you use me thus?/ I lov'd you ever" (5.1.283–85). For Hamlet, the shock of Ophelia's death is intensified by the shock of Laertes' hatred. Oddly enough, he cannot seem to imagine why Laertes is so unfriendly. Ironically, however, the very circumstance that might have united these men (the shared loss of beloved fathers at the hands of killers) prevents their friendship.

When Hamlet reappears in 5.2 with Horatio, he is recounting a different battle against different former friends—Rosencrantz and Guildenstern. He reports how, having stolen the secret death-warrant they carried to the English king, he forged a substitute letter, full of friendly phrasing (5.2.39–42) but ordering that his two old chums be "put to sudden death,/ Not shriving-time allow'd" (5.2.46–47). Horatio's response—"So Guildenstern and Rosencrantz go to 't (5.2.56)—is wonderfully cryptic and can, of course, be interpreted in varying and contradictory ways.[23] It seems to register shock, especially when we realize that Hamlet has now treated his two old friends precisely as Claudius treated his murdered brother. Hamlet himself seems to interpret Horatio's comment as an implied criticism, or perhaps his conscience is bothered even though he claims it isn't (5.2.58). If the first interpretation is correct, then Horatio seems to be a good friend by being willing to question his friend's behavior; if the second interpretation makes more sense, then Hamlet demonstrates a continuing capacity for friendship by showing that he is not completely ruthless. Although he claims his conscience is untroubled, his very need to claim this may paradoxically suggest the opposite. In any case, he at least feels a need to explain to Horatio, who in a sense functions (here and elsewhere) as the play's embodied conscience. Curiously, Horatio never directly responds to Hamlet's self-justification but instead shifts subjects (5.2.62). Perhaps he realizes that there is no point in arguing (the deed, after all, is done); perhaps he is *afraid* to argue; perhaps he even approves the prince's conduct. Shakespeare wisely leaves all options open: Horatio's reticence adds to the rich ambiguity of the drama. If Horatio had openly approved the killings, he might seem less a friend than a toady. By instead keeping him relatively silent, Shakespeare here (as usual) gives us plenty to think about.

As if to see how and why Horatio is *not* a toady, we now

meet the real thing: Osric. He appears just after Hamlet has re-
gretted quarreling with Laertes and expressed his intent to
"court" the latter's "favours" (5.2.78). Osric, however, is a court-
ier in the more obvious sense and thus serves as a foil to both the
prince and Horatio. His pliability helps emphasize, by contrast,
Horatio's plain-spokenness, and Hamlet's playfully contemptuous treatment of the fop is, in part, a show staged to amuse his
comrade. Uncharacteristically, Horatio even joins the mockery
(5.2.129–30, 152–53, 183), although he seems rather to tease
Hamlet than openly torment Osric. Such intellectual and verbal
fencing (not only Horatio's with Hamlet but also Hamlet's with
the unarmed Osric) ironically precedes the real fencing in 5.3,
and by lampooning Osric Hamlet implies at once his ideals *of*
friendship, his capacity *for* friendship, but also his continuing
capacity for aggression. The fact that courtiers such as Osric are
now generally doted on (5.2.184–91) makes Hamlet's choice of
Horatio as a friend seem all the more worthy. His own character
is implied by the friend he selects.

Hamlet's decision to fight Laertes before the court shows,
paradoxically, his public respect for the other man and willingness to treat him as an equal; their fencing will potentially help
renew their bond. By dueling with Laertes, Hamlet seeks to make
amends for their earlier public confrontation; at the same time, of
course, by accepting the challenge he also helps display his self-
respect and protect (and repair) his reputation. Disciplined
swordplay will ideally function, for both of them, as ritualized
atonement (to each other and the court) for their earlier chaotic
fight. Gertrude even wants Hamlet to offer Laertes an open show
of friendship *before* they fight, and Hamlet's willingness to do so
shows his own capacity for amity—both to her and to Laertes
(5.2.202–04). Horatio, meanwhile, speaks with a true friend's
bluntness when he unflatteringly predicts that Hamlet will lose
the duel (5.2.205),[24] but he can have no idea, of course, just how
prophetic he is. Similarly, Hamlet shows his trust in and comfort
with his friend when he confesses misgivings about the fight
(5.2.208–12), while Horatio's willingness to lie for Hamlet
(5.2.213–14) shows that he values his private friend more than
the public truth.

When Claudius places Laertes' hand into Hamlet's before
the duel, he perverts one of the most symbolic gestures of friendship. This act becomes an emblem of his role as corrupt mediator
between the younger men. Hamlet's public apology to Laertes,
meanwhile, sounds almost too glib to strike Laertes as sincere,

however sincerely Hamlet may have intended it. Once more the potential for misinterpreting even truly friendly gestures arises: *we* have reason to believe (from the recent exchange with Horatio) that Hamlet does genuinely want to make amends with Laertes; but to Laertes, Hamlet's words may sound either ironic ("Was't Hamlet wrong'd Laertes? Never Hamlet") or sardonic ("Hamlet is of the faction that is wrong'd; His madness is poor Hamlet's enemy," 5.2.229, 234–35). This public apology is inherently ambiguous: by speaking before the court, Hamlet can be seen either as seeking to make truly open amends or as engaging in public relations (or both). Little wonder that Laertes seems unsure about how to respond until he consults some trusted friends (5.2.244). In the meantime, he is willing to receive Hamlet's "offer'd love like love/ And will not wrong it" (5.2.247–48). This whole exchange shows the complications that result when private friendships are negotiated in public.

No sooner do Hamlet and Laertes reach apparent accord, in fact, than the latter suspects the former of mocking him (5.2. 252–55), while the apparently friendly words between Hamlet and Claudius can be seen either as a brief cessation of hostilities or as disguised verbal jousting (5.2.256–60). Meanwhile, once the real fighting begins, Laertes' eventual willingness to confess to being hit (5.2.288) seems to show a capacity for honor and friendship even in the thick of combat. This appearance is complicated, though, by our knowledge that he is Claudius's willing instrument, yet we begin to doubt our doubts when Laertes confesses (in an aside) to a troubled conscience—just before he nonetheless strikes the fatal blow (5.2.300). Shakespeare thus goes out of his way to make Laertes (and nearly all the characters) difficult to judge simply: instead, they easily seem as complex as our own friends or ourselves. Ironically, the final reconciliation between Hamlet and Laertes is preceded by apparently real hatred (5.2.306), but in his dying moments Laertes shows himself capable of real friendship not only by forgiving Hamlet (and seeking Hamlet's forgiveness) but also by accusing himself (5.2.332–36). His self-condemnation paradoxically functions as self-praise: the more he denounces his own "treachery" (5.2. 313), the more worthy he seems. One aspect of the play's tragedy, indeed, is that these young men feel a kind of friendship just when real friendship between them becomes impossible.[25]

Meanwhile, although "friends" is almost Claudius's final word (5.2.329), such phrasing seems wonderfully ironic. The king appeals to friends to defend him, yet no one moves: instead, he is now almost completely friendless. The man who sought to win, keep, and manipulate friends dies alone, even though surrounded by fellow-revelers and erstwhile drinking companions. Their final disloyalty is no surprise: they are largely friends of pleasure. Openly denounced by his co-conspirator and recognized as a murderer by his dying wife, Claudius dies suddenly, his throat flooded by wine, no shriving time allowed. Hamlet, in contrast, dies a slower death that allows him to speak final friendly words to Laertes, his dead mother, the court, and especially Horatio (5.2.337–45). Horatio's desperate effort to act as a true friend by dying with Hamlet is prevented by the prince himself, who claims to interpet the apparently selfless gesture as a sign of selfish weakness. Ironically, one of Hamlet's last physical acts is to duel with his friend for possession of the poisoned cup (5.2.347–48). From Hamlet's perspective, Horatio's willingness to suffer the pain of living, not any willingness to end pain by death, will truly show him a friend (5.2.351–54).

This final conflict between Hamlet and Horatio paradoxically signals the depth of their mutual love, but it also shows the extent of Hamlet's dependence. He needs Horatio now more than ever, and he needs him particularly to help Hamlet win and keep friends even after the prince is dead: "O God, Horatio, what wounded name,/ Things standing thus unknown, shall I leave behind me" (5.2.349–50). Even as he leaves the world, Hamlet is concerned with his worldly reputation—with having friends, with being well regarded and truly respected. He therefore implicitly challenges the sincerity of Horatio's friendship (thereby, ironically, showing his real trust in it): "If ever thou didst hold me in thy heart,/ Absent thee from felicity awhile" (5.2.351–52). Hamlet is now a totally dependent and vulnerable friend, and Horatio now, unusually, has nearly total (but *not* total) power in their relationship. Even as he dies, Hamlet tries to control his friend's future words, conduct, and status. He publicly appoints Horatio his spokesman, just as he publicly nominates Fortinbras (once an enemy) as the new king. Although physically weak, Hamlet still wields power, particularly over his once and future friends.

Horatio's famous words ("Good night, sweet prince,/ And flights of angels sing thee to thy rest"; 5.2.364–65) are ironically juxtaposed with sounds of drums. These might normally signal war but now symbolize a kind of peace. The very brevity of Horatio's reaction to Hamlet's death makes it seem more powerfully heartfelt and sincere than any long, rhetorical speech could be, while the adjective "sweet" suggests how their friendship has ripened into love. Horatio's last image of Hamlet depicts the prince surrounded by true spiritual friends who will properly appreciate and love him and who, almost by definition, are incapable of doing him any harm. This image of ministering angels, though, is soon contrasted by Fortinbras's image of "proud Death" as an enemy feasting on the scattered bodies (5.2.369–72). And that image is complicated, in turn, when the English ambassadors appear, expecting friendly welcome (and reward?) for announcing the deaths of Hamlet's old chums, Rosencrantz and Guildenstern.

The ambassadors' arrival and their news might seem an odd distraction or an obvious bit of irony, but perhaps this touch is Shakespeare's way of emphasizing, one last time, the theme of friendship and the enormous complexities that theme often involves. The closing reference to Rosencrantz and Guildenstern helps complicate any simple judgments we might wish to make. If we think of them as wronged friends, we must also think of them as Claudius's inadvertent tools. If we think of them as Hamlet's victims, we must also think of them as victims of Claudius and of fate. If we think of them as disposable fools whose deaths finally do not matter, we probably cheapen the play. We view Hamlet as a victim just as we hear of the old friends he has helped victimize. In this play, few matters (including friendship) are ever simple.

Horatio, the one-time outsider, now takes partial charge and also center stage. As Hamlet's friend and as the only survivor who knows the whole truth, he is now positioned to serve as a friend both to Denmark (by explaining truly what has happened) and to Fortinbras (by legitimating the new ruler's claim to power). By acting as Hamlet's voice, Horatio will win friends for the new king and may even, ironically, become one of the new ruler's closest Danish advisors. Fortinbras, meanwhile, speaks words of friendly tribute to Hamlet (5.2.400–05)—words which, like so many other friendly words in this play, can seem merely politic, truly sincere, or both at once. Even in these final lines Shakespeare refuses to simplify the friendship theme. The play closes with sounds of thundering canons—sounds of war transformed into sounds of tribute, sounds of power transformed into sounds of love and honor, sounds of violence transformed into sounds of peace, sounds of hatred transformed into final peals of friendship.

Auburn University at Montgomery

NOTES

[1] *The Question of Hamlet* (Oxford: Oxford University Press, 1959), 3-4.

[2] "Friendship" does not appear, for instance, as a separate subject in the indices of either Randal F. Robinson, *Hamlet in the 1950s: An Annotated Bibliography* (New York: Garland, 1984) or Julia Dietrich, *Hamlet in the 1960s: An Annotated Bibliography* (New York: Garland, 1992). Inevitably it is discussed to one degree or another by various scholars whose work is cited in these books. In Robinson, for example, see entries 317 (Leo Kirschbaum) and 438 (Abbie Potts). In Dietrich, see such entries as the following: 103 (Curtis Watson); 651 (Heinrich Straumann); 665 (Fermin de Urmeneta); and 1033 (Howard Feinstein). Even more helpful is Bruce T. Sajdak's *Shakespeare Index: An Annotated Bibliography of Critical Articles on the Plays 1959–1983*, 2 vols. (Millwood, New York: Krause International, 1992). The following items in Sajdak's work are particularly helpful: U40 (Isadore Traschen); U238 (Howard Feinstein); U272 (Bridget Gellert); U345 (James I. Wimsatt); U364 (Robert Willson); U496 (Kristian Smidt); U376 (Joseph Meeker); U403 (Thomas Nelson); U494 (Andrew J. Sacks); U606 (Leo Rockas); U610 (Pierre Sahel); U714 (Ilona Bell); U772 (Charles Haines); U793 (Michael Taylor). Although I do not agree with the arguments of all these scholars, I have found all their ideas suggestive.
Also helpful have been the following: Julia Lupton, "Truant Dispositions: Hamlet and Machiavelli," *Journal of Medieval and Renaissance Studies* 17 (1987): 59–82, and (most recently) Keith Doubt, *"Hamlet* and Friendship," *Hamlet Studies* 17 (1995): 54–62. However, none of the studies mentioned in this note, nor any others of which I am aware, undertake the kind of detailed, almost scene-by-scene approach to the theme of friendship I hope to offer here.

[3] My original intent, when I first conceived this article, was both to theorize and historicize Shakespeare's treatment of friendship in *Hamlet*, but as I worked on the piece, one problem kept arising: the sheer richness of the play kept intruding on any sustained effort to pull back from the work itself. I have opted here instead, therefore, to work my way minutely through the drama, saving explicit theorizing on Renaissance friendship for another forum. I do already offer some historical and theoretical comments about the topic in chapter 6 of *Ben Jonson and the Poetics of Patronage* (Lewisburg: Bucknell University Press, 1989), 192–221. For a useful guide to general discussions of friendship, see J.L. Barkas, *Friendship: A Selected, Annotated Bibliography* (New York: Garland, 1985). Among the items listed by Barkas, the following have proven most helpful: 9 (Aristotle); 11 (Augustine); 23 (Robert R. Bell); 36 (Peter M. Blau); 41 (Lawrence A. Blum); 49 (Robert Brain); 63 (Cicero); 78 (Steve Duck); 116 and 117 (Erving Goffman); 124 (Andrew M. Greeley); 135 (George Homans); 188 and 189 (George J. McCall and J.L. Simmons); 194 (Gilbert C. Meilander); 208 (Friedrich Nietzsche); 222 (Plato); 225 (Plutarch); 227 (John M. Reisman); 263 (Jeremy Taylor); 311 (Sir Francis Bacon); and 504 (Montaigne). For more recent work see, for instance, Neera Kapur Bahwar, ed., *Friendship: A Philosophical Reader* (Ithaca, New York: Cornell University Press, 1993); Leroy S. Rouner, ed., *The Changing Face of Friendship* (Indiana: University of Notre Dame Press, 1994); and the special issue on friendship (edited by Peter Murphy) of the *South Atlantic Review* 97:1 (1998).
Jacques Derrida's book *The Politics of Friendship*, trans. George Collins (London: Verso, 1997) appeared too late (and seemed perhaps a bit too opaque) for me to make much use of it here.

[4] See *"Timon of Athens:* The Iconography of False Friendship," *Huntington Library Quarterly* 43 (1980): 181–200, esp. 185. I am honored to acknowledge here the true friendship Cliff Davidson has always shown, not only toward me and many other colleagues (such as his long-time collaborator John S. Stroupe), but also toward the numerous scholars he has generously helped over the years. Cliff's encouragement and assistance

will be greatly missed but never forgotten.

One of the most valuable studies of Renaissance concepts of friendship remains the venerable study by Laurens J. Mills, *One Soul in Bodies Twain: Friendship in Tudor Literature and Stuart Drama* (Bloomington: Principia, 1937). Mills surveys (and quotes extensively from) all the standard sources. One of these is William Baldwin's 1547 *Treatise of Morall Philosophie*, which was subsequently enlarged by Thomas Palfreyman and reprinted in 1620. This text quickly summarizes nearly all the most typical Renaissance ideas about friendship (mostly borrowed from classical precursors). These include the beliefs that friendship is a "vertue" rooted in virtue; that it involves "perfect consent in all things"; that "there is nothing giuen of God (except wisedome) that is to man more commodious"; that friendship makes "of two persons one"; that it is "small pleasure to haue life in this world if a man may not trust his friends"; that friendship "is to be preferred before all worldly things"; that "where equality is not, friendship may not long continue"; that a "true friend is more to be esteemed, then kinfolke"; that one should be "slow to fall into friendship, but when . . . in [should] continue"; that one should not trust friends won during prosperity; that "friends lightly taken, are likewise lightly left again"; that the "iniury of a friend is much more grieuous than the iniury of an enemy"; but also (paradoxically) that there "is so little [obvious] difference between our enemy and our friend" that it is "hard to know the one from the other." See the edition of Baldwin's treatise edited by Robert Hood Bowers (Gainesville: Scholars' Facsimiles and Reprints, 1967), 174–79.

For more recent discussions of Renaissance friendship see, for example, Lorna Hutson, *The Usurer's Daughter: Male Friendship and Fictions of Women in Sixteenth-Century England* (London: Routledge, 1994), as well as Laurie J. Shannon's "'Soveraigne Amitie': Friendship and the Political Imagination in Renaissance Texts" (Ph.D. diss., University of Chicago, 1996) and the secondary works cited therein.

⁵ This is not the place to discuss the complicated texts of *Hamlet*. Suffice it to say that I have elected to use the Arden edition, prepared by Harold Jenkins (London: Methuen, 1982). I have also consulted other editions and have found particularly helpful *The Three-Text Hamlet: Parallel Texts of the First and Second Quartos and First Folio*, ed. Paul Bertram and Bernice W. Kliman (New York: AMS Press, 1991). Unless otherwise noted, any italics in quotations are mine and have been added to emphasize particular words.

⁶ In addition to the Arden notes and the works cited in my first two endnotes, I have also found the following scholarship particularly helpful in thinking about the play in general and especially about the theme of friendship: Paul S. Conklin, *A History of Hamlet Criticism* (London: Routledge and Kegan Paul, 1947); Arthur G. Davis, *Hamlet and the Eternal Problem of Man* (New York: St. John's University Press, 1964), esp. 137–66; John W. Draper, *The Hamlet of Shakespeare's Audience* (Durham, North Carolina: Duke University Press, 1938), esp. 17–53, 70–82, and 152–244; Harold Fisch, *Hamlet and the Word: The Covenant Pattern in Shakespeare* (New York: Unger, 1971), esp. 44–57; Walter N. King, *Hamlet's Search for Meaning* (Athens: University of Georgia Press, 1982); Marvin Rosenberg, *The Masks of Hamlet* (Newark: University of Delaware Press, 1992); Bert O. States, *Hamlet and the Concept of Character* (Baltimore: Johns Hopkins University Press, 1992), esp. 147–89; and Morris Weitz, *Hamlet and the Philosophy of Literary Criticism* (Chicago: University of Chicago Press, 1964).

⁷ See States, *Hamlet and the Concept of Character*, 152.

⁸ See Shannon, "'Soveraigne Amitie'," *passim*.

⁹ See Davis, *Hamlet and the Eternal Problem of Man*, 154.

¹⁰ See also Draper, *The Hamlet of Shakespeare's Audience*, 22.

¹¹ This encounter is greatly expanded in the folio version; see Bertram and Kliman,

eds., *The Three-Text Hamlet*, 96–100.

[12] See States, *Hamlet and the Concept of Character*, 149.

[13] See Draper, *The Hamlet of Shakespeare's Audience*, 19.

[14] For an effective analysis of this entire scene, see James I. Wimsatt, "The Player King on Friendship," *Modern Language Review* 65 (1970): 1–6.

[15] See Fisch, *Hamlet and the Word*, 48.

[16] See Rosenberg, *The Masks of Hamlet*, 559.

[17] See Davis, *Hamlet and the Eternal Problem of Man*, 155.

[18] See Rosenberg, *The Masks of Hamlet*, 560.

[19] But see King, *Hamlet's Search for Meaning*, 82.

[20] See Mills, *One Soul in Bodies Twain*, 134–44; and Draper, *The Hamlet of Shakespeare's Audience*, 282.

[21] See Doubt, "*Hamlet* and Friendship," 59.

[22] See Joan Larson Klein, "*Hamlet* IV.ii.12–21 and Whitney's *Choice of Emblems*," *Notes and Queries*, n.s. 23:4 (1976): 158–61.

[23] See Rosenberg, *The Masks of Hamlet*, 865.

[24] See Draper, *The Hamlet of Shakespeare's Audience*, 157.

[25] See Doubt, "*Hamlet* and Friendship," 61.

Alfieri's *Saul*
as Enlightenment Tragedy

Jerome Mazzaro

Vittorio Alfieri's *Saul* was written in 1782, six years after the American colonies declared their independence from England and while the Italian playwright was involved with the Countess of Albany, wife of the aging Young Pretender to the British crown, Charles Edward Stuart. Alfieri had already written *Of Tyranny* (1777), assisted the Countess in her escape from her raving husband, and had as well composed the first four odes of *All'America libera* (1781). This last had been dedicated to George Washington and affirmed the Italian writer's support for the principles of political freedom that underscored the American Revolution. Like other intellectuals of his day, Alfieri opposed oppression and superstition, advocating right reason and political freedom; given the circumstances of his personal life and perhaps rumors of King George's incipient madness, it is not surprising that, having been led into a view of art as political action, he should choose a mad king for a subject. Like so many Enlightenment figures, he was interested in the human drives and larger principles upon which various forms of government were created and supported, in particular the form of government that most suited his needs. Nor is it surprising that, as a writer born and brought up in Piedmont with French as a first language, he should be influenced in the development of his art by the "rules" of French classical tragedy. *Saul* in its investigations of oppression and monarchy under assault observes the unities of plot, time, and action first established by Scaliger and Castelvetro and brought into prominence by the dramas of Racine. In so doing, the work compresses ideas and events surrounding the reign of the first king of Israel into 24 hours, locates them in an Israelite camp at Mt. Gilboa, and restricts its incidents and characters to a single action. In keeping with Tasso's recommendation, history is preferred to fiction and, perhaps as a consequence of his involvement with the Countess, a Cornellian love interest, absent from Alfieri's earlier works, appears.

125

Along with these Renaissance "rules" of drama, *Saul* sub-
scribes to Aristotle's notions of tragedy's involving the purga-
tion of pity and fear.[1] Pity, which for the Greek philosopher was
"the affective meaning of present incidents as they are related to
the past," involves in Alfieri's work "sufferings which arise in
friendships, as well as killing or something else of this sort" occurring among family or near-family relations.[2] Fear, which for
Aristotle was "the affective meaning of present incidents as they
are related to the future," is intertwined in Alfieri and other writers of his day with the essence of tyranny.[3] For Alfieri as for
Montesquieu earlier, a tyrant was anyone who "obtained the absolute reigns of government and believed [himself] to be and
[was] above the law." He was both a source and an object of fear,
and in the course of his tragedies, Alfieri's dominant central
theme involves conflicts between this tyrant and a hero, the aim
of their struggle being "political and personal liberty."[4] By
watching the actions being staged, audiences were to be purged
until they were themselves capable of heroic deeds in pursuit of
their own liberty. These elements of tyrant and hero appear in
Saul as an individual internal struggle to control and redirect irrational instincts by belief in a force that allows improvement of
oneself. The struggle takes place on two planes, inwardly in the
mind of Saul and outwardly in the conflict between high priest
and prince over right action and jurisdiction that had analogues
in the contemporary struggle between Pope Pius VI and secular
governors like the Emperor Joseph II. Despite Alfieri's own hatred of religion and its tyranny, he hoped at one time to dedicate
the play to Pius VI and read it "to an assembly chiefly formed of
high dignitaries of the Church" for their approval. "The Holy Father," Alfieri writes in his *Vita*, "excused himself by saying that
he could not agree to have any theatrical pieces dedicated to him
of whatever kind they might be."[5]

The usual practice that Alfieri followed when composing a
drama was threefold. As he describes it in his *Vita*, he maintained
a plan of conception, development, and versification in order to
adhere to Horace's warning against excessive haste in a work's
realization. By conception, he intended "the distribution of the
subject into acts and scenes, fixing the number of [characters]
and tracing in two pages of careless prose a summary of the
plot." This distribution within a standard five-act play included
the limiting of principal characters to four or five and an action
that was propelled by incident rather than narrative description.
Confidants which abound in French classical tragedy give way to

soliloquies as the means of revealing one's inmost thoughts, and no hero is to be introduced in an opening act by a character created for that purpose, nor is narrative to be used in the last act for what could be shown on stage. By development, Alfieri meant the writing of dialogues in prose for the different scenes indicated in the rough draft. By versification, he meant the conversion of the prose of these speeches into poetry, "selecting the best thoughts and clothing them in poetic language." This verse, as he indicates, is shaped partly by the translations of Ossian and of Voltaire's tragedies into Italian by Melchiorre Cesarotti and partly by his own reaction to Seneca's Latin iambics, whose "boldest and most virile strokes . . . derived half of their sublimity from broken and disjointed metre." The verse would present "an arrangement of words, of sounds perpetually varied and broken, of phrases short and energetic, which [would] distinguish tragedy from all other kinds of blank verse, as well as from every species of rhyme, whether epic or lyric." It would aim at its climactic moments "to astonish and strike terror into the hearts of its listeners" and its semblance to Alfieri's own voice and manner has led critics at times to confound Alfieri with his creations, whose roles he often played in private productions. Saul's rage and despair have been equated with Alfieri's own.[6]

Alfieri was drawn to the subject of the first Israelite king by his readings in the Bible. He was impressed by the richness of the account's imagery, its uses of simile, its almost classical instances of *harmartia* and *hubris*, and Saul's Cato-like end in suicide. In addition, the biblical account contained arguments for and against monarchy as a divinely sanctioned form of government. Years before Saul's coronation, Gidean had refused the crown, saying that neither he nor his sons would rule over Israel, but that the Lord alone was monarch (Judges 8:23). However, the demoralizing defeat of the Hebrews at Aptek (1 Samuel 4) brought about an increased pressure for a king to unify the Israelite league for its continuing existence. In one of two conflicting versions, the prophet Samuel, under whose judgeship this pressure came, resented the pressure, and God, though affirming a king was an offense, nevertheless instructed him to accede to the people's demand (1 Samuel 8:5–22). Samuel does so, warning the people of God's displeasure and the evils that will befall them. In a parallel, older pro-monarchist account, Saul is chosen king by designation and popular affirmation. He is anointed secretly by Samuel before being presented to the people and affirmed by sacred lot (1 Samuel 10). His selection appears to be ratified when the Israelites defeat the Ammonites a month later. All the same, as Samuel had foretold, disfavor eventually comes.

Two different offenses are given for this disfavor, both of which find their ways into Alfieri's drama. One offense concerns Saul's offering of the holocaust when Samuel's promised arrival does not occur and a sacrifice is needed before the Israelites confront the Philistines. For this usurpation of the priestly function, Saul is told that his office will be taken from him and his heirs (1 Samuel 13). The other, completely unrelated offense concerns Saul's failure to carry out fully the destruction of the tribe of Amalec as Samuel tells him that the Lord commands. For this disobedience, he incurs rejection (1 Samuel 15), and it is this offense which Alfieri makes paramount in his tragedy. Alfieri sees in Saul's act of mercy toward Agag an adumbration of the lessening of animal ferocity and impulse toward betterment that he makes central to man's relationship to God; in the play it defines Saul's refusal to accept Samuel's view of an unmerciful God as well as his wish for a more temperate deity.

In the biblical account as in the Alfieri drama, Saul is joined in his decisions by the figures of David, Jonathan, Michal, Abner, and Ahimelech. Of them, the most important figures are David, Jonathan, and Michal. Abner is merely an instigator of evil, playing upon Saul's jealousies and fears to what he believes is his own advantage, and Ahimelech a victim of Saul's madness in his support of a vengeful God, assistance to David, and echoing disobedience. David is important historically and theologically, as well as being central in a mythology of artist and monarch that Alfieri articulates in *The Prince and Letters*, begun in 1774 but not completed until 1786. In David, one has a king who resolves the differences between state and church by embodying in himself the authorities of both and, for Christians, prefiguring, as Saint Augustine says in *De civitate Dei*, on a worldly level Christ and his eternal reign.[7] In *Saul*, he supports the view of a more merciful God while preserving his biblical trait of doing no injury to the Lord's anointed. In David, one also has a masterly poet, who with the rationality of his music is able to calm the madness of Saul and, for Alfieri, confer fame on both the king and himself. In accepting the prince's favors and protection and, with them, a form of slavery, the artist must never forget—as Alfieri's David does not with his merciful God—that in upholding Horace's *delectare* a poet's true task is setting before the people "love of truth, a thirst for glory, [and] a knowledge of their rights."[8] Along with Jonathan and Michal, he forms part of a young generation which critics of Alfieri's play see as opposing the old one embodied in an aging Saul (and by extension, perhaps the Young Pretender?),[9] and certainly Jonathan, Michal, and David represent individuals who do not let their instinctive needs overcome their reason and who, as distinct from Abner and Ahimelech, are vital, fully drawn characterizations.

Nor in going to the Bible for his subject and characters and in mediating the Bible's differing views on monarchy does Alfieri wholly abandon his Enlightenment views on government. His travels and readings disposed him in *Of Tyranny* toward a constitutional monarchy, where, besides a king and government by law, there would be a body of representatives or nobles in whom intermediate and subordinate powers were vested. He believed that no king should be above the law, that absolute monarchs like Saul were despotic, and that the function of government was to insure personal liberty. In his belief, he was particularly drawn to England and Holland for their equitable governments, wise laws, and true liberty, as well as to accounts of the Roman Empire, where polytheism "turned heaven into a kind of republic." By its pluralism, paganism avoided the tyranny of a single ruler in worldly imitation of an otherworldly deity on whose model contemporary monarchies rested. In especial, Alfieri disliked having to seek permission from his king to travel abroad and from his king and church censors to publish his works. Alfieri, moreover, saw the Christian religion of his day aiding tyranny by commanding "only the blind obedience" of its believers, "never utter[ing] the word liberty," and "liken[ing] the tyrant, cleric or lay, to God."[10] His Saul seems to believe in a monarchy independent of church dominance and, once having been sanctified, an office existing in perpetuity beyond church interference for himself and his descendants. Ann Hallock sees in the play seeds of Alfieri's subsequent affirmation of the important relationship between man and God for man's release from suffering and attainment of peace as well as his defenses of God against other Enlightenment figures like Voltaire, who sought to eliminate all religious belief. He characterizes God's force as "generat[ing] piety and good works and eliminat[ing] man's ferocity."[11]

The play opens much like other Alfieri dramas on a soliloquy. In it, David establishes the setting, his faith in God, and his standing with Saul, who, as in the Bible, has called for David's death. God has left Saul to the mercy of an "evil spirit," and David wonders pointedly what man is, "se Iddio ci lascia" ("if

God deserts us," 1.20).[12] David will surrender himself to Saul and assist him in beating back the Philistines that are about to attack, referring twice in his decision to "il brando" ("sword"), once as its possible victim and then as its wielder (1.6, 30). His words are overheard by his brother-in-law Jonathan, to whom he willingly reveals himself and, in Alfieric fashion, expresses his eagerness to fight with those "under the sword" (1.51) for country and king. In acknowledging David's virtue and election by God, Jonathan ponders how he will present this outcast to his father, since David has spent time with Israel's enemies. David's opposite Abner now holds Saul's heart,[13] and at mention of his sister and David's wife, David experiences elation. Jonathan recounts for him the bad times suffered by Michal and Israel since his departure and recommends patience and stealth. David prefers openness and indicates that Saul may yet seek pardon and reconciliation with God, whose judgments are sometimes terrible. Jonathan promises that, so long as he lives, no sword of Saul's will fall on David. As is her habit, Michal approaches, lamenting her state and resolving to find her husband. Jonathan tells her to wait. David will come to her, drawn there by his heart. Jonathan relates their father's present state of paralysis that David's arrival might end. David reveals himself and reunites with Michal, both of whom rejoice as the darkness of the night and their lives turn to dawn. Jonathan and Michal bid David hide until they are able to present his case to their father.

Act 2 opens with Saul and Abner at another part of the Israelite camp. Saul fears the outcome of the upcoming battle and is consoled by Abner's assurance that delay will insure him victory. He reminisces on his lost strength, God's lost favor, and David's absence, and echoing David's earlier question on what man is without God, Abner counters that without David Saul's army will prove victorious. Saul's divided state since being cast off by God is explained as the result of high priests who are upset with the king's no longer being subordinate to them and that this and the reputation of David have caused his condition. Abner describes David as a tool of Samuel and, at heart, a priest who cannot succeed except at Saul's expense. Abner greets Saul's account of the events and voices that led to his becoming king with the statement that his "sogni, sventure, visïon, terrori" ("dreams, mishaps, hallucinations, terrors," 2.121) will cease with David's death. At that moment, Jonathan and Michal arrive to plead David's case. Jonathan, too, assures his father of victory, but Saul remains only partly persuaded and asks why they came. Michal reminds him of David's ability to calm his moods and Jonathan of David's worthiness in battle. Brought back by their words to past glory, Saul slips again into despair as Abner pronounces, "nulla è in David" ("nothing is in David," 2.211). David enters, and in his voice Saul hears divine purpose. At first, he is satisfied at David's rehearsal of his achievements in service of God and king but soon recalls David's eclipsing popularity. David lays blame for its damaging effects on Abner and his kind, and Abner responds by accusing David of conspiring with priests and Philistines to gain power. Michal defends her husband, and Saul asks David to account for his time among the Philistines. David responds by showing a piece of cloth that he had cut from the king's robe while the king was sleeping and could easily have been murdered. Reassured of David's loyalty, Saul bids him, Jonathan, and Michal join him in his tent.

Act 3 sees the emergence of more of Alfieri's political views. It opens with a meeting of David and Abner to discuss battle strategy. Again they air their differing perspectives on God and king, and king and family, some of Abner's positions being those Enlightenment views contained in *Of Tyranny*.[14] A battle plan is agreed upon, and David assumes leadership of the army. After Abner's departure, he notes Abner's inability to gain the soldiers' hearts, important if one is to win. Michal arrives to tell him that Abner has undermined his standing with Saul. David offers to go into exile after the battle, and Michal expresses her unwillingness to be again separated from him. Jonathan and Saul arrive, Saul being once more deeply depressed. Jonathan and Michal try to revive his spirits, but he demands David, whose prompt mention of God Saul takes as an insult. Implying that in rejecting God Saul has lost that force to betterment and peace of mind, David answers that God does not dwell with those who do not love Him and that God's love is shown in Saul's office and existence. Saul asks David to approach so that he might determine whether he is David or Samuel. In doing so, David reveals that he has Goliath's sword, and Saul asks how he came into possession of that holy object. David tells him that it was given him at Nob by the high priest Ahimelech. Saul explodes and, calmed by Jonathan and David, again laments his age and now accuses his children of wanting his death. Michal and Jonathan deny these thoughts and ask David to calm him with song. In anticipation of *The Prince and Letters*, David begins a celebration of the king's fame in four songs. The first is an invocation of God, the second describes one of the king's early victories, the third recounts the return of his soldiers to domestic peace, and the last numbers the dreams of the sleeping king. His mention of two swords in the final song, however, revives Saul's fury, and Michal tells David to flee. She and Jonathan in the meantime try to appease their father's anger.

At the start of act 4, Jonathan reveals to Michal that, although their father has regained his reason, he is still too jealous of David to allow a reconciliation. Saul enters and, despite Jonathan's defense, repeats his fear of David's becoming king as an instrument of priestly malice, since it signifies the destruction of his line. He sends Michal to fetch David. Abner arrives and reports the disappearance of David and his capture of Ahimelech. Saul accuses the high priest of treachery in having aided David, and Ahimelech responds by reciting for authority a line of priests going back to Aaron that rivals the descent that Saul hopes for his line. Because of his irreverences to Samuel and other high priests, this line is being threatened by God. Saul orders Ahimelech to confess the aid and Ahimelech does, adding that his loyalty and Israel's victory lie not in Saul but in God and David. Saul blames Samuel's antipathy jointly on his refusal to accept a bloodthirsty God and slay Agag as Samuel indicated was God's will, and on the desire of the priestly class ultimately to rule over the throne. Ahimelech is astonished at Saul's arrogance and asserts man's insignificance as compared to God. He predicts Saul's imminent death and pronounces Abner "di Satàn fratello" ("Satan's brother," 4.226). As proof of his significance, Saul responds by condemning Ahimelech to death and altering agreed-upon battle plans so as to prevent the possibility of David's disclosing them to the Philistines. Thinking that Ahimelech's death is not enough, he then extends, as in 1 Samuel 22:16–19, the death sentence to all of Nob, saying that, in doing so, his importance is proven. Jonathan registers his objection to the spilling of sacerdotal blood but agrees to join his father in the next day's battle. Michal returns and says that she cannot locate David. Disappointed, Saul proclaims himself alone, no longer certain even of his children's loyalty.

Act 5 begins with a meeting between Michal and David at David's hiding place. She has decided to accompany him into exile. He objects, and in her effort to persuade him, she tells him of Ahimelech's death, Abner's being ordered to kill him on sight, and Jonathan's intent to die in battle. David acknowledges that he can no longer serve Saul because of the king's shedding of priestly blood and must leave, but he is insistent that Michal not join him. She must stay behind so as not to impede his escape. She is needed, moreover, by Saul. He will send word of his whereabouts when he is settled. They embrace, and he departs, leaving her to face her father, who has come on the scene lost in hallucination. He believes that he sees the ghost of Samuel and wishes to hide from it. Watching him, Michal finds she cannot penetrate his thoughts. He asks Samuel to take the crown from him but not the office from his offspring. He thinks that David can rescue him from his fate, much as he had rescued him earlier from his madness. Images of blood and destruction continue to fill his sight, including the ghosts of Ahimelech and his children, to make him aware that he will soon be among the dead. The sound of battle breaks him from his hallucinations. Recovered, he calls for his arms. Abner arrives with news that the Philistines have attacked unexpectedly and that his sons have been killed. Saul orders him to guide Michal out of the battle area, and left alone, no longer fearful, he commits suicide rather than allowing himself to be taken. No more will he submit to the Philistines than he had to the high priests.

The compression needed to retell these events surrounding Saul's suicide at Mt. Gilboa in less than twenty-four hours requires that elements of the action proceed differently from those of the Bible. So, too, do the requirements of drama and tragedy. Alfieri, for example, invents the story of David's being in the Israelite camp shortly before the battle to externalize and heighten Saul's internal conflicts and prevent what could have been reduced to a long, agonizing monologue. In 1 Samuel, David is in pursuit of the Amalekites for their destruction of Ziklag and capture of David's wives (1 Samuel 30). Alfieri invents as well the passionate romance between David and Michal to show David's character as divided between love of God and love of Michal in echo of Saul's similarly divided state. At the time of her father's death, Michal is already married to Phalti (1 Samuel 25:44), and in exile, David has married Abigail and Ahinoam (1 Samuel 25:42–43). Ahimelech, whom Alfieri includes to show the vengeful side of God and, by extension, the vengeful side of Saul and, presumably, the vengeful sides of his own age's interfering church and state, is long dead before the events at Mt. Gilboa (1 Samuel 22:17). There is, in addition, no biblical basis for David's being at Ramah, for Samuel's deathbed blessing, or for the antithetical natures of David and Abner which Alfieri depicts, though all add to the work's dramatic impact. In keeping with Horace's stricture against showing on stage

actions which might be more tastefully carried on behind the
scenes, Alfieri's Saul is not mortally wounded in battle as he is
in 1 Samuel 31:3 before he commits suicide; perhaps to keep the
number of characters small, Alfieri excludes the Witch of Endor,
preferring to have Saul's final encounters with Samuel and
Ahimelech occur as hallucination. Earlier biblical incidents
which do make it into the play do so eloquently in speeches as
recollections or diversions to enrich or explain relationships and
situations. So, too, phrases from 1 Samuel skillfully enter the text
to intensify Saul's envy of David's favor with God and the people and his own fears of having lost favor with God and of losing
the crown for his heirs.

Indeed, the hallmark of Alfierian drama, like that of French
classical theater, is an intensity brought about by this compression; in the case of *Saul*, this intensity is increased by the urgency of the play's fugitive David avoiding capture and death,
and an Israelite army about to attack or be attacked by an enemy.
In this intensity, worldly place gives way to moral position in
respect to God. The intensity allows for the play's rapid shifts
from exposition to assertion, rage to calm, battle strategy to romance, outdoors to indoors, and hope to despair. In these shifts
the play demonstrates some of the same effects that Alfieri finds
in Seneca's dramas and that audiences are likely to encounter in
Renaissance music and poetry, especially in Petrarch, whose
work Alfieri admired. Consistency dictates, moreover, that the
exposition and action occurring with these shifts be heightened
to a degree that, except for opera, modern audiences are no more
likely to find congenial than the abstract, no-place, nowhere setting that allows Saul in the midst of a siege to send a large
enough contingent of troops to Nob to slaughter the family, kin,
and kind of Ahimelech and return miraculously, as if no distance
but the sound of words existed between Mt. Gilboa and Nob, and
none of the enemy could see or take advantage of the maneuver.
The vagueness of the setting also allows Michal to rendezvous
with a supposedly distant, hidden David in a spot where, after
David's departure, Saul immediately enters. Nor does the imagery—especially strong, rich, and varied in *Saul*—lessen the intensity with its interplays of dark and light and age and youth
and its simultaneous evocations of inherited literary and biblical
pasts and, for modern audiences, foreshadowings of Freudian
father-son antagonisms and sibling rivalries between Saul and
David; among Saul, David, and Samuel; and Saul, David, and
God; as well as Freud's sense (common in French classical trag-

edy) that the remembered context or history of a situation, however disguised, is its meaning.

Enlightenment tragedy as it emerges in *Saul* is a reexamination of the bounds of necessity and convention. Classical tragedy is a tragedy of necessity. Fate is determined, as W. H. Auden says, not by one's actions but by one's name or being. The feeling it arouses in audiences is "What a pity it had to be this way!" It differs from Christian tragedy or tragedy of possibility by the audience's belief in free will and "pity that it was this way when it might have been otherwise."[15] In Enlightenment tragedy this possibility is muted by the illusion of necessity, often realized as lingering myth or what Francis Bacon calls "idols of the tribe." In *Saul*, this "idol" is that of an immanent God and worldly existence as a shadow-play of divine will and favor. It is best articulated by the common thread underlying the differing views of David and Ahimelech, but it also underlies Saul's view of himself. It turns what in classical tragedy is accepted, powerful external forces into internal psychological forces. As Alfieri notes, audiences do not have to accept Saul's end as divine punishment. For the purpose of the play what matters is that Saul believes that he has fallen from divine favor; this is enough to initiate his troubled state of mind.[16] Thus, one might say that Enlightenment tragedy is a tragedy of failed myth, differing from the *idées fixes* of more modern tragedies by being tribal rather than individual, though its challenges to myth are, likewise, often individual. In the play, these challenges extend as well to superstition and the Bible's "evil spirits," whose powers are given over to the very human Abner and the Witch of Endor. Her ability to summon the dead Samuel is turned into one of Saul's several self-generated hallucinations. The challenges extend as well to the sense that what passes as revelation might be distorted by priests into positions that minimize mankind's achievements in favor of its own self-interests.

In Saul's refusals to give into the separate pleas of David and Ahimelech to return to God's grace by submitting to Him and the authority of His high priests, audiences have precursors of Hegel's concept of the essence of classical tragedy in *The Philosophy of Fine Art* (1835) as well as the Romantic "Satanic Hero." Saul clearly sees a partial good—the separation of the state from church interference—as an absolute good. The self-division and intestinal warfare which he undergoes in the course of the drama provides the Hegelian "collision" or "conflict" that leads to the work's unhappy end. While based upon the biblical account,

Saul's suicide—that he not become a trophy for the Philistines—is less a direct act of freedom than is his defiance of Samuel's pronouncements. This defiance is an equivalent to Satan's *non serviam* in John Milton's *Paradise Lost* (1667, 1674), taken up by English Romantic poets like William Blake and Percy Shelley as an embodiment of rebellious energy against oppressive limitation. While it exists, Saul's flawed grandeur—his passions and strength surpassing all but David's—provides what is in the nineteenth century to become the Byronic hero. All the same, not the defiance but the suicide complementing it is what critics emphasize, casting it in terms of Cato's suicide as that was presented in Cicero's *Tusculan Disputations*, Plutarch's *Lives*, and Dante's *Divine Comedy*. It is the ultimate worldly sacrifice to political freedom. Since the writers of the Old Testament did not censure any of the five suicides that occur there, one suspects that they did not consider Saul's death as cowardly. Nor is Seneca less sympathetic. He considers suicide proof of an individual's inability to be held against his will. It is the act *par excellence* of the free man. Not until Augustine does Christianity move to define the act as sinful.[17]

However much Saul's suicide can be seen as an extension and externalization of the defiance he shows to Samuel's image of an unmerciful God, modern audiences are likely to see it as the result of self-consciousness and paranoid schizophrenia. Saul conceives of his difficulties as troubles focused squarely on him and his relations to God and God's high priests, rather than as politically and militarily generated challenges. Every experience is weighed in terms of how it affects him, and eventually nothing exists for him but himself. Reason for his continuing existence and interactions diminishes. It is this state that psychologists believe prompts the act and that Alfieri seeks elsewhere to avoid by upholding the importance of the relationship between God and man. It is this state, too, that Alfieri may have glimpsed in his own nature and in the rages of the Young Pretender. It is, likewise, this state which writers like Augustine and Saint Thomas Aquinas seek to discourage with their beliefs that to sever the soul prematurely from the body usurps a privilege that belongs only to God and that self-preservation is a primary universal natural law. If committed while one is sane, self-murder would be open to charges of cowardice rather than heroism. In the play, Alfieri's masterly, almost clinical depiction of paranoid vacillation, paralysis, delusions, jealousies, and hallucinations has prompted critics like Vernon Lee to charge that Saul is a "suspicious madman" and, therefore, neither heroic nor morally responsible for his statements or actions.[18] To counter this impression Alfieri goes to an inflated diction, recollections of past heroic actions, assertions of sanity, and respect for Saul from David, his children, and Abner.

In the instances within the play involving swords—"il brando," "il ferro," and "la spada"—audiences have adumbrations of Alfieri's belief that expression can lead to political action. Their combination occurs at least forty-one times. 1 Samuel records twenty-four occasions when "sword" is used, and the weapon is fitting in any account dealing with battle plans and war. "Sword" is used literally at times to refer to a weapon; it is also used metonymically to suggest troops or army and the retributory power of God. It is used emblematically in *Saul* in expressions like "il sacro brando" ("the sacred sword," 4.150), "la infuocata spada" ("the flaming sword," 5.132), and "il brando sanguinoso" ("the bloodied sword," 3.9–10), and it is twice addressed directly, once by Michal (1.283) in regard to David and once by Saul (5.220) as he is about to commit suicide. Also evident is Alfieri's effort to locate man within the province of nature's laws by using metaphors of nature. Saul's various rages are "tempeste" ("storms"), and he sees himself as a "quercia antica" ("old oak"), who shows his "squallide radici" ("squalid roots") where once he had lifted branches (2.157–59). His "trunk" is rotten (3.235), and David's decision to attack the Philistines in the afternoon indicative of his "declining arm" (4. 244). His "house" is spent (4.91), bereft of splendor (2.49), and soon to be uprooted (4.91–92). This natural decline infuses the play's accusations and Saul's fears of lost divine favor with variations of "fuoco" ("fire") and "sangue" ("blood") calibrating man's instinctual ferocity. Finally, underlying the play's language is Alfieri's concept of liberty as a balance of one's instinctive needs to be greater and better than the next man and the arresting or restrictive drives of society, here personified in the high priests because, as king, Saul is above the law.

It is unfortunate that a play as interesting as *Saul* should for most non-Italian readers be subordinated to Alfieri's anticipations of Hegel's tragic conflicts, the Romantic Byronic hero, and nineteenth-century Italian politics. There is no doubt that the moral positions taken in Alfieri's works are those needed "to become the Italy of [Giuseppe] Mazzini and [Giuseppe] Garibaldi . . . [and Ugo] Foscolo and [Giacomo] Leopardi."[19] They shamed Italians of the latter eighteenth century into the gestures of car-

ing, strength, and heroism that helped found a nation. The play
offers a degree of "Oriental splendor" and "lyrical sublimity,"
especially in the king's troubled utterances,[20] but as importantly
it shows how communal stories like those of the Old Testament
can be successfully modernized, as external forces are internal-
ized and subject, thereby, to individual control. In doing so, it
adds to the century's concern with "conscience" and the paralyz-
ing impacts of competing duties by seeming to promote both
sides of a central issue. One may side with David, Samuel, and
Ahimelech in believing that Saul's defeat and suicide are divine
just punishment for his rejection of the Lord of Israel and spilling
of priestly blood; or, in accepting the possibility of Samuel's
God as Saul does, one might sympathize with his need for a less
restrictive God to achieve personal liberty and admire his willingness to face destruction rather than submit to tyranny. Like
Cato in defeat, who refuses to owe his life to Caesar, Saul does
not so much lessen his greatness as raise questions about his fate.
His last act before his suicide is an act of mercy toward his
daughter Michal, which exposes audiences to the betterment that
Alfieri associates in different ways with God and constitutional
government. Not chiefly a theorist, Alfieri is, nonetheless, a
playwright who, as E. R. Vincent says, "knew how to get his
ideas on to the stage."[21]

Buffalo, New York

NOTES

[1] Aristotle, *Poetics*, 1449b.

[2] Ibid., 1453b.

[3] Kenneth A. Telford, "Analysis" in Aristotle, *Poetics* (Chicago: H. Regnery, 1961),
108.

[4] Vittorio Alfieri, *Of Tyranny*, trans. and ed. Julius A. Molinaro and Beatrice Corr
igan (Toronto: University of Toronto Press, 1961), 9; E. R. Vincent, introduction to
Vittorio Alfieri's *Memoirs* (London: Oxford University Press, 1961), xvii.

[5] Beatrice Corrigan, introduction to Vittorio Alfieri's *The Prince and Letters*, trans.
and ed. Beatrice Corrigan and Julius A. Molinaro (Toronto: University of Toronto Press,
1972), xxiii; Alfieri, *Memoirs*, 210.

[6] Vittorio Alfieri, *Memoirs*, 161, 163, 169, 177. *Encyclopaedia Britannica*, 14th ed.,
s.v. "Vittorio Alfieri." In *The Countess of Albany* (Boston: Roberts Brothers, 1884),
Vernon Lee cautions that in an Alfieri play, "there may be two or three Alfieris, good and
bad" (164), and it is indeed dangerous to make any single one of his creations his only
spokesperson.

[7] Augustine, *De civitate Dei*, 17:6–7.

[8] Beatrice Corrigan, introduction to *The Prince and Letters*, xxi.

[9] Charles Edward Stuart was elderly when he married the young Countess of Albany, and as Lee notes, he was not only given to rages but like Saul in regard to David, he was very jealous of the younger Alfieri and even tried to have him murdered. Like the Israelite king, Charles, too, was preoccupied with preserving his royal line.

[10] Vittorio Alfieri, *Of Tyranny*, 41.

[11] Ann Hallock, "The Religious Aspect of Alfieri's *Saul*," *Forum Italicum* 18 (1984): 55.

[12] All citations are to Vittorio Alfieri, *Il Saul*, ed. Rosolino Guastalla (Milan: Carlo Signorelli, 1965). The translations are mine.

[13] Alfieri sets up this opposition by having David's voice "penetrate" to the heart of Jonathan (1.31–32) and Abner's "invade" the heart of Saul (1.69–70).

[14] Again, although critics usually see Saul as the mask for Alfieri, Alfieri's ideas are filtered through several characters in the course of the play.

[15] W. H. Auden, "The Christian Tragic Hero," *New York Times Book Review*, 16 December 1945, 1.

[16] Vittorio Alfieri, "Parere" in *Il Saul*, 68.

[17] A. J. Droge, "Suicide," in *The Anchor Bible Dictionary*, ed. David Noel Freedman, et al. (New York: Doubleday, 1992), 6:225–27.

[18] Vernon Lee, *The Countess of Albany*, 163.

[19] Ibid., 164–65.

[20] Vittorio Alfieri, *The Tragedies*, ed. Edgar A. Bowring (1876; reprint, Westport: Greenwood Press, 1970), 2:109.

[21] E. R. Vincent, introduction to Vittorio Alfieri's *Memoirs*, xviii.

Ibsen's Cycle as Hegelian Tragedy

Brian Johnston

I

The Inutility of Tragedy. Tragedy, in the modern theater, is a genre more honored in repute than in performance, and Ibsen, inasmuch as he is admired, is not admired generally as a tragedian. In college courses tragedy, in various guises, is taught respectfully; and having a "tragic vision" is always considered an impressive cachet for a dramatist to possess. But the creation of a full scale, multidimensional tragic argument about the modern world (of Aristotelian "magnitude") does not appeal to theatergoers, (still less to film-goers) nor to modern playwrights. It goes against the thrust of current actor training, too, which is to keep the actor reassuringly close to the same level of experience as audiences, to get audiences to find themselves on familiar ground with the actor and the world of the play and not to establish the undemocratic aesthetic distance that the scale of action and the expanding perspectives necessary to tragedy insist upon. Revivals of Greek tragedy, like those of Serban, Suzuki, Sellars or Mnouchkine[1], reveal the power of ancient tragedy to speak effectively through specially devised new theatric conventions: but the exoticism of these productions keeps the details of our own contemporary world unrealized from tragic perspectives. The same goes for Elizabethan revivals: even in modern dress, the terms of these tragedies are not those of our modern world so that the experience of the tragic becomes part of an exotic excursion into foreign, and so safer, territory. As George Bernard Shaw remarked, "Shakespeare has put ourselves on the stage, but not our situations. . . . Ibsen supplies the want left by Shakespeare. He gives us not only ourselves, but ourselves in our situations."[2] Or, rather, our situations transfigured by tragic perspectives.

Perhaps the most compelling tragic vision in twentieth century drama is that of Samuel Beckett, which recovered a tragic voice for the modern theater often through the devices of comedy. The tragic argument of Beckett's later plays, by increasingly narrowing the focus of the dramatic *agon* to a single, inward, particular state of agonized consciousness, attained a form of tragic universality much like *Everyman*: each of us ultimately is alone with his or her particular and personal devastation. But no more than the Greek and Elizabethan revivals did this theater organize the objective concerns of our complexly experienced contemporary world and its cultural conflicts into a tragic art in the way in which the concerns of the Athenian *polis* or the Elizabethan world-view were so organized. T. S. Eliot's *The Family Reunion* is an honorable exception to the rule that the concerns of modern culture seem unfavorable to a full-scale tragic argument.

The arena of contemporary cultural conflict attracts adherents of many social projects who believe drama is doing its best work when advancing one or another of these agendas. It clearly is extremely desirable that we should be conscious of, for example, the failure of our social systems and the injustices suffered by one or another group through the insensitivities of the culture at large. To what better task can serious drama set itself, it might be asked, than to make the public more conscious of these shortcomings and eager to do something about them? To counter with the argument that the purpose of a tragic art is to be adequately tragic—convincingly, devastatingly tragic—might seem a copout from the urgent demands of the culture. This is what proponents of Enlightenment "serious drama" (*drames*)—Diderot, Beaumarchais, Mercer, Marmontel—believed; it is what George Bernard Shaw proclaimed in *The Quintessence of Ibsenism*—a brilliant handbook for the practical application of Ibsen's plays.

Shaw's is still the prevalent view in interpreting the Ibsen who, we are asked to believe, gave up the huge mythopoetic, metaphysical, and tragic perspectives of his middle-period plays, *Brand, Peer Gynt, Emperor and Galilean*, to address instead "the problems of the present." His plays, from this view, are utilitarian: ferreting out shortcomings in the bourgeoisie to guide that troubled class towards leading freer, less problematic lives— which is as far from the hazards of the tragic vision as it is possible to go. Even comedy, in its strictest form, plays a more unsettling game than this, leaving as insolubly problematic the fate of its misfits: Socrates, Shylock, Malvolio, Alceste, Tartuffe.

In the poem, "To My Friend Who Talks of Revolutions" (1870) Ibsen described the Flood as the only revolution "that was not scamped half-heartedly"—except for the deplorable survival of Noah and his family! He calls for a replay of the botched event in which he would be around to set a torpedo under the Ark.[3] This is the Ibsen who has been transmogrified by his interpreters from a grimly tragic skald to a basically benignant scold, reconstituted as the operator of a moralizing (and psychologizing) gladiatorial peepshow who casts variously defective specimens of humanity into his theatric arena to be doomed or reprieved according to our moral predilections. Viewing or reading Ibsen's twelve-play Cycle thus has come to resemble visits to Bedlam by the fashionable sane in eighteenth-century London: edifying excursions into the realm of the Deplorable or Unfortunate Other. The gatherings of modern Ibsenists all too often resembles a pharisaic festival for vaunting one's morally or politically correct credentials—what Oscar Wilde called simply washing one's clean linen in public.[4]

This also is a teachable Ibsen, easily assignable in anthologies of modern drama as "the father of modern realism," to be followed by his more or less similarly sober progeny. In the U.S. this practically ensures that the only texts to appear in repertory and in college anthologies, with dreary regularity, are *A Doll House* and *Hedda Gabler*, on which the seal of at least partial political correctness has been stamped. In Europe, true, Ibsen is appreciated and performed more variedly and more adequately —though the twelve realist dramas beginning with *Pillars of Society* and ending with the "dramatic epilogue" *When We Dead Awaken*, still are not recognized as a great, interconnected tragic Cycle. There has been no attempt to take up Ibsen's injunction, seconded by Shaw, to read or perform the plays in the order in which they were written, to discover what Ibsen insisted were the mutual connections between the plays. Ibsen, on such a scale, still proves difficult for the modern theater—or modern scholarship—to accommodate.

II

The Realist Cycle as an Archetype-filled Tragic Space. In *The Ibsen Cycle* I argued that the twelve plays constituted a single tripartite Cycle whose subject was modern humanity undergoing (in Hegelian terms) a great journey of spiritual recollection.[5] On this audacious journey, the modern scenes, characters, and actions recall archetypal forces and presences from the cultural/historical past of the race—at least, of the Western tradition of that race. The whole sequence of such actions is dialectical, each play uncovering the fatal contradictions inhering in each stage of the journey and thus tragically self-destructing, so that there can be no going back in the evolutionary winding stairway of despair performed by the Cycle as a whole. And each play in itself is such a dialectical action: the Nora Helmer of *A Doll House*, act 2, for example, can not return to the condition of consciousness of act 1; nor, after act 3, to the condition of act 2, and so on, through play after play up to the "Epilogue." The "mini-Nora" at the opening of *A Doll House* will discover the "super-Nora" awaiting her at the close of act 3. And this is true not only of Nora but also, to a lesser though still notable extent, of the other accompanying characters in the play whose actions and speeches similarly evolve with the evolving dialectic. In the beginning of *Ghosts*, the confident, joyful, self-justifying Helene Alving is ineluctably journeying towards the distraught and horrified tragic figure of the final curtain in a play as dialectically relentless as *Oedipus Tyrannos*. Yet the devastating action also is a *tragically* transfiguring one, as archetypes from Greek drama and other spiritual streams (*åndelige strømninger*) crowd back onto the modern stage and provide a more adequate, even if a more desolating, *agon* of the human condition. In the Cycle, Ibsen created a space in which his imagination, crammed with cultural and historical content, could find room to explore fully.

This program of the Cycle resembles similarly audacious projects for the redemption of our modern identity by such post-Romantic contemporaries of Ibsen as Richard Wagner and Friedrich Nietzsche—a program continued by modernists like T. S. Eliot and James Joyce. Joyce's lifelong admiration for Ibsen, I claimed, was due to a similarity of purpose in the two artists. The tragic *agon* that Ibsen invented for modern drama includes: (a) the dialectical subversion of modernity's claim to adequacy as human identity; (b) the archetypal recollection, beneath the images of modernity, of more adequate, though suppressed or evaded, forces and ghosts of the past—like a collective séance of modern consciousness. His archetypes are vehicles of the inherited and unresolved spiritual conflicts within the Western mind which have gone into the formation of our modern identity. Such archetypal presences within the plays, as in the work of Joyce and Eliot, gives them the spiritual dimensions necessary for a modern *tragic* argument, transcending the immediate problems of the present—as those problems usually are envisioned.

Tragedy, on this scale and in this sense, is not serviceable to any pragmatic agenda. It does not proclaim we would be better off if men were forced to be more accommodating, women more empowered, politicians made honest, or social injustices ended, admirable though these nostrums are. Tragedy has the more awkward intention of transporting our imaginations, if and when we dead awaken, into more liberating but also more desolate dimensions. The tragic experience is supremely inutile—which is why, in the utilitarian Enlightenment culture of the eighteenth century, the almost universally accepted Horatian formula—that the purpose of drama was "to please and instruct"—proved so fatal to the tragic genre. This nostrum gave us both moralizing and laughter-defying "weeping comedy" (*comédie larmoyante*), and such frigid exercises in tragic attitudinizing as Addison's *Cato*, the only British tragedy allowed by Voltaire to have achieved aesthetic adequacy.[6]

Utilitarian attitudes to art (Enlightenment, Liberal, Marxist) are anti-tragic, are, indeed, deeply discomfited by the premises of tragedy. For Enlightenment thinkers, who discerned the clear obligations artists had towards the improvement of society, tragedy signally failed to serve a useful social purpose, as Beaumarchais insisted:

> . . . the inevitable blows of fate do not offer the mind any moral lesson. When one can only shudder and be silent, is not the act of reflection the worst thing one might do? If a morality were extracted from this genre of play, it would be a dreadful one which might lead many souls toward crime, since its fatalistic vision would provide them with a justification; it would discourage many from following the ways of virtue, and all such efforts, according to this system, would be for naught. If there is no virtue without sacrifice, so too there is no sacrifice without hope of reward. Any belief in fatalism degrades man by depriving him of the freedom without which his actions reveal no sense of morality to him.[7]

Marxism inherited from the Enlightenment, along with much else, its insistence on the social utility of art and, along with it, Enlightenment's hostility to tragedy:

> . . . the Marxists do not like the tragic, hence not tragedy either, as long as it shows human failure as an eternal category of human existence. It is their firm belief that mankind has introduced the tragic into the world and that human effort can, therefore, remove it as well. So they see the tragic as a historical category of the *condition humaine* rather than an existential one. . . .Thus tragedy appears to be unresolved alienation. Tragedy makes man enter the "realm of necessity" consciously for the first time.[8]

Enlightened social and political causes are unquestionably worth fighting for: economic justice, feminism, hominism, gay rights, ecological sanity, the strictest gun laws, the abolition not only of capital punishment but of the barbarism of prisons and of all punitive law—together with many other attempts to improve and prolong our brief existence in the cosmos. It is good that playwrights effectively address these issues in the theater and bring home to us the urgency of reforms. Some of the best and most acclaimed plays of our time do just this. Many of his interpreters insist that concerns of this nature are the major purpose of Ibsen's art and that, in fact, this is where his real strength lies. They see him inheriting and continuing the unfinished agenda of the Enlightenment theater: of Lillo, Moore, and the *drames* of Beaumarchais Diderot, Mercer and Lessing. This would not be a bad job for a playwright. But Ibsen, as a *tragic* dramatist, is not furthering this agenda which, from his *tragic* perspective, merely is re-arranging the deck chairs on the Ark before his torpedo hits. In his major work, which includes the Realist Cycle, he is performing the odder and less alluring task of rendering a tragic portrait of modern humanity, of getting his contemporaries to see themselves through a tragic perspective. Without such a perspective, our vision is not adequately, or authentically, human.

Getting us to take in the tragic perspective might be one way of snatching a shred of utility from the devastation of tragedy: but it is a fairly tough-minded concession. In *Ghosts*, tragedy is the privilege of only Osvald and Helene Alving, spiritual aristocrats who refuse the wary ethical myopia of Manders, Engstrand and Regina, and are transfigured but devastated in consequence. Tragedy is something one would never wish on one's friends, but which one demands for one's most admired dramatic characters. No one wants Antigone to give in to Creon and avert the calamity that comes down on her and upon so many others; nor do we side with Tiresias, Jocasta and the old shepherd, wanting Oedipus to stop his investigation even as we see, and reluctantly admire, the infernal machine that is being so superbly assembled against him. We go along with the obstinate suffering of these figures, and even with those of Euripides—who clearly seem more sinned against than sinning—because of the way such suffering opens up a clarifying, if bleak, perspective on the human condition.

Ghosts, a bigger play than *A Doll House*, is less often anthologized because, like *Rosmersholm* or *John Gabriel Borkman*, it is more difficult to misread as meliorist and therefore intrinsically optimistic. The optimists, in fact, once declared the play redundant, from a utilitarian point of view, because of the discovery of penicillin—though a rescue operation now is being mounted for its new relevance to the AIDS crisis. The path Ibsen is taking us down in *Ghosts*, however, is a metaphysical, not a medical one. The grim game the tragedy is tremendously playing demonstrates that modern reality, under imaginative and rigorous analysis, reveals a tragic structure, an inescapable clash of irreconcilable imperatives. In *Ghosts*, I have suggested, the Cycle recollects and re-enacts our Hellenic heritage, whose supreme artwork was tragedy. The horror and execration with which the play was received shows how unprepared the nineteenth century was for the Greek tragic vision when stripped of classicizing costume and applied directly to the texture of the modern world. But that near-hysterical reaction to the play on its appearance in Europe—especially to the notorious performance at the Independent Theatre in London on Friday the 13th of March, 1891—showed a better sense of what it actually was about than current respectful attitudes that see it as a worthy classic somewhat dated by medical progress. In *Ghosts*, more starkly perhaps than in the rest of the Cycle, Ibsen presents our humanity as an inchoate identity made up of an uncertainly recollected and conflicted past voyaging to a problematic future within a cosmos we still cannot comprehend; one by one the sustaining fictions we have constructed as faith, morality, truth, are stripped away. The sun that rises at the end of the play illuminates a total multiperspectival devastation.

III

The Conditions for the Game of Modern Tragedy. Ibsen's uningratiating tragic vision is inseparable from an equally unsettling comic one, as *Ghosts*, for one, attests. Audiences often are surprised to discover how deliberately funny much of the play is, and many productions, convinced that an Ibsen play must be pervasively solemn, especially one with such a title, seem uncertain how to handle the comedy—especially as Ibsen's comedy springs from the same essentially anarchic vision as his tragedy. Tragedy and comedy, at their purest, are equally uncompromising and equally discomforting; in fact, comedy often is the crueler genre. The story of *Oedipus Tyrannos*, of the young hero who leaves home, encounters and defeats a violent opponent, and then outwits a monster by answering a riddle—for which he is given the hand of the princess and made king—is really a comedic-fabulous archetype which would usually end with "and they lived happily ever after." The plot that *then* follows, the devastation of the triumphant hero, unfolded with supreme irony, is a cosmic joke from the divine perspective which Sophocles allows us to share disquietingly. Shaw observed of Hamlet, Othello and Macbeth: "The plays in which these characters appear could be turned into comedies without altering a hair of their beards."[9] At the same time there clearly are tragic perspectives in comedies like *The Misanthrope* or *Peer Gynt*. It might be that, at their most authentic, both tragedy and comedy takes in the other's perspective and survives it, as in *King Lear* and *John Gabriel Borkman*. In tragi-comedies like *The Wild Duck* and the work of Samuel Beckett the distinction between tragic and comic evaporates without lessening the bleakness of the result.

Events that get a tragic rhythm going can usually be set right pragmatically in everyday life. A more adequate provision for superannuated monarchs might prevent the conflict of *King Lear*, and *Ghosts* might be only a condom away from happiness. But once the tragic rhythm takes over, usually by stubbornly disregarding everyday common sense, the audience finds itself submitting to this rhythm, and disregarding pragmatist objections —those, for instance, Thomas Rymer very sensibly made against the plot of *Othello*. We play the tragedian's game, forgiving sleights of hand if they work into the action another kind of logic, the thematic logic of tragedy, creating that conviction of the necessity of the events that Aristotle commended. The medical causes of Osvald Alving's collapse become totally subordinate to the metaphysical logic of devastation his situation sets in motion—its larger, metaphoric argument. We expect tragedy to validate, by the exploration it undertakes, such bleak music as, "best of all is not to have been born"; "Men must endure/ Their going hence, even as their coming hither;/ Ripeness is all"; "I almost believe we are ghosts, all of us . . ."; "You're on earth; there's no cure for that!" These are painfully earned moments or stages in the progress of the tragic *agon*.

We recognize the rules of the game of tragedy and expect them to be obeyed. Any dramatic performance is a meeting ground where author, performers, and audience sort out what kind of game is being offered. If it is tragedy, we don't ask the play to provide the satisfactions of another genre—a drama of warm human sympathy, or engaged proselytizing or moralizing, for example. For though tragedy may contain these elements, it must override them. We recognize the attainment of the genre, whatever the *style*,when it (relatively rarely) occurs. If a tragedy's great effects come from language worked up to high levels of poetic and rhetorical force—as in the eloquent aria-like monologues and soliloquies of Elizabethan drama, or the *tirades* of French neoclassical tragedy—or from a thematic plotting in the linkage of themes and imagery, we are likely to forgive realistic implausibilities in the plots. Thomas Rymer, refusing to go along with the game Shakespeare was offering, condemned the plot of *Othello* as "a bloody farce" (Voltaire was even more dismissive: "his monstrous farces that are called tragedies").[10]

For a realist tragedy in modern dress (the immensely difficult game Ibsen is playing) Elizabethan or neoclassical rhetoric would be out of place; and the art will shift instead to careful analytic plotting, a method of revealing immense implications beneath the frugal-seeming terms of a modern realism. In Ibsen's analytic method, the thematic and realistic plots are closely linked; and it is this rhetorical frugality that has led some to deny the plays a tragic status. To compare a rhetorical passage from Shakespeare with a "prosaic" passage from Ibsen and then to declare the latter lacking in tragic heft is to fail to see the new terms under which, alone, tragic pity and terror can be achieved in a modern drama. (Enlightenment bourgeois tragedies fail by preserving the rhetorical force of verse in a new overwrought prose.) The tragic rhythm has to reveal itself through an art of plausible factuality; through a theatric semiotics that indicates *modern* minds in conflict or under duress: through pauses, sudden accelerations or amplifications of everyday speech, half finished sentences, and a subtle pattern of submerged imagery and ambiguity. What we lose in amplitude of emotional rhetoric we gain in the precision and alarming closeness of tragic analysis.

IV

The Comfortless Zone of Tragedy. Tragedy lures us into an arena where we have to give up the defenses we otherwise use to protect ourselves. It creates a thematic logic so imperative that (the opposite of our reaction in everyday life) we would be indignant if the catastrophe were somehow pragmatically averted. Tragedy, in this (Greek) sense, is tough for a culture to assent to. Samuel Johnson, along with his contemporaries, famously could not bear to let the conclusion of *King Lear* stand:

> A play in which the wicked prosper, and the virtuous miscarry, may doubtless be good, because it is a just representation of the common events of human life: but since all reasonable beings naturally love justice, I cannot easily be persuaded, that the observation of justice makes a play worse; or, that if other excellencies are equal, the audience will not always rise better pleased from the final triumph of persecuted virtue.
>
> In the present case the publick has decided. Cordelia, from the time of Tate, has always retired with victory and felicity. And if my sensations could add any thing to the general suffrage, I might relate, that I was many years ago so shocked by Cordelia's death, that I know not whether I ever endured to read again the last scenes of the play till I undertook to revise them as an editor.[11]

That last sentence pulls us up before we start to laugh at eighteenth-century squeamishness. Johnson obviously responded to the tragic situation more keenly than most of us, and took its moral implications very seriously. There was a point in which he could no longer go along with the rules of the game Shakespeare was offering. He could not enter a tragic space that asked him to set aside his deepest moral feelings. Unlike the Greek audiences, sincere Christians such as Johnson could not believe that the cosmos, created by a God expressly for the benefit—or at least the fair trial—of humanity, ultimately could not satisfy a human sense of justice. It is why they (along with Enlightenment rationalists like Voltaire) found it so hard to follow the Greek example of allowing tragedy to open onto an abyss where human rationality and divine or cosmic reality no longer coincided: where an Ajax could be cruelly toyed with and destroyed by Athena, an Oedipus made the object of a ghastly cosmic joke, or a Hippolytus, Pentheus or Phaedra hideously destroyed by unjustly indignant deities. (The formula of the "tragic flaw" seems a desperate misreading of Aristotle's *harmartia* to inject some moral comfort into the bleak zone of Greek tragedy.) The gods of Greek tragedy are amorally powerful forces and, like the cosmic forces of modern scientific thinking, they ultimately elude the human categories by which we try to identify them. This is the vision so unsettlingly recovered in *Ghosts*, where the tragic nemesis lies waiting in the blood of its innocent victim, and an indifferent sun rises to illuminate the scene of human devastation.

The understandable tendency of modern audiences is to protest, like Johnson, against the tragic rhythm taking over events. It simply is not fair that Helene or Osvald Alving, the most admirable characters in *Ghosts*, should suffer so appallingly even as the play builds up the logic that requires them to. Tragedy requires us to override moral perspectives and to recognize the tragic structure ultimately underlying reality. Tragic impartiality goes against the way in which we react to events in the world. John Adams' opera *The Death of Klinghoffer* caused indignation among many (including members of the Klinghoffer family) because this is how it represented a situation usually described in passionately partisan terms. There is a natural tendency to pull tragedy down from its uncompromising stance, to rehabilitate it in our world where we sensibly resist it by all means possible: moral, medical, legal, social, financial; or by anodynes (we should all understand and love one another).

Roland Barthes describes the French interpretation of Racine which seeks

> to domesticate Racine, to strip him of his tragic elements, to identify him with ourselves, to locate ourselves with him in the noble salon of classic art, but *en famille*; it seeks to give the themes of the bourgeois theatre an eternal status, to transfer to the credit of the psychological theatre the greatness of the tragic theatre. . . . [It is necessary] to renounce looking for ourselves in this theatre: what we find of ourselves there is not the best part, either of Racine or ourselves As with the ancient theatre, Racine's theatre concerns us much more, and much more valuably, by its strangeness than by its familiarity: its relation to us is its remoteness. If we want to keep Racine, we must keep him at a distance.[12]

The idea of Ibsen that emerges from much well-intentioned interpretation is of a troubled photographic recorder of nineteenth-century Norway and its social ills. The Norway he presents to us for deprecation, with some aesthetic license conceded to the constraints of the theatrical medium, is, we often are told, one that would have been recognized by any similarly shrewd and concerned observer of the scene (the enlightened commentator, perhaps?). The actual absurdity of this should be apparent to anyone who reflects on the plays and what they are depicting. Knock on any Norwegian door, the claim seems to say, and it will be opened by a haggard Karsten Bernick, a distraught Torvald Helmer, a devastated Helene Alving, a beleaguered Thomas Stockmann, a messianic Gregers Werle, a suicidal Rosmer and Rebekka, a near-schizophrenic Ellida Wangel, or a Hedda with her gun, and so on, all caught in mid-peripety-and-anagnorisis, perhaps—even without including a wandering cast of ghostly white horses, drowned sailors (called Johnston), uncannily summoned sirens, Rat Wives, and walking statues.

V

Ibsen's Invented Norway: a Metaphoric Stage Space. Ibsen's dramatic artistry is not the attempted accurate recreation of everyday reality onstage: everyday reality, on the contrary, is ruthlessly rifled by him only insofar as it helps his art to come into perfected being. Like all major artists, he reorganizes appearances—his experience of the world—into aesthetic significance. For someone concerned mainly with drawing faithfully the lineaments of his country's contemporary society, Ibsen went to extraordinary lengths to keep away from it, spending all but the last few years of his major creative life in self-imposed exile from Norway. It is obvious that in the Realist Cycle, as in *Brand* and *Peer Gynt*, Ibsen did not *imitate* his Norway, he *invented* it—as an adequately metaphoric space for his tragic vision.

This metaphoric space extends into a metaphysical landscape from "the depths of the sea" which will claim certain characters, to earth-transcending heights "towards the mountains. Towards the stars. And the great silence" (the invocation in *Little Eyolf*) towards which other characters yearn. This vertical external landscape is echoed, or mirrored, as an internal landscape within characters, as in the Romantic art and literature that Ibsen inherited and adapted. The light and darkness, seasons, sunrises and sunsets, storms and avalanches, undertows, and planetary pulls of this landscape operate on cue with movements within the internal landscapes of the characters. In *Brand*, *Peer Gynt* and the Realist Cycle, Ibsen furnishes the landscape with a ventriloquism whereby it speaks through the dramatis personae, just as he creates characters that earn the right to speak such language. A tragically eloquent cosmos emerges through the modern realism of Ibsen's drama.

The human habitations within this landscape, like the houses of Greek drama, gather together a crux of conflicts containing fateful histories and memories; or they evolve, in the course of the dramatic action, into alien, constraining environments, peopled by watchful, constricting communities. The only characters allowed to enter that metaphoric space are those who earn their right to be there—by carrying a cargo of archetypal identity under their modern appearance; and this larger identity is released, imagistically, in multilayered speeches and actions that gradually build up and sustain the dramatic dialectic—of the "magnitude" necessary for tragic significance. Unlike real life characters, they perform only those actions and speak only those lines which advance the tragic argument that moves, in each act, to its prepared crisis of anagnorisis and peripeteia. That this is an accurate imitation of the rhythms and texture of everyday Norwegian life is as preposterous a notion as that the characters and actions of Greek tragedy are faithful representations of the everyday domestic and civic life of fifth century B.C.E. Athens.

The difference between Punch and Judy and Rosmer and Rebckka West is not that one pair is artificial and the other "real life": the second pair is equally as much a construct of art, but conceived with a greater degree of aesthetic complexity. The protagonists are designed to bring out a more elaborate argument and aesthetic structure than a Punch and Judy show (itself capable of different levels of complexity)—a structure whose model ultimately is Greek tragedy. Jan Kott, for one, noted the resemblance between Ibsen's dramatis personae and those of the Greek tragedians:

> Into the houses of Ibsen's imagination descend the ghosts of Oedipus, Electra, Orestes and Iphigenia. . . . The summoning of Greek shadows reveals . . . parallels between Ibsen and Freud.[13]

There are more than Greek ghosts in the Hegelian recollection, or *temps retrouvé*, undertaken by the Cycle, however, as Ibsen sets in tragic motion our entire human identity as it has revealed itself in the past as well as in the present. This is modern tragedy as a hugely recollective art where, in a resurgence of the repressed, archetypes of our human history and culture repopulate the stage. The Hegelian nature of this art of recollection does not mean that Ibsen's Cycle is ideologically Hegelian: only that he was imaginative and intelligent enough to recognize, with many artists, the possibilities within the Hegelian vision for a significant modern art and literature. Such a recollective art, in fact, is the major achievement of Modernism.

The archetypal identity of an Ibsen character emerges from its interaction with other, similarly conceived identities in the ensemble of each play. Each character study, while interesting in itself, gains its full metaphoric stature only when juxtaposed with and put in action with others, marking out the lean logic of Ibsen's realism from the realism of others in the modern theater. Beyond individual identity, gender, and generation, characters onstage establish cultural, historical, ideological and archetypal dimensions. (See my schematic below.) Osvald Alving in *Ghosts* is the vehicle for a cluster of active metaphoric associations: sexuality, Parisian joy of life, artistic creativity, Greek paganism (his Orestean elements), Dionysian wine, Apollonian light, the sun (Julian's Helios in *Emperor and Galilean*)—which bring him in conflict with Pastor Mander's equally multilayered hostility to all of these and to the intellectually inquiring and significantly named *Helene* Alving. Engstrand, Regine and the dead Alving and Johanna are equally essential components of the total concept of the play.

Beyond the multilayered human and cultural conflict, dispersing the rain shrouding the metaphysical landscape, rises the sun, mentioned throughout, an emblem of so many levels of the conflict; at the same time the sun is the reminder of an indifferent, cosmic perspective on the tragic human scene. This powerful juxtaposition of metaphoric characters, action, and scene creates a form of symbolist shorthand allowing the confined space and time of the stage to contain, in each play and in the Cycle as a whole, the same vistas as the three middle-period plays, *Brand*, *Peer Gynt*, and *Emperor and Galilean.* The conflict widens and transcends the particulars of individual persons and place, an aspect of Ibsen's art commented on by the young James Joyce:

> Ibsen's plays do not depend for their interest on the action, or on the incidents. Even the characters, faultlessly drawn though they be, are not the first thing in his plays. But the naked drama—either the perception of a great truth, or the opening up of a great question, or a great conflict which is almost independent of the conflicting actors, and has been and is of far-reaching importance—this is what primarily rivets our attention.[14]

The great conflicts of the plays require a selective dramatic method less minutely detailed and less casual than that of many realists not concerned to keep Ibsen's tragic and multiple perspectives in view. Not to see these perspectives is to compare Ibsen disadvantageously with writers not engaged with his artistic difficulties. A contrast of any passage in the Cycle with any passage from a realistic dramatist (for example, Harley Granville-Barker), will reveal the same difference in method as that between, say, Edouard Manet and the meticulously rendered realism of a conventional salon painter. Ibsen's thematic selectivity must impose distortions, economies, on the appearances and rhythms of everyday life much in the way Manet must do. Reality is rendered only as it serves the austere thematic requirements

of the art. The *metaphoric* time of *Ghosts*, for example, requires
that an action occurring between mid-day and sunrise the next
day be encapsulated in less than three hours of almost uninter-
rupted *realistic* action. The change in the set from gloom to
starkly brilliant light, like the lamp and champagne brought in
for the joy-of-life dialogues, or the carefully calibrated collapse
of Osvald precisely at sunrise and at the conclusion of the the-
matic/dramatic argument, is set to a metaphoric, not a realistic,
clock—the same accelerating clock, in fact, that Greek tragedy
kept time to. The metaphoric-tragic imperative driving the action
of *Ghosts* is so compelling that few audiences notice the temporal sleight-of-hand that Ibsen is practicing on them.

VI

Creating the Dimensions of a Modern Tragic Drama. Not
every play in the Cycle is tragic, any more than in a Greek
tetralogy,[15] but the Cycle as a whole creates a space in which
tragic forces and a great tragic argument can come into being and
from which elements of everyday life irrelevant to that argument
are cleared away. The Cycle sets out to be (a) modern and (b)
tragic—a combination more intractable than might be supposed.
To be *tragic* Ibsen's cycle must be the imitation of an action that
is serious, complete, and possessing magnitude: to be *modern*, it
would need to set into tragic motion an adequate representation
of our modern identity. After the mid–nineteenth century this
identity was understood as having evolved over long biological
and cultural time and to have accumulated the results, including
the conflicts, of this history. An adequate, modern, tragic drama
would have to encompass this. To take up a limited area of modern reality and then to offer an impassioned but partisan and partial account of it is the way the discourse of the world is conducted; but such partiality has to be discarded for tragedy, which
requires more of a doomsday account, a Judgment Day upon the
soul, as Ibsen said of his poetic vocation.[16] Ibsen's is a judgment
not just of others' individual souls—for that would lack magnitude as well as honesty—but of the psyche of our modern humanity itself, filled with all the dimensions of its cultural past, in
which the dramatist is as involved as his creatures; for each one
of us, Ibsen said, shares the guilt of his/her people. There is no
such thing as a guiltless class, race or gender—another currently
unpopular idea.
    Nineteenth-century middle class humanity was an ideal

tragic subject: it was the class in power and a deeply guilty class. Its supremacy rested on a betrayal of the principles of the French Revolution and of almost every universal value earlier proclaimed when the bourgeoisie was seeking to end the oppressive hegemonies of the old order of monarchy, church, and aristocracy. In that Rousseauist dawn it may have been bliss to be alive: but by Ibsen's time that same middle class, empowered, had set up hideous industrial cities with their proletarian slums; had dispossessed and annihilated the native Americans; had supported the colonial seizures, massacres, and exploitations in Africa, the middle east, and Asia, and had lost all sight of its living spiritual heritage through a cynical materialist exploitation of the world— all this was cloaked in a conveniently indulgent religiosity and celebrated, conventionally and opulently, in non-subversive, visionless art.

Even before it sought the séance or the psychoanalytic couch, this was a class deeply uneasy about itself, attacked from the right for its crass materialist values and tastes and from the left for its gross injustices. This, however, made it an extremely interesting class; its tortuous complexities were good fictional and dramatic material. The proletariat has not been able to rival it in interest, however much it might surpass it in virtue.[17] This guilt-ridden class whose passing the Cycle seems to envisage, also carried, if only unconsciously, a huge cargo of archetypal memory, the reproachful ghosts that erupt continually to the surface of the psyche and extend the scale of the modern drama. As each individual, in Hegel's formulation, is a "world soul" containing these immensities, tragedy no longer is the prerogative of a prince but a possible fate for anyone, regardless of social station. Ibsen's most imposing tragic protagonist, Brand, is a peasant's son. Another aspect of a modern tragedy, then, is that it is classless: a universal tragic action can be enacted as plausibly in a bourgeois drawing room as in the antechamber of a monarch.

To be tragic in this modern—or modernist—drama, the individual must be awakened into becoming a vehicle for the ghosts on which the modern world, for the most part, has turned its back. Ibsen's plays, in fact, have as much the nature of séances as of psychoanalyses. The awakened individual becomes the medium through which the banished powers speak. This makes the Ibsen scene haunted ground where inadvertent actions can trigger off the archetypal drama. Ibsen's son, Sigurd, wrote of art that it "gives liberty of action to forces and possibilities to which life does not grant the chance of coming into their rights."[18] Being

vehicles of forces essential to our human wholeness (rather than
to our happiness) they exist in a context beyond our usual moral
categories. Ibsen's major characters, it must be admitted, behave
extravagantly, alarmingly, often unpleasantly. It is in the nature
of tragic individuals to be uningratiating; even, I have argued
elsewhere, to be immature and irresponsible (a frequent charge
of psychologizing critics):

> An Antigone, well adjusted to her family history and to the new polity
> of Creon, happily marrying Haemon (and this, it seems, *was* the
> mythic story that lay to Sophocles' hand) was of no use to Sophocles'
> tragic purpose. An Antigone such as Sophocles reinvented her, ob-
> sessed with a corpse and the world of the dead, rating brothers higher
> than husbands, though abnormal and even pathological from the mor-
> alizing, psychoanalytic point of view, was perfect for Sophocles' pur-
> pose of demonstrating a heroic norm from which we, in our daily pu-
> sillanimity, have fallen. . . . The passionate Achilles, the hot-tempered
> Ajax, the stubborn Philoctetes, the extravagant Lear, and the malcon-
> tent Hamlet . . . all do much and say much that mature and responsible
> middle-class citizens would not and could not say and do—and are all
> the more impressive for it. . . . The concern that the cosmos should
> conform to our moral predilections is an attitude antithetical to trag-
> edy.[19]

Much commentary on Ibsen's plays still seems less interested in the plays as carefully shaped and extended metaphors
realized only in stage time and space than as real-life case histories. It is a better critical discipline to see the plays as realizing
and extending the requirements, thematic and formal, inherent in
the genre. They perform the difficult and delicate task of keeping
all dimensions of the dialectical action in play while advancing
the plausible modern story. *Thematically*, the plays are dramatized concepts about the human condition, guiding the argument
of each drama to a new level of awareness; *aesthetically*, they are
beautifully controlled and shaped movements, as in contrapuntal
music, moving, in each act in each play, to their powerfully prepared moments of peripeteia and anagnorisis, and attended by an
imagery that gives them their poetic resonance; *imaginatively*,
the characters in these plays, their fates and their worlds, take
hold of our minds and emotions as they are gradually realized in
formal terms. To ignore this considerable aesthetic achievement
and engage in moralistic judgment or partisan partiality—as if
the characters were presented, with their histories, in a police
line-up or a psychoanalyst's casebook, and not in shaped dramatic structures—is to be operating altogether in the wrong area

of interest.

VII

The Modern World a Defective Work of Art; The Theme of Alienation. Everyday modern life is not a natural truth the artist is obliged to imitate: it is always, already, itself a bad work of art, an artifice, a distortion of our humanity, created over time by our alienated, bungling consciousness and not in itself worth imitating. It becomes the artist's worthwhile subject only if its inadequacy is the starting point for exploring the extent of the error' and loss entailed by human history. Any natural identity of our humanity, as the Romantics have insisted since Rousseau and Schiller, has long been lost sight of (if it ever existed) by an alienating and disfiguring cultural-historical process; by oppressive traditions and institutions; by superstitions; by corruption of the truth. We receive a disfigured and corrupted inheritance as our human identity and we disfigure and corrupt it further. There is a moment in *When We Dead Awaken* when the artist Arnold Rubek tells how his work, under the guise of contemporary human portraits, has smuggled into it the "dear domestic zoo. . . . All the animals which man has distorted (*forkvaklet*) into his own image. And which have distorted him in return."[20] Against this ongoing cultural corruption Rubek set up, in statue form, the image of a naked young woman "awakening to light and glory with nothing ugly or tainted to shed"—but he is speaking of this to the former model of that image, a woman whose subsequent history in the world, in her own manic account, has been one of self-annihilation, madness, and multiple murders. The gulf between the image and the irreparably damaged human model seems to encapsulate that between a potentially free humanity and its actual contemporary existence—the ground, I would claim, of Ibsen's tragic vision.

The world, its institutions and its history, is to a humanity seeking authenticity and freedom a hostile, alien space, as Schiller insisted in *Letters on the Aesthetic Education of Mankind*; the individual, the product of this alien space, is therefore self-alienated and must undergo a crisis that reveals both the repressing and inhibiting environment it takes for reality, and the falsity of the self that has, at the cost of its own truth, adapted to that so-called reality.

He comes to himself out of his sensuous slumber, recognizes himself

as Man, looks around and finds himself—in the State. An unavoidable
exigency had thrown him there before he could freely choose his station; need ordained it through mere natural laws before he could do so
by the laws of reason.[21]

The dialectical detection of an alienated condition is the action of all the plays in the Cycle; the one most familiar to American readers is *A Doll House*, in which the initially desirable
environment, the charming home and family for Nora, the good
new job and salary for Torvald, and so on—all carefully quaran-
tined from such contamination as a Krogstad might threaten—
represent the investment towards "the wonderful" (*det vidunder-
lige*) which modern bourgeois humanity is seeking as its fulfill-
ment. In the course of the play "the wonderful" is repeated, mul-
tiplied, right to the closing lines, undergoing its own dialectic
transformations: the home and family become an intolerable
prison to a self (Nora) just becoming aware of its own unreality
within an unreal world. The same revelation awaits Torvald, who
is as much a victim of alienating history as Nora—something
partisan appreciation of the play often overlooks.

This confrontation, where a human identity seeks to realize
its authenticity within an environment whose very values, loyalties and virtues are lethal impediments to self-determination, sets
up the terms of an Hegelian tragic action of the greatest serious-
ness and magnitude, especially when carried out on the scale of a
twelve-play cycle. The modern mind's fateful encounter with its
ghosts, with its suppressed, evaded, or forgotten identity, is just
the action and imagery to sustain a dialectic on such a scale. This
would be the *Zeitgeist*'s interrogation by the *Weltgeist*, of particular culture by universal history—and vice versa. As an account
of the human condition, this was a somber corrective to the nineteenth century's optimistic faith in Progress, its confidence that
modern reason, through legislation and technology, could liber-
ate humanity. In a group of notes to *Ghosts* Ibsen contrasted "the
luxuriant growth of our culture, in literature, art, etc.—and by
way of contrast: the whole of mankind on the wrong track. . . .
The fault lies in the fact that the whole of mankind is a failure. If
a man demands to live and develop as a man should, then that is
megalomania . . ."[22] These are not considered and well-honed
apothegms in the Nietzschean manner; but their perspectives are
Nietzschean. In the same spirit the Greek tragedians, especially
Sophocles, confronted their confident, rationalist democracy
with the challenging ghosts of a distant, heroic, aristocratic, and

decidedly non-democratic past. Oedipus, the supreme rationalist who yet unconsciously confirms the mantic prophecy of Tiresias, is the classic emblem of this confrontation. Roland Barthes wrote that the Greek theater

> is always a triple spectacle: of a present (we are watching the transformation of a past into a future), of a freedom (what is to be done?), and of a meaning (the answer of gods and men). . . . Already mythology had been the imposition of a vast semantic system upon nature. The Greek theater seizes upon the mythological answer and makes use of it as a reservoir of new questions: for to interrogate mythology is to interrogate what had been in its time a fulfilled answer. Itself an interrogation, the Greek theater thus takes place between two other interrogations: one, religious, is mythology; the other, secular, is philosophy.[23]

In Ibsen's Cycle the spectacle undertaken by the plot of each play takes place between the interrogation of a mythology constructed out of cultural history, and the interrogation of a modern, scientific/technological materialism. The opening play of the Cycle sets this out forcefully: Bernick's bid for supremacy in his society is to happen by means of the materialist-technological enterprise of the railway and attendant projects he wishes to bring about and control; but this is disrupted by the emergence from the past of the semi-mythological Lona (her name deriving from Apollonia, follower of Apollo) arriving with a Dionysian circus and music to inaugurate another enterprise altogether—the beginning of the modern spirit's tragic journey to spiritual authenticity which the rest of the Cycle will undertake.

The use of cultural history as "a reservoir of new questions" was begun by Friedrich Schiller, who lamented the modern dramatist's lack of mythological sources such as the Greek dramatists could employ: in his plays he set about converting history and its prominent individuals and events into a new mythological system, a mythology of service to the post-Romantic, post-Revolutionary spirit. Don Carlos, King Philip, Posa, the blind Grand Inquisitor, the Duke of Alba, Wallenstein, Mary Stuart, Elizabeth, Demetrius and so on, are made, with a liberal rendering of historical facts, into metaphysical agents of freedom and repression, light and darkness, truth-bringers and truth-deniers, whose victories and defeats (in *tragic* drama it is the positive forces who are defeated) help us understand the structure of our inherited spiritual reality. With *Don Carlos*, Schiller inaugurated the supertext of modern dialectical drama. In the dialectical tradition continued by Ibsen, Shaw, Brecht, Genet, these archetypal agents of progress or regression, light and darkness, take on innumerable modern guises.

What was new about this Romantic/post-Romantic supertext or mythological system was that, unlike the Greek, it was from the start militantly subversive of the mainstream orthodoxy. It emerged at the point where the modern world divides between mainstream and minority cultures (and theaters). It is at this moment that the tragic hero (of minority literature and theater) emerges as the wanderer, outsider, outcast, rebel—even criminal—and where the old tragic concern with Integrity, (adherence to conventional heroic norms) now gives way to concern with Authenticity (rejecting conventional norms as inauthentic). The Byronic criminal-outcasts such as Cain or Manfred; Schiller's "interestingly guilty" Mary Stuart, Wallenstein, or Demetrius; Ibsen's Brand, Peer Gynt, Julian, Rebekka West, Hedda Gabler, Halvard Solness, or John Gabriel Borkman; Dostoevsky's, Raskolnikov, Stavrogin, Ivan Karamazov; Shaw's St. Joan; Kafka's alienated K; the Outsider and Caligula of Camus; Jean Genet's Blacks or the Said of *The Screens*, (and Genet himself)—to name only a few—are all examples of the variously subversive alienated consciousness of modern tragic literature.

The Romantics made Prometheus their hero and rehabilitated Milton's Satan. These and more realistically localized alienated characters become vehicles that better can express the nature and extent of our spiritual malaise than "the normal ego, that false self competently adjusted to our alienated social reality" described by R. D. Laing in *The Politics of Experience*.[24] This cultural divide, clearly perceived by Schiller, created the terms of all subsequent dialectical drama from Byron, through Ibsen, to Jean Genet.[25] It was a form of tragic drama and tragic hero that Hegel commended in the early plays of Goethe and Schiller.

In his historical dramas, Schiller selected certain transgressive individuals and certain critical turning points in history in which the origins or manifestation of modern conflicts could clearly be set out. He never claimed to be presenting accurate history but, in Kantian terms, an arena of conscious play or self-conscious illusion, in which the material and sensuous world could be illuminatingly reshaped through rational and aesthetic form—an aesthetic education. The modern audiences, aware of this aesthetic reshaping of reality, would be alerted to identify the conflicting forces going into the formation of misshapen modern consciousness. It was a method developed more complexly and massively by Hegel in his own philosophy. *The Phenomenology of Spirit* is such a succession of dialectical dramas of our universal humanity recovered from the past—both within and yet above cultural history. In both Schiller and Hegel, this action of cultural recollection takes place within a modern mind (the poet's, the philosopher's, or the audience's). It is only another step to set the dialectical dramas, not in past historical time and place, but in the familiar contemporary world where the actions of archetypal recollection can take place in a modern drawing room—in a form of psychoanalysis of the *Zeitgeist*. And this is the step Ibsen takes in his Cycle.

VIII

Addressing the Scale of Modern Alienation; Archetypal Recollection. Ibsen's tragic drama, which takes up as well the ahistorical, mythopoetic dimensions Richard Wagner explored in his music-dramas, is one in which archetypal forces erupt into, transfigure, and devastate, modern (nineteenth-century) identity and the world created by that identity as a self-sustaining but repressive inner and outer environment. This idea of his tragic subject was explored by Ibsen in his three great middle-period plays, *Brand*, *Peer Gynt*, and *Emperor and Galilean*. Since these plays were not written for theatrical performance he was free to extend to their limits the temporal and spatial metaphors of his argument (in the sense of Milton's "great Argument" in *Paradise Lost*) through an active vertical landscape and through the huge historical collision of Hellenism and Christianity in Julian's Byzantium. (I am not claiming all this was a conscious program: artists mostly discover such a pattern or program while at work on it.) These three plays, I would claim, shape Ibsen's dramatic cosmos; afterwards he would devise the means of staging it as a tragic, recollective drama of modern, urban, bourgeois humanity. The result was to be a portrait of humanity in nineteenth-century costume as compelling as any in the history of drama. The humdrum identities of modern urban life (ourselves and our situations) are enlarged and galvanized by archetypal forces that extend the dimensions of human identity through individual, familial, communal, national, historical, cultural, natural, and supernatural circumferences of meaning (see my schematic below).

If, as Nietzsche claimed, it is only as aesthetic phenomena, as works of art, that we are finally justified, and if, as he further claimed, tragedy is the highest form of art, then Ibsen has offered a magnificent justification of nineteenth-century life. The portrait that emerges is of a humanity whose contemporary agitations and conflicts awaken and stir into life dormant and primordial layers of our identity; a "mine" containing "an infinite host of images of the past slumber[ing] . . . lying hidden in the dark depths of our inner being," as Hegel describes the Unconscious in *The Philosophy of Mind*.[26] When we recognize that the hero/ine of the Cycle is the human spirit itself made up of the wonderfully varied myriad of individual characters, major and minor, we will see there was no drawing in of artistic ambitions between the plays of the great middle period and the inauguration of the Cycle with *Pillars of Society*.

In *Brand* and *Peer Gynt* Ibsen had placed his alternate "galilean" and "emperor" identities within a metaphorically charged vertical landscape. This landscape changed with the changing terms of the protagonists' drama, serving as a responsive mirror that extended the hero's action into the cosmos. From the recidivist trolls in the depths of the sea in *Brand*, or the depths of the earth in *Peer Gynt*, to the lethal Ice Church and mountain peaks, the landscape of the two plays clearly is a symbolic as well as a natural terrain. This same vertical, symbolic-natural-metaphysical landscape would be explored in the Cycle, from sea-depths and mine-depths to mountain peaks and beyond.

The humanity inhabiting this landscape is extended in time as well as in space. In *Emperor and Galilean* these temporal perspectives are gathered around the collision within fourth-century Byzantium between a declining Hellenism and a triumphant, but corrupted, Christianity. Similar forces might have been summoned by other cultural situations. They would have taken on different ideological aspects but they would express the same recurring collision of worldly and other-worldly, life-affirming and life-denying, free and dogmatic forces, within humanity. Julian's failure to undo the Christian revolution or to impel the human spirit beyond this conflict into a new synthesis, is, I believe, an emblem rather than the cause of the spiritual *malaise* pervading the Cycle. Nevertheless, characters, situations, and imagery from the middle period plays, especially from *Emperor and Galilean*, reappear throughout the Cycle. Such an ironic, blasé production as *Hedda Gabler*, for example, re-enacts in miniature, within the drawing room of the Falk mansion, the whole huge spiritual conflict of Ibsen's world-historical drama.

Each play in the Cycle enacts a resurrection day. The ghosts are summoned for an exorcism as well as for a recovery of the repressed, in much the same way—if not with the same intention —as in *The Phenomenology of Spirit*. Ibsen's Faustian role *vis-à-vis* his society can be seen to resemble that of Ibsen's own Maximos, the magus of "the third empire" in *Emperor and Galilean*, which raises the spirits in the cause of human wholeness. The Cycle traverses a long night of the soul—in the last four plays literally, in the last act sequence, *evening, late evening, night, dawn before the sunrise*[27]—while ascending in higher stages, sequentially, to "the peak of Promise" of the last. Like Maximos, the cycle cannot deliver the liberation it envisages (Ibsen insisted his work represented a closure), only the sacrifice and suffering necessary to prepare for it. Without this sacrifice and suffering, however, the prospect of liberation could not be adequately— that is tragically—affirmed.

IX

A Schematic: Dimensions of Reality. Like Peer Gynt's onion, the dimensions of reality and conflict encompassed by an adequate tragic art can be set out in multiple layers, peeling "right to the centre."[28]

Supernatural/metaphysical
Natural world
Historical/cultural forces
National identity
Social interactions: local time and place
Generational conflicts
Familial loyalties/conflicts
Male/female identities
Individual ego/libido
Unconscious realm

Not every tragedy will reveal all these dimensions—but the greatest generally do, trying to activate all layers in its single action. So integrated are all these layers that, like a spider's web (to change the metaphor), the shaking of any one strand causes the convulsion of the whole. Slice of life realism usually keeps to the "lower" levels of action; abstract allegory to the "upper." Of course, this is not a test to apply to plays, but rather only an aid to help detect the possible dimensions of the tragic art.

Carnegie Mellon University

NOTES

[1] See Marianne McDonald, *Ancient Sun, Modern Light: Greek Drama on the Modern Stage* (New York: Columbia University Press, 1992), for an account of the adaptations of Greek drama by Peter Sellars and Suzuki Tadashi. Mnouchkine's *Les Atrides* was first performed in Paris in 1990 and subsequently visited New York and Montreal.

[2] George Bernard Shaw, "The Technical Novelty in Ibsen's Plays," in *The Quintessence of Ibsenism*, 3d ed. (New York: Hill and Wang, 1957), 182.

[3] Cited in Michael Meyer, *Ibsen: A Biography* (New York: Doubleday, 1971), 329–30.

[4] The recent *Cambridge Companion to Ibsen* (Cambridge: Cambridge University Press, 1994) reveals, in most of its critical essays, only too drearily how academic Ibsen interpretation actually has regressed from the early days when first-rate imaginations such as Henry James, Bernard Shaw, James Joyce, Thomas Mann, Rainer Maria Rilke, Hugo von Hoffmanstahl and their peers responded to his plays. On washing clean linen, see Algernon Moncrieff in Wilde, *The Importance of Being Earnest*, ed. Peter Raby (Oxford: Clarendon Press, 1995), 1.244.

[5] Brian Johnston, *The Ibsen Cycle: The Design of the Plays from* Pillars of Society *to* When We Dead Awaken, rev. ed. (University Park: The Pennsylvania State University Press, 1992).

[6] Voltaire, *Appel à toutes les nations*, in *Oeuvres complètes de Voltaire*, ed. Louis Moland (Paris: Garnier Frères, 1983), 24.201.

[7] Beaumarchais (Pierre Augustan Caron), *Essai Sur Le Genre Dramatique Sérieux*, trans. Thomas B. Markus, in *Dramatic Theory and Criticism: Greeks to Grotowski*, ed. Bernard F. Dukore (New York: Harcourt Brace Jovanovich, 1974), 300.

[8] Ernst Schumacher, "Again: The Marxists and Tragedy," *Theater Three* 8 (Spring 1990): 7. Marxism's aversion to tragedy may explain why Bertolt Brecht so stubbornly denied any tragic perspective to such plays as *Mother Courage and Her Children* or *The Life of Galileo*.

[9] Shaw, *The Quintessence of Ibsenism*, 179.

[10] Thomas Rymer, *A Short View of Tragedy*, cited in Dukore, 351; Voltaire, "Sur la tragédie," in *Lettres Philosophiques*, trans. William D. Howarth, in *French Theatre in the Neoclassical Era, 1550–1789: Theatre in Europe: A Documentary History* (Cambridge: Cambridge University Press, 1997), 592.

[11] Samuel Johnson, "Notes on Shakespeare's Plays: *King Lear*," in *Johnson on Shakespeare*, ed. Arthur Sherbo, The Yale Edition of the Works of Samuel Johnson, 8 (New Haven: Yale University Press, 1968), 704.

[12] Roland Barthes, *On Racine*, trans. Richard Howard (New York: Hill and Wang, 1964), 149.

[13] Jan Kott, "Ibsen Read Anew," in *The Theatre of Essence and Other Essays* (Evanston: Northwestern University Press, 1984), 58–9.

[14] James Joyce, "Ibsen's New Drama," in *The Critical Writings of James Joyce*, ed. Ellsworth Mason and Richard Ellmann (New York: Viking Press, 1959), 63.

[15] It is my conviction that the twelve-play cycle consists of three tetralogies, with the fourth play as a comedy or satyr play, making the Cycle an intellectualized (i.e. modernist) festival of Dionysos.

[16] "Writing means summoning oneself/ To court and playing the judge's part." Ibsen to Ludwig Passarge, Munich, 16 June 1880, *Ibsen: Letters and Speeches*, ed. Evert Sprinchorn (New York: Hill and Wang, 1964), 187.

[17] Brecht's proletarian or peasant figures are what William Empson would have called "versions of pastoral" devoid of potentially tragic (guilty) motivation, and so denied a fully adult identity.

[18] Sigurd Ibsen, *Human Quintessence* (New York: B. W. Huebsch, 1911; Books for Libraries Press, 1972), 93.

[19] Brian Johnston, *Text and Supertext in Ibsen's Drama* (University Park: Pennsylvania State University Press, 1989), 62–3.

[20] *Ibsen: Four Major Plays*, trans. Brian Johnston (Lyme: H. H. Smith and Kraus, 1995), 195.

[21] Friedrich Schiller, *On The Aesthetic Education of Mankind, In A Series of Letters*, trans. Reginald Snell (London: Routledge & Kegan Paul, 1954; New York: Frederick Ungar Publishing, 1965), 28.

[22] "Draft Manuscripts: Preliminary Notes," in *The Oxford Ibsen*, trans. and ed. James Walter McFarlane (London: Oxford University Press, 1961), 5.468.

[23] Roland Barthes, *The Responsibility of Forms: Critical Essays on Music, Art and Representation* (New York: Hill and Wang, 1985), 68.

[24] R. D. Laing, *The Politics of Experience* (New York: Pantheon Books, 1967), 144.

[25] The terms of this dialectic are clearly set out in the quarrel between Edmund Burke's *Reflections on the Revolution in France* and Tom Paine's *The Rights of Man.* Both writers draw on imagery of the *theater*, Burke on the old theater of Garrick and Siddons, Paine unconsciously creating a new imagery of the revolutionary theater. This dialectic and its images are taken up, after Schiller, by Shaw, Hauptmann, Gorky, Brecht, and culminate in Genet. Cf. Brian Johnston, "Revolution and the Romantic Theater," *Theater Three* 4 (Spring 1988): 5–20.

[26] Georg Wilhelm Friedrich Hegel, *The Philosophy of Mind*, trans. William Wallace and A. V. Miller (Oxford: Clarendon Press, 1971), 205.

[27] Cf. Brian Johnston, *The Ibsen Cycle*, 160.

[28] Ibsen, *Peer Gynt: A Dramatic Poem*, in *The Oxford Ibsen*, English version by Christopher Fry based on a literal translation by Johan Fillinger (London: Oxford University Press, 1972), 3.396–97.

Some Late Reflections on Tragedy and Its Theatrical Chemistry

J. L. Styan

All criticism likes to classify, but in the case of dramatic criticism classification is an essential operation, since the decision whether a play is a tragedy or a comedy, a farce or a melodrama, has crucial implications for the director and his actors. An implicit decision about genre, its nature and purposes, indeed, has its effects upon a whole production, upon its conventions and all that go with it—costume, setting, lighting, style of speech and movement, music. The determination is fundamentally one about the desired control of, and effect upon, the audience itself. Nevertheless, classification is far from straightforward. Over a period of some two thousand years the pressures of widely different cultures and conventions on the stage have brought about sweeping changes in practice.

The student of drama who is curious about the problem of dramatic kinds will encounter a forest of different genres and sub-genres, and each in its own way will differ according to its historical and topical context. However, there is a way into the maze. Every dramatic genre must answer two questions: *the why* —what is the intended effect of this genre upon the given audience? and *the how*—what qualities of style and performance are accordingly demanded? To seek to answer these questions is to try to identify the characteristics of the genre, and the key to the answers is to be pragmatic, testing theory against practice.

That said, the ancient division of drama into tragedy and comedy still provides a first guide to the activity of the theater: the division points to the enduring alternatives in people's attitude to life, and the beginnings of drama reveal that its basic features persist.

I

Tragedy, historically the most dignified and ritualistic of dramatic genres, calls for the spectator's most passionate response.

166

Nevertheless, in the last three hundred years it is not so easy to find a true and rigorous example, and modern discussion tends to turn on our suppositions about the tragedy of the remote past, specifically that from ancient Athens, Elizabethan and Jacobean London, the Golden Age in Spain, and the neoclassical theater of seventeenth-century Paris under Louis IV. Even then, these periods differ greatly from one another, and even among the tragedies of, say, Euripides or Shakespeare no two are alike. Nevertheless, their best examples cannot be ignored and must provide our starting point.

The tone and effect of tragedy were long ago identified by Aristotle as those of pain, usually of punishment for sin. In his *Poetics* he points to both the purpose and the method, writing that a tragedy is the imitation of an action with incidents arousing pity and fear;[1] thereafter the critical debate has been ceaseless. It was pain felt by the central character, but shared between the stage and the audience, and made worse because its source was mysterious. Tragedy also implied a struggle within that character, an act of self-knowledge which was inescapable, brought about by forces beyond its control. Cocteau introduced his version of the Oedipus story, *La Machine infernale*, with the words,

> Watch now, spectator. Before you is a fully wound machine. Slowly its spring will unwind the entire span of a human life. It is one of the most perfect machines devised by the infernal gods for the mathematical annihilation of a mortal.[2]

Moreover, the emotions of pity and fear were painful because they were also in conflict with one another: pity involves the urge to approach and share, and fear the urge to retreat and evade. Watching great tragedy, therefore, the spectator was torn apart.

To achieve these extraordinary and powerful effects, the style of tragedy was traditionally one of grandeur: it has always adopted a non-naturalistic, penetrating, lyrical mode of speech and movement. It has also assumed a ritual quality that was repeated with each performance: highly conventional, it spoke for the community and for mankind, so that its subjects acquired a mythical status. It aimed at universality, as Allardyce Nicoll insisted in *The Theory of Drama*, with symbolic and moral implications for all who saw it.[3] For that reason, its hero and heroine were commonly accorded noble stature, great in their guilt and seen at the limits of their endurance. It is not surprising that the best actors of history have therefore excelled in the magnificent, undying parts of tragedy—Oedipus, Lear, Macbeth, El Cid, Phèdre, and many more. Yet the traditional style of tragedy was to change, and such great parts would become rare.

II

If to generalize about the elements of tragedy is a thankless task, it is always necessary to focus upon the particular periods which gave rise to the great prototypes. At this point it will be helpful to recall one or two of the theater's finest tragedies, and to observe that even in its beginnings and at its height this apparently inflexible genre showed signs of what might be its subsequent development.

In the festivals of ancient Greece myths and legends were repeated with variations again and again, each well known to the citizen audience. Far from boring it, this repetition of subject was acceptable because the stories were hallowed by the religious tradition in which they were performed, the familiarity with the stories actually permitting the smallest changes of emphasis to be both subtle and effective. But at all times the ritual of performance seemed essential to the sacred atmosphere and, although this cannot be recreated for today's audiences, nevertheless something of the original spirit of the occasion may be recaptured when some of the impressive ingredients of Greek tragic performance—chorus, costume and mask, speech and gesture, music and dance—are in place.

The range of Greek tragedy is greater than appears. Euripides created characters more vivid and realistic than his predecessors, and his central figures were frequently "psychological" studies of women under stress, as in *Electra*, *Hecuba*, and *Medea*, even though the eponymous heroine was played by a man. These creatures continued to inhabit a world of myth and legend, of gods and goddesses, even though their plays touched human problems closely. Aristotle emphasized the primacy of "plot," but this hardly applies to Euripides's anti-war play, *The Trojan Women*, which offered an essentially lyrical image of a cruel world, unified only by its emotional incidents of suffering and sorrow. The captive Queen Hecuba of Troy is its chief character, and she is accompanied by a chorus of captive women, while Cassandra, the enslaved concubine of Agamemnon, and Andromache, the enslaved widow of Hector, contribute to the terrible occasion. In tone and style the play is wholly a lament, and it grieves for mankind, all through the eyes of women.

In the new, secular playhouses of Elizabethan and Jacobean London, tragic drama assumed an even more human aspect, and it is critically astonishing that the most weighty and intense tragedies of Shakespeare are sufficiently modern in feeling and natural in style to enable them to be sympathetically received by today's audiences everywhere. His four central masterpieces in the tragic vein (*Hamlet*, *Othello*, *King Lear*, and *Macbeth*) probe the presence and mystery of evil in the universe, yet in notably particular and human terms, and are often unrestricted in their contrasting use of humor and satire. The human elements so conspicuously present amidst such profound material make these plays unique.

Even a tragedy of the stature of *King Lear*, apparently set in ancient Britain and seeming to deal with a society remote from our own, is totally accessible to modern audiences worldwide, and its strong tragic pattern, while retaining its symbolic strength, continues to be recognizable and to carry meaning on a simple and unpretentious level. The play tells the story of a tyrant whose pride and arrogance as both ruler and father reduce his rich and orderly world to one of chaos, beggary, and madness. Nevertheless, throughout the action the presence of the redeeming characters Cordelia and Edgar enable the tyrant to recover an enlightened sense of humility, and through his new humanity the play reaches for a new harmony. The poetic structure of *King Lear* insists that the spectator sees life as a circular journey, one on which man is "bound/ Upon a wheel of fire,"[4] and the detail of human relationships guides the audience every step of the way.

With the classical stage of seventeenth-century France, tragedy returned to ritual and resumed its rigidly conventional style. At first sight it seems that never on the stage had there been so much to say but so little to do—and when they were not alone and speaking in soliloquy, the French characters confronted one another endlessly in formal duologues. Yet the vitality of the masterpieces of Corneille and Racine actually derived directly from this fierce conventionality. Written in formal Alexandrines and arranged in formal couplets, the speech of the French tragedies enjoyed a rhythmical intensity that endowed the drama with a sense of finality. The stage image was remorselessly stylized: bound by the artificial conventions of the three unities, the dialogue was kept busy indeed, and since there was no allowance for comic relief or physical activity, the scenes resembled inflexible *tableaux*. In pace and movement the stage was not unlike a chessboard set about with characters who behaved with the limitations of chessmen.

The neoclassical plots again drew upon myth and legend, beginning at the crisis of a story and presenting it as a series of predicaments. Corneille's *Le Cid* exhibited the lovers Don Rodrigue and Chimène, characters who were abstractly idealized as hero and heroine. All is well until their fathers quarrel and Rodrigue's father asks his son to avenge him. Dilemma! The hero will lose his honor if he does not kill the heroine's father, and lose her love if he does. In this way the play was arranged for powerful speeches of exalted passion and self-destructive agonizing. The implicit tragedy lay in the clash between love and honor, between the idealized code of duty and loyalty (*gloire*), and the forces of human reason and feeling.[5] It seems that Aristotelian pity and fear were still present in the audience's understanding of, and horror at, an impossible situation. Yet such a mechanical situation could serve to disclose exquisite subtleties of human feeling.

Racine's outstanding *Phèdre* also dealt in the conflict between love and honor, now more pointedly between the rational and the irrational. The plot, one of almost architectural symmetry, is again simplicity itself: Phèdre is all but dying from incestuous love for her stepson Hippolyte, but when he learns of this, he rejects her in disgust, and she poisons herself. Nevertheless, with Racine human emotion took on full dramatic force, and the rupture between Phèdre's infatuation and her conscience was the source of the tension in the play and of the power of her characterization: she is both a monster and a victim of inexorable circumstances. Racine was famous for his tirades, and on an almost bare stage (the French *décor unique*), his words weighed momentously; at the same time they enjoyed a remarkable musical texture which can bear notably subtle psychological analysis.

In *Phèdre* 2.5, the Queen, thinking her husband Thésée dead, slides involuntarily into confessing her feelings to Hippolyte, a man so much younger than she is. Racine is concerned about revealing her divided mind, torn between her passion for the youth and her duty to her husband; and the dialogue of the scene, its tenor and rhythm, carries an extraordinary tension, its complexity reflecting her anguish. She at first contrives to speak of Hippolyte in the glowing terms she should have kept for Thésée:

He had your eyes, your bearing, and your speech.

His face flushed with your noble modesty.

Then she thinks of the time when Thésée slew the Minotaur, and Ariadne guided him from the labyrinth with the help of a thread. In a kind of ecstasy she imagines what she herself would have done had Hippolyte been Thésée and she Ariadne:

A thread would not have reassured my fears.
Affronting danger side by side with you,
I would myself have wished to lead the way,
And Phaedra, with you in the labyrinth,
Would have returned with you and met her doom.

The audience is by now well aware that she is thinking only of Hippolyte, and anticipates and observes his horror and disbelief as he slowly realizes what she means:

What do I hear? Have you forgotten that
King Theseus is my father, you his wife?. . .
Forgive me. Blushing, I confess your words
Were innocent, and I misunderstood.
For very shame I cannot bear your gaze.
I go . . . [6]

He finally understands, and is utterly revolted.

In all its neoclassical decorum, the duologue is characteristically static for the spectator, but it is evident that Phèdre is looking hard at Hippolyte as she confesses her love, and that in the confusion and embarrassment of his slow recognition of her lust with its incestuous and adulterous implications, he is turning and moving away, trying to escape his repugnance ("I cannot bear your gaze./ I go . . . "). The stiff Racinian stage could in fact be fully alive and even quite physical. In self-loathing she will shortly offer her breast to him ("Here is my heart") and even seize his sword as if to kill herself. Moreover, the Queen's nurse and confidante Oenone is, like the spectator, a public witness to events, so that Racine creates a stunning emotional crisis in which Phèdre is physically seen and felt to have suffered complete humiliation in the face of Hippolyte's contempt. The audience may have been expected to respond with intense compassion and horrified dismay—perhaps, indeed, with Aristotle's pity and fear.

III

After signs of such an exemplary compromise between the ritualistic and the realistic, what occurred? In the long progress of western drama the stage suffered a kind of metamorphosis. The aims and effects of classical high tragedy did not recur, and Western society seemed not to recognize the same values. Symptomatically, the stage grew less ritualistic and a greater naturalism in manner and purpose governed such plays as Ibsen's *Ghosts*, Strindberg's *The Father*, Brecht's *Mother Courage and Her Children*, O'Neill's *Long Day's Journey into Night*, Williams's *A Streetcar Named Desire*, and Miller's *Death of a Salesman*. There are other distinguished plays of this essentially domestic kind that vaguely and ambiguously border on the tragic, but it remains a matter for uncomfortable debate whether any of them actually touch the same genre as their tragic predecessors.

In his preface to *Bérénice*, Racine had himself argued that it was not necessary for there to be blood and corpses in a tragedy,[7] and certainly the classical unities and any ritual of presentation have since disappeared. Then, nearly 300 years later, Arthur Miller followed his *Death of a Salesman* with his own apologia, "Tragedy and the Common Man," in which he declared that the rank of the protagonist was merely one of the outward forms of tragedy, and that any man might acquire tragic stature in his search for personal dignity and integrity.[8] Aristotle has been ostracized for a while now.

In recent times the academic systemization and classification of the stage has shown itself to be caught in an even more tangled web, and notions of "tragicomedy," that most elusive and ironical of dramatic concepts, has been claimed to be the embarrassing recourse for virtually any play whose particular mix of ingredients was uncertain. As the tragic impulse absorbed, blended with, and subverted the myriad forms of comedy that readily sprang up on the modern stage, ideas of tragicomedy offered the basis for every critical excursion.

It is arguable that tragicomedy is not a genre at all, but down the years its existence has pointed out a direction of *escape* from the formal and conventional. If the dramatic unities and expected rules of the stage were too restrictive, if tragedy or comedy aspired to realism, if melodrama or farce grew too thoughtful, the urge was towards tragicomedy. Every audience knows that in life tears admit laughter, and that laughter can bring tears; and if drama to be good must touch life, every audience will tolerate the unpredictable freedom and indirection of tragicomedy.

It has been acceptable to think of a comedy like Shakespeare's *Troilus and Cressida* or Molière's *Le Misanthrope*, or a potential tragedy like Shaw's *Saint Joan* or O'Casey's *Juno and the Paycock*, as inhabiting the grey area that is neither tragedy nor comedy. At the curtain, such "problem" plays are deliberately ambivalent in thought and feeling, and a delightfully ambiguous indeterminism is the name of the game. Their lapse into tragicomedy is not taken to be a failure, a concession, or an evasion, but a direct and hearty encounter with teasing reality.

Examples are legion. In Shakespeare a pointed instance of this is the careful manipulation of the audience at the end of *Measure for Measure*. At the last the Duke of Vienna offers his hand in marriage to the chaste novice Isabella; but she has been mortified first by the sexual advances of the judge Angelo and then by her brother Claudio's refusal to defend her virtue. Therefore, for a conclusion, Shakespeare deliberately refuses to convey any hint of her answer to the Duke. For years it was assumed that she would automatically obey the conventions of romantic comedy and gratefully accept him, but performance studies have confirmed that Shakespeare's ending is hugely and naughtily ambiguous.

These are the Duke's words, significantly the last words in the play:

> Dear Isabel,
> I have a notion much imports your good;
> Whereto if you'll a willing ear incline,
> What's mine is yours, and what is yours is mine.
> So bring us to our palace, where we'll show
> What's yet behind that's meet you all should know.[9]

Will she accept his offer? She does not answer, and in the Folio text no stage direction for her is given. Editors and directors have variously resolved the matter, most commonly by inventing a processional exit led by the Duke with the lady on his arm, thus implying her tacit consent. Happily, recent productions have shown that for Isabella to deny the Duke a clear answer is to keep open the dramatic issues and associate her decision with the moral paradox of the whole play. If on his words she walks away and then turns back to him, her divided mind is seen, but the challenge is over. If she turns away from him as if in disgust, she seems to paint the world wholly evil and to have chosen her nunnery as a final refuge from men and society. If, however, she does nothing, makes no motion but simply stands silent and alone, *she has passed her difficulty and the issue of the play to the audience*—which presumably is what Shakespeare's sly absence of direction implies.

It may be that this comedy can admit a romantic ending and simultaneously suggest its tragic irony. Down the ages the stage has confirmed that the problem is always more stimulating than the solution, and in performance indeterminacy—a superior form of suspense—always provokes new interest. In *Measure for Measure* the spectator's conflicting positions are at cruel variance.

IV

The characteristics of "realism" and "naturalism" have presented new challenges to the critic. Paradoxically, Aristotle may well have been responsible for the dramatic thinking behind the realism of tragicomedy. When he urged unity of action in tragedy—not unambiguously he wrote that the story must represent one action, a complete whole, with its several incidents so closely connected that the transposal or withdrawal of any one of them will disjoin and dislocate the whole[10]—it was in order to avoid any adulteration of the tragic spirit, and for many years it was the neoclassical idea that kings and clowns should not mingle. Nevertheless, in *An Essay of Dramatick Poesie* John Dryden was among the first to recognize that such diversity was in fact "natural," and in the next century Dr. Johnson declared in his *Preface to Shakespeare* that Shakespeare was "the poet of nature" holding up "a faithful mirrour of manners and of life."[11] Johnson was acknowledging that since Tudor times the English stage had been taking every kind of liberty with the rules of dramatic composition, not as an act of rebellion, but in simple and honest pursuit of the possibilities of the medium.

In more recent times the instinct for tragicomedy has been thought to be the impulse behind the "problem play" or "play of ideas" which the modern prose masters—Ibsen, Strindberg, Chekhov, and Pirandello—made their own. Plays like *The Wild Duck* and *Uncle Vanya* touched a nerve of social realism, and probed a human problem by maintaining a careful comic distance from what would otherwise be appallingly tragic. Is it because Chekhov uniquely dealt only in the tiny details of life—Trigorin's impulse to go fishing rather than be a romantic hero, Gaev's habit of sucking a candy and doing so while allowing his cherry orchard to be sold—that their author can never be accounted a creator of tragedy? The bitterly ironic *Six Characters in Search of an Author* and *Enrico IV* of Pirandello also hold tragedy in check by mixing and manipulating reality and his own clever brands of illusion, each essentially a calculated comic undercutting.

On the stage today it is amusing to see that serious, open-ended tragicomedy is widely called "drama," but if nothing else this confirms that expectations of genre remain uncertain and shifting: the modern stage deals less in different kinds of play and more in gradations of audience response. Horace Walpole famously believed that "this world is a comedy to those that think, a tragedy to those that feel," but nowadays we can see that there can be a good deal of thinking in tragedy and of feeling in comedy, which leaves Sidney's "mongrel tragi-comedy" liberty to play over the whole range of human experience.[12]

Today the aspiring dramatist also has an infinite choice of styles and forms of staging, drawn from what Andrew Kennedy called, in *Six Dramatists in Search of a Language*, "the imaginary museum" of tried and tested examples from past theater,[13] and ranging from the abstract and symbolic to the realistic and pedestrian. It could certainly be argued that the realistic styles which burgeoned towards the end of the nineteenth century are at the heart of any development of the contemporary tragic. Realism is now the modern way to reach out to less traditional audiences and less ritualized procedures and situations. In the best of Ibsen and Chekhov, the scene and its action are now domestic and particular, humanized and balanced, but in spite of these apparently trivializing tendencies, it is noticeable that symptoms of the grand surges and reactions of classical tragedy remain.

We may conclude that the tragic mode is still alive, and continues to shift and change. In my first ramble through its modern territory in *The Dark Comedy*, I quoted García Lorca in the introduction to his tragedies: "If in certain scenes the audience doesn't know what to do, whether to laugh or to cry, that will be a success for me."[14] He confirmed that although the genre we associate with Oedipus and Hamlet may seem to have grown remote and elusive, the forces of tragedy are imperishable.

Milford on Sea, England

NOTES

[1] Aristotle, *Poetics*, Loeb Classical Library (1927), 6.2.

[2] Jean Cocteau, *The Infernal Machine*, trans. Albert Bermel, in *The Infernal Machine, and Other Plays by Jean Cocteau* (Norfolk, Connecticut: New Directions, 1963), 6.

[3] Allardyce Nicoll, *The Theory of Drama: Introduction to Dramatic Theory*, rev. ed. (New York: B. Blom, 1966), 98–174.

[4] William Shakespeare, *The Tragedy of King Lear*, ed. Jay L. Halio, The New Cambridge Shakespeare (Cambridge: Cambridge University Press, 1992), 4.6.43–4.

[5] See, e.g., Louis Auchincloss's study *La Gloire: The Roman Empire of Corneille and Racine* (Columbia: University of South Carolina Press, 1996), *passim*.

[6] Jean Racine, *Phaedra*, trans. John Cairncross, in *Iphigenia, Phaedra, Athaliah*, rev. ed. (Harmondsworth, England: Penguin, 1970), ll. 641–70.

[7] Jean Racine, Preface to *Bérénice*, in *Oeuvres Complètes* (Paris: Editions du Seuil, 1962), 165–66.

[8] Arthur Miller, "Tragedy and the Common Man," in *The Theater Essays of Arthur Miller*, ed. and with an introduction by Robert A. Martin, foreword by Arthur Miller (New York : Viking Press, 1978), 3–7.

[9] Shakespeare, *Measure for Measure*, ed. Brian Gibbons, The New Cambridge Shakespeare (Cambridge: Cambridge University Press, 1991), 5.1.526–31.

[10] Aristotle, *Poetics*, 8.4.

[11] John Dryden, *An Essay of Dramatick Poesie*, The Works of John Dryden, 17, ed. Samuel Holt Monk (Berkeley: University of California Press, 1971), 44–9; Samuel Johnson, *Preface to Shakespeare*, The Yale Edition of the Works of Samuel Johnson, 7, ed. Arthur Sherbo (New Haven: Yale University Press, 1968), 62.

[12] Horace Walpole to the Countess of Upper Ossory, 15 August 1776, *Horace Walpole's Correspondence with the Countess of Upper Ossory*, The Yale Edition of Horace Walpole's Correspondence, 32, ed. W. S. Lewis (New Haven: Yale University Press, 1965), 315; Philip Sidney, *A Defense of Poetry*, in *Miscellaneous Prose of Sir Philip Sidney*, ed. Katherine Duncan-Jones and Jan van Dorsten (Oxford: Clarendon Press, 1973), 114.

[13] Andrew K. Kennedy, *Six Dramatists in Search of a Language: Studies in Dramatic Language* (London and New York: Cambridge University Press, 1975), 39.

[14] García Lorca to his brother Francisco, introduction to *Three Tragedies of Federico García Lorca*, trans. James Graham-Luján and Richard O'Connell (New York: New Directions, 1955), 13; cited in J. L. Styan, *The Dark Comedy: The Development of Modern Comic Tragedy*. Cambridge University Press, 1962), 1.